Put Emotional Intelligence to Work

EQuip Yourself for Success

JEFF FELDMAN

AND

KARL MULLE

P R E S S

Alexandria, Virginia

ASTD Press is an internationally renowned source of insightful and practical information on workplace learning and performance topics, including training basics, evaluation and return-on-investment (ROI), instructional systems development (ISD), e-learning, leadership, and career development.

Ordering information: Books published by ASTD Press can be purchased by visiting our website at store.astd.org or by calling 800.628.2783 or 703.683.8100.

Library of Congress Control Number: 2007921486

ISBN-10: 1-56286-482-3
ISBN-13: 978-1-56286-482-8

ASTD Press Editorial Staff
Director: Cat Russo
Manager, Acquisitions & Author Relations: Mark Morrow
Editorial Manager: Jacqueline Edlund-Braun
Editorial Assistant: Maureen Soyars
Retail Trade Manager: Yelba Quinn
Cover Design: Ana Ilieva
Cover Illustration: Jonathan Evans
Editing and production by IGS, Inc.

Printed by Victor Graphics, Inc., Baltimore, Maryland, www.victorgraphics.com.

Contents

Preface

Thirty-five people gathered in Room 10 that morning. The classroom was designed to hold only 30 comfortably. We were at 3M, our largest corporate client at the time, one we had been serving for the past several years with a training curriculum called Personal Leadership. We were launching a new course in the PL series and apparently it addressed a topic that was generating quite a bit of interest.

This occurred in 1996, a year after Daniel Goleman had published his now landmark book, *Emotional Intelligence: Why It Can Matter More than IQ*. The book created a tremendous buzz in the business world; organizations everywhere were clamoring for more insight into this thing called emotional intelligence.

From our first EI course that day at 3M through the work we've done presenting this topic to Johnson & Johnson, General Electric, the U.S. government, and a host of other organizations large and small, the interest in and perceived value of emotional intelligence has not waned. Research in the field has grown tremendously, various models have been developed, new questions have been raised, lines of thinking have diverged, and we all still have a lot to learn.

Daniel Goleman didn't invent emotional intelligence; rather, he very nicely packaged and built on some work done by others in the field. Psychologists Peter Salovey and John Mayer are often credited as having coined the term "emotional intelligence" in an article by the same name they co-authored in 1990. Five years before that though, Reuven Bar-On, a psychologist at Haifa University in Israel, was seeking to isolate and identify the factors that determine one's ability to be effective in life. Based on his research findings, Bar-On introduced something he called the emotional quotient or EQ. This abbreviation, of course, was a pushback against the long-running notion that a high IQ was a predictor of success in life. Bar-On and many who have researched, written about, and taught the concepts of emotional intelligence after him believe that although intellect is certainly important, intellectual capacity alone is not enough. Other critical factors need to be considered. These factors, an interrelated group of competencies, are collectively known as emotional intelligence.

Definitions and models for framing EI continue to be refined by both the pioneers of the field and those who have followed in their footsteps. There are several different versions, and each camp likes to put on its own spin. For our purposes here, we choose to apply a fairly general definition to the term:

> Emotional intelligence is using your emotions intelligently to gain the performance you wish to see within yourself and to achieve interpersonal effectiveness with others.

Our placement of the emotional intelligence competencies as a component of overall performance aligns us most closely with Daniel Goleman's framework for EI. Goleman's model consists of four major EI domains:

+ Self-Awareness
+ Self-Management
+ Social Awareness
+ Relational Skills.

Within each of these domains, Goleman describes related competencies. You'll find these domains and many of the competencies within each described in detail in the pages ahead.

WHY WE WROTE THIS BOOK

A number of important questions need to be asked about emotional intelligence. Primary among them is: Can the competencies of emotional intelligence be developed? IQ is often thought of as being static—you score what you score on the IQ test and that's about where it stays throughout your life. So what about growth opportunities for one's EQ?

Most researchers and practitioners in the field believe that emotional intelligence is something that can be developed. We agree of course, thus we offer this book on the topic. Granted, some people may be more naturally gifted at certain EI competencies than others, but competencies consist of behaviors that can be developmentally scaled. This means that with training and practice we can all become *more* competent over time. Therefore, we believe that all people have EI within them and can develop their EI abilities more fully if desired.

A second important question then follows—can EI be measured? Again, many of those in the field believe that it can be. Goleman, Bar-On, and Salovy and Mayer along with their colleague David Caruso have all developed EI (or EQ in the case of Bar-On) assessment instruments. Some of these are self-scoring instruments requiring a high degree of self-insight and honesty, whereas others are 360-feedback designs inviting input from those with whom you work or otherwise interact. See the Resources section of the book for an overview of some of the various EI assessment instruments.

Today many individuals and organizations are doing good work in the field of emotional intelligence research, promotion, and education. We feel that these efforts have significant value both for enhancing the lives of individuals and for contributing to organizational effectiveness. We applaud the work being done and are proud to be a small part of it. We offer this book to you as a launching-off point. Allow *Put Emotional Intelligence to Work* to serve as your introduction to and overview of the concept of emotional intelligence. We hope it provides valuable insight, presents pathways for growth, and provokes you to further exploration both within yourself and ever deeper into the realm of emotional intelligence.

HOW THIS BOOK WILL HELP YOU

The question: *"What is emotional intelligence?"* does not necessarily have a basic answer. We have suggested a simple definition, but in reality emotional intelligence works more like a construct, a comprehensive model that is used to understand how cognition and emotion affect both personal and interpersonal behaviors. *Put Emotional Intelligence to Work* therefore offers these tools:

- It concisely explains the EI model.
- It translates the current EI research into practical, relevant understanding.
- It focuses on the relevance of EI for personal and interpersonal success.
- It offers practical application exercises.
- It teaches the reader how to manage impulsive, unpleasant, and disruptive emotions that often lead to unwanted behaviors.
- It teaches the reader how to tap into self-motivating emotions like confidence, passion, enthusiasm, desire, happiness, and anticipation.
- It demonstrates how emotional intelligence learning applies to influencing people, managing change, dealing with conflict, building teams, and developing others.
- It provides insight into what it means to be an emotionally intelligent leader.

WHO SHOULD READ THIS BOOK?

We have written this book for people who want to develop their own emotional competency and for training, learning, and development professionals who are committed to building emotionally intelligent organizations. This group might include:

- trainers who want to learn more about how to apply emotional intelligence research to practical learning
- organization development professionals
- human resource professionals
- managers who need emotional intelligence training to enhance leadership and coaching skills

- anyone who wants to understand how the various components of emotional intelligence work together to form a comprehensive model of effective living
- anyone who wants to translate the current EI research into practical and relevant applications
- faculty members and school teachers who want to integrate emotional intelligence concepts into their teaching materials.

CHAPTER-BY-CHAPTER HIGHLIGHTS

As trainers, we seek to create opportunities in the training classroom for participants to experience the content we are exploring together. We work hard to take the theories of something like EI and bring them to life through activities and exercises. Through these efforts, we seek to both engage our training participants more deeply in the content as well as to help them to build a bridge of relevancy between these theories and their real lives.

Here now, as we seek to express EI in book form, we find ourselves another step removed from being able to truly bring this content to life and help you, the reader, make a connection to it. To resolve this, at points throughout the book, we lean back on our EI-training-classroom experiences. Every so often in a chapter, you'll come across something called "A Glimpse into the Classroom" in which we tell the story of how we explore one aspect of EI in a training session. We include these little vignettes as a way of helping you "experience" EI as we often present it in the training sessions, allowing you to live vicariously through the classroom-based experience of our training participants. We hope you find these glimpses both interesting and helpful.

Our exploration of emotional intelligence begins with self-awareness. Research supports that self-awareness is foundational to both self-management and social awareness. Self-management and social awareness then determine relationship effectiveness. A summary of the chapter-by-chapter content follows. We begin with self-awareness, move on to self-management, then consider social awareness, and relationship management.

Preface

Chapter 1. Emotional Intelligence: The New Science of Success

This chapter introduces the concept of emotional intelligence, examines why it is important to success, and explores EI basics.

Chapter 2. Emotional Self-Awareness

This chapter defines self-awareness as an effortful activity that includes not only recognition of emotional states, but also an awareness of why the emotion is present and an acceptance of the emotion as a source of helpful feedback.

Chapter 3. Confidence, Self-Esteem, and Peak Performance

A component of self-awareness includes an awareness of one's personal strengths, self-worth, capabilities, and even purpose in life. This chapter shows how your confidence and self-esteem are developed through a healthy and accurate assessment of your true giftedness.

If self-awareness provides us with accurate feedback, then self-management is our response to that feedback. Chapters 4, 5, and 6 focus on self-management.

Chapter 4. The Anatomy of an Emotion

The first step to managing your emotions is to understand why emotions can often be so impulsive, reactive, and disruptive. This chapter explains how the brain processes emotions and that you have the ability to use your unique human intelligence to manage disruptive emotions proactively.

Chapter 5. Cognitive and Behavioral Strategies for Managing Your Emotions

This chapter explores both cognitive and behavioral strategies for managing disruptive emotions.

Chapter 6. Achieving Goals and Overcoming Adversity

Part of managing emotions includes learning how to tap into emotional energy and employ it in the direction of achieving goals. This chapter discusses the kind of emotional energy that we all want to leverage—enthusiasm, motivation, passion, desire, and optimism.

Chapters 7 to 10 move us from the personal competencies of self-awareness and self-management to the social competencies of social awareness and relationship management.

Chapter 7. Social Awareness

Perhaps the most important skill to developing effective interpersonal relationships is empathy. This chapter explains why empathy is so important, how to do it well, and how to avoid some common pitfalls surrounding it.

Chapter 8. EI and Workplace Issues

Relationship management is where your self-awareness, self-management, and social awareness get put to the test. This chapter explains how emotional intelligence helps you deal with the potentially more emotional challenges of work life—navigating change, resolving conflict, and interacting with teams.

Chapter 9. Emotional Intelligence and Influence

Influence is the result of a kind of emotional energy that occurs between two or more people who resonate with one another. This chapter explores the concept of resonant leadership and how to create resonance in your interpersonal relationships.

Chapter 10. Putting It All Together—Your EI Plan of Action

This chapter provides a framework for clarifying your intentions concerning growth and development of your emotional intelligence and offers a structure for creating an action plan for implementing your development goals.

In addition, the book includes an Additional Resources section that lists many sources to support your further exploration and continued growth and development of your emotional intelligence.

HOW THIS BOOK CAN HELP YOU TO *EQUIP YOURSELF* FOR SUCCESS

Emotional intelligence is something we all have within us. We have no doubt that you are already strong in certain aspects of EI. We also have no doubt that there are elements of emotional intelligence that you need to be reminded of and in which you could focus some energy toward becoming more secure. That's what your journey through this book and this work is all about. Our challenge to you as you turn these pages and engage this exploration is this:

- Recognize, acknowledge, and celebrate your strengths with regard to EI. Leverage these gifts to their fullest potential.
- Identify areas of EI in which you need to grow. Focus some energy on this by putting in place an action plan for development in these areas.

We need to add the disclaimer that when you've turned the last page of this text and set this book aside fully read, you will not necessarily be more emotionally intelligent than you were when you began reading. Sorry, it just doesn't work that way! Leveraging, honing, and improving the skills of EI requires practice and focused effort. It requires real-world application and cannot be gained by simply reading "How to . . . "

We can promise that when you finish this book, you'll know what EI looks like, you'll understand why it's critical to your success in life. You will have some foundation for applying and growing it as needed. At that point, we'll have done our job; the rest is up to you.

ACKNOWLEDGMENTS

We dedicate this book to our spouses, Kristin Alexander, and Jessica Mulle. Their support and encouragement gave us the emotional nourishment we needed to complete this book even when we both had too many irons in the fire. We also thank our colleague and friend, Bruce Christopher, who was in Room 10 with us when we first started this journey.

Chapter 1

Emotional Intelligence: The New Science of Success

.... **In this chapter, you will learn** ....

- ◆ why emotional intelligence is so important for success
- ◆ the definition and components of emotional intelligence
- ◆ the basic framework for discussing emotional intelligence in this book
- ◆ how this book can help you *EQuip Yourself* for success.

Jimmy's mom glanced at his report card and frowned. "Look at these grades! Do you realize that this is going into your permanent school record?" The dreaded parental warning played over and over again in Jimmy's 10-year-old mind. "Have I really just blown my opportunity to be successful in life?" he wondered.

Do you recall your school report cards? If you attended grammar school before the 1980s you likely would not have received quarterly progress updates via the electronic, computer-generated version so familiar today. Certainly grades for each course were issued, but they were handwritten in black, blue, or red ink. The long journey home from school even found some youngsters frantically trying to find the right color ink, so that the C in Social Studies could be converted into a B, or possibly even an A. Of course the hope was to avoid whatever the inevitable punishment was going to be for achieving grades lower than expected. Unfortunately, these report cards contained something much more difficult for these children to deal with, something that no one could change or avoid—the teacher's comments scrawled in the margins of the report.

Who knew then, that the most important predictor of young Jimmy's success had little to do with the grade itself, but was more a factor of those handwritten notes in the margin?

> Jimmy plays well with all the students and is the most popular boy in school. He is a natural leader. Unfortunately, he is using his popularity to influence other children to stay late on the playground during lunch, instead of coming to math class on time. His grade in math has slipped to a "C."

If Jimmy was slightly more precocious and allowed to get away with it, he could turn to his parents and say, "Did you know that getting along well with others is a component of emotional intelligence, which research shows is more important for success than my 4th grade math scores?"

Unfortunately, Jimmy can't quite pull that off, and his low grade in math may lead him to be grounded from playing with his friends for a few days. The truth is that the life skills Jimmy learns on the playground are just as important as his academic training in helping him to successfully achieve his goals and get what he wants out of life. When Jimmy is older and enters the workforce, he will discover that a basic level of technical skill and academic achievement are necessary to get his "foot in the door." He will realize that in some ways school never ends. *All* employees are expected to develop expertise by learning and improving on the job. But beyond these basic, *threshold* requirements, the crucial skills that are necessary for his achievement and success are all related to *emotional intelligence* (Goleman, 1998):

- ♦ listening and oral communication
- ♦ adaptability and creative responses to setbacks and obstacles

- personal management, confidence, motivation to work toward goals, a sense of wanting to develop one's career and take pride in accomplishments
- group and interpersonal effectiveness, cooperation, and teamwork; ability to negotiate disagreements
- effectiveness in the organization, wanting to make a contribution, leadership potential.

Daniel Goleman (1998), who has conducted studies in over 200 large companies, says: "The research shows that for jobs of all kinds, *emotional intelligence is twice as important* an ingredient of outstanding performance as ability and technical skill combined. The higher you go in the organization, the more important these qualities are for success. When it comes to leadership, they are almost everything."

Emotional intelligence then, is the *x-factor* that separates average performers from outstanding performers. It separates those who know themselves well and take personal responsibility for their actions from those who lack self-awareness and repeat the same mistakes over and over. It separates those who can manage their emotions and motivate themselves from those who are overwhelmed by their emotions and let their emotional impulses control their behaviors. It separates those who are good at connecting with others and creating positive relationships from those who seem insensitive and uncaring. It separates those who build rapport, have influence, and collaborate effectively with others from those who are demanding, lack empathy, and are therefore difficult to work with. Above all, emotional intelligence separates those who are successful at managing their emotional energy and navigating through life from those who find themselves in emotional wreckage, derailed, and sometimes even disqualified from the path to success.

EMOTIONAL INTELLIGENCE: THE DIFFERENCE BETWEEN SUCCESS AND DERAILMENT

Two stories will be presented. One ends successfully; the other does not. Both of these stories represent emotionally charged situations in which the primary difference between one's success and the other's derailment is *emotional intelligence*. In each situation, emotional arousal offers two possible outcomes:

Success = Being aware of your emotions and managing them so your behaviors are intelligently and proactively driven, resulting in intentional and successful outcomes.

Derailment = Losing control of your emotions so your behaviors are impulsively and reactively driven, resulting in unintended and potentially costly outcomes.

A Success Story

Sarah was 22 years old and had somewhat limited business experience. She was now living on her own, so finding a job (and a source of income) was very important to her. After a series of four interviews for an inside sales and customer service position with a new company, she finally got the call that offered her the position. In her own words she describes the experience:

"I was very excited! This was a new industry in an area of computer technology I was unfamiliar with. It would be an exciting new challenge. Five days before my official start date, I unexpectedly received a plane ticket in the mail from the CEO of the company. I contacted him and asked what it was regarding and was told he would like me to go to Washington, D.C., and assist him with selling the company's computer software at a major tradeshow.

"Initially, I was taken aback with the proposition. I had never met the CEO. I hadn't yet set foot in the office to do even a minute of training. I had no idea how to sell software I had never seen . . . much less fly to D.C. and sell it there!

"I was nervous. My emotions were telling me to figure out some way to avoid this trip. My gut feeling, however, told me that my decision to go on this trip as requested would set the tone for the rest of my career with this company. It would also establish the CEO's perception of me. Despite feeling scared and quite unprepared for this role, I determined to make the best of it and told the CEO I would be happy to assist him.

"I only had four days to get ready and did not even own a decent business suit. I was on a very limited budget, so I went to a thrift shop to look for an appropriate business outfit. I found the perfect suit. Then I went to the dollar store and found some fake jewelry that looked real enough. I put it all together and managed to look very professional for less than $15.

"When the big day arrived, I flew to D.C. Taking my first taxi ever, I headed downtown to one of the most upscale hotels in Washington. Feeling way out of my league, I checked in and called the CEO to let him know I had arrived. We met at a restaurant in the lobby of the hotel. He was tall and dressed perfectly. My impression was that he set high standards for how he expected others to look. He was professional, friendly, and extremely intelligent. I could tell immediately that he had a low tolerance for incompetence.

"We had a nice dinner meeting, but he offered little in the way of training or information about what I was expected to do. As our dinner ended, he handed me a folder that contained information about the products I would be selling the next morning. It was 11 p.m. I was exhausted and had to go right to bed without time to look over the materials.

"The show started at 7:30 a.m. and I was up at 5 a.m. to give myself enough time to get ready. With little time to spare, I propped up the papers he gave me in front of the bathroom mirror and managed to study the materials while blow-drying my hair! I did the best I could to learn about the software and its features, compatibility issues, technical support solutions, and other details. I relieved some of my nervousness by reminding myself that the CEO would be there to work with me.

"When we met in the tradeshow hall, there were several thousand professionals ready to ask us questions. As it turned out, there would be no "us." The CEO said I would have to run the show on my own because he had to attend meetings all day. In that moment, I actually wanted to cry! I had no idea what I was doing, and these people all wanted answers.

"By about mid-morning, I began to feel more confident. My crash course with hairdryer in hand turned out to be very helpful. Most of the tradeshow attendees showed understanding if I didn't have an exact answer to their questions, and accepted my offer to follow-up with them later.

"At the end of the day when my new boss came back, I was full of smiles. I was proud of myself for all of the accomplishments—arriving, quickly learning the job, and actually selling some software! He inquired, "How did it go?" "Excellent," I replied. "I did great and we made a lot of money!" His face lit up and he was eager to hear the details. I told him that I sold a $200 piece of software. His face formed a funny smile, the way a parent smiles when a child does something wrong but is too cute to reprimand.

"Now, 10 years later with the same company, I know that $200 for a day is a terrible show. The goal is about $5,000 a day. But in my blissfully ignorant excitement, the CEO was too nice to burst my bubble. It was the foundation for a wonderful 10 years at his company. I am now Director of Operations and oversee a multimillion-dollar business.

"I learned many lessons from that experience in Washington, D.C. Perhaps the most important being that no matter who you are, stretching outside your comfort zone is a formula for success and confidence. Even if I had failed (which in terms of sales numbers I did), I would always be proud that I got on the plane and with a positive, optimistic attitude tried my best! Doing so then and since has ultimately led to a level of achievement I had only imagined."

A Derailment Story

Ron Artest Jr. was born and raised in the largest public housing development in the United States, the Queensbridge Projects of Long Island City, New York. His success in basketball provided him with his ticket out of the projects. After becoming an NCAA All-American in 1999, he joined the professional ranks, and by 2004, was considered one of the best defensive players in the National Basketball Association. In fact, he was voted the NBA's Defensive Player of the Year for the 2003-2004 basketball season. Unfortunately for Artest, his on-court success has often been be overshadowed by his reputation for having a short fuse.

On November 19, 2004, Artest took center stage in arguably the most infamous brawl in professional sports history. With less than a minute left in the game, Artest's Indianapolis Pacers were well on their way to victory with an insurmountable 97-82 lead over the Detroit Pistons. The brawl began when Artest fouled Piston's Ben Wallace. A frustrated Wallace, upset at being fouled so hard when the game was effectively over, responded by shoving Artest hard with both hands, accidentally hitting him in the nose. A number of Pacers and Pistons squared off, but Artest actually walked away from the fracas and lay on the scorer's table in order to calm himself down. At this point *cooler heads could have prevailed*, but Wallace continued to instigate. He walked over to the scorer's table and threw his armband at Artest. One of the Piston's fans followed suit by throwing a cup full of ice and liquid that hit Artest on the chest and in the face.

One could argue that Artest was *provoked*. In his own words, Artest said: "I . . . was lying down when I got hit with a liquid, ice and glass container on my chest and on my face. After that it was self defense." In self-defense mode, Artest snapped to attention and jumped into the front-row seats, confronting the man he believed to be responsible. But in the chaos of the moment, he actually confronted the wrong man. The situation quickly erupted into a brawl between Piston's fans and several of the Indiana Pacer players. Artest returned to the basketball court, where he managed to deck a Piston's fan, who apparently was taunting him. The mayhem ended with Detroit fans throwing chairs, food, and other debris at the Indianapolis players while they walked back to their locker room.

In the aftermath, each participant could easily replay the blow-by-blow details that explained and even provoked each successive act of aggression. A flagrant foul provoked a push, a soda-and-ice shower, and some name-calling. A push, a soda-and-ice shower, and some name-calling provoked a brawl in the stands and a fan getting punched. Maybe on some level of playground justice, everybody got what he deserved; perhaps all of the impulsive, uncontrolled emotional behaviors should cancel each other out. After all, it is much easier to critique the actions of others than it is to actually do the right thing in the heat of battle. In moments of honesty we all must admit times when our emotions have unraveled us. It hardly seems fair to single out one player or fan's lack of self-control as being more egregious than the next.

The NBA, however, has rules, and the brawl became a classic case of *two wrongs do not make a right*. Players are expected to use emotional self-control and rational behavior to maintain the immutable boundary that separates the fans from the court. Given this expectation, the list of guilty participants was indeed extensive. But when the penalties were finally doled out, Artest's penalty was the most severe because of his past history of losing control. He was suspended for 73 games plus playoff appearances, the longest nondrug- or gambling-related suspension in NBA history. NBA Commissioner, David Stern, administered the penalty, stating: "I did not strike from my mind the fact that Ron Artest had been suspended on previous conditions for loss of self-control."

Regardless of how harsh or unfair this penalty may seem, it serves as a poignant reminder to those who are interested in the field of emotional intelligence. Unmanaged emotional behaviors can be very costly and can derail you from fulfilling your true intentions.

Not only did Ron Artest confront the wrong guy, at the wrong time, and in the wrong way, but that one impulsive act turned out to be tremendously costly. Financially, the suspension cost him $5 million in salary as well as potential endorsement earnings. Emotionally, the suspension cost him an opportunity to compete for a possible NBA championship with a team that might have made it to the finals.

> **Guiding Principle**
>
> *Unmanaged emotional behaviors can be very costly and can derail you from fulfilling your true intentions.*

In our success story, Sarah not only recognized the affect that her feelings of anxiety, fear, and insecurity were having on her, but she also managed these emotions in a way that helped her to gain confidence as well as valuable experience in her new job. Had anxiety taken control, she might have missed her flight, offered excuses, pretended that there was a death in her family, or created any number of other reasons for avoiding the very thing that she needed to do in order to be successful.

In our derailment story, Ron Artest actually did recognize that he was agitated and tried to manage his emotions by resting on the scorer's table. This worked until a fan threw a drink on him. Artest defended his actions by claiming self-defense, but there is one significant flaw to this argument—*being hit in the face with a cold liquid is not really a severe threat.* In fact, many coaches can testify that they have safelysurvived being doused by an entire bucket of ice-cold liquid. There was actually a lesson to learn from this incident and a much more emotionally intelligent way for Artest to have handled this situation. He could have continued to manage his anger and then ask security personnel to escort the offender out of the stadium. Perhaps this alone would have been sufficient to satisfy his anger, but if his anger required even more justice, then he still had the option of pressing charges in a court of law.

There are at least two significant differences between these two stories. First, it is more difficult to manage your emotions when someone is deliberately hostile or offensive as opposed to when someone is simply challenging you to step outside of your comfort zone. Second, there will always be a healthy debate about how ethically right or wrong it is to lose control of your emotions in certain situations. In fact, there is often understanding, not punishment, when you lose control of your emotions because a projectile is thrown at you. At any rate, this book is not concerned with either difference. In other words, it makes sense to live your life in an emotionally intelligent way: *No matter how intensely difficult it may be to manage your emotions in certain*

> **Guiding Principle**
>
> *Out-of-control emotions can have a tremendous affect on your performance, on how others perceive you, and on how those in power ultimately judge you.*

situations, and no matter how justified you believe it is to lose control of your emotions in certain situations.

Out-of-control emotions can have a tremendous affect on your performance, on how others perceive you, and on how those in power ultimately judge you. The more successful outcome is accomplished when emotional intelligence is applied. This book, then, is all about understanding how to develop into a more fully emotionally intelligent person. In the coming chapters we will guide you through an exploration of the important competencies that are reflected in all emotionally intelligent behavior.

COMPONENTS OF EMOTIONAL INTELLIGENCE

Describing an emotionally intelligent person is like describing a wonderful teacher, an effective counselor, or a successful politician. An entire range of qualities, skills, and behaviors need to be delineated to fully comprehend what the individual is really all about. After all, emotional intelligence, like teaching, politics, or counseling, is *a way of being*. Concise definitions are possible, but not adequate. We have concisely defined emotional intelligence as:

Using your emotions intelligently to gain the performance you wish to see within yourself and to achieve interpersonal effectiveness with others.

This definition is sufficient as a starting point for understanding EI, as long as one places special emphasis on each component of the definition. *Emotional intelligence* therefore is

- ◆ *Using your emotions*—implies both awareness of and the ability to manage your emotions.
- ◆ Using your emotions *intelligently*—implies that you can consciously reflect on your emotions and then choose appropriate responses.
- ◆ *To gain the performance you wish to see within yourself*—implies that our emotional energy can serve a special purpose in both motivating and helping us to achieve our goals.
- ◆ *To achieve interpersonal effectiveness with others*—implies that our intelligence and sensitivity about emotions can help us achieve better results when relating to others.

There is both a personal and interpersonal or social component to emotional intelligence. Daniel Goleman, Richard Boyatzis, and Annie McKee (2002) have introduced a model for understanding emotional intelligence that divides personal and social competence into four basic domains. The first two domains are *self-awareness* and *self-management*. These domains relate to personal competence. The second two domains are *social awareness* and *relationship management*. These domains relate to social competence. According to this model, each domain contains a set of behaviors that can be developed in order for one to become more emotionally intelligent (see Figure 1-1).

UNDERSTANDING AND GROWING YOUR OWN EI

This four-domain model of understanding emotional intelligence will serve as a basic framework for how emotional intelligence is discussed in

EI	**Personal Competence (Self)**	**Social Competence (Others)**
Recognition	**Self-Awareness** • Emotional Self-Awareness • Accurate Self-Assessment • Self-Confidence	**Social Awareness** • Empathy • Organizational Awareness • Service Orientation
Regulation	**Self-Management** • Emotional Self-Control • Transparency • Adaptability • Achievement • Initiative • Optimism	**Relationship Management** • Developing Others • Inspirational Leadership • Influence • Change Catalyst • Conflict Management • Teamwork & Collaboration

Figure 1-1. Goleman, Boyatzis, and McKee's four domains of emotional intelligence; each domain contains a set of emotional competencies.

this book. Each chapter provides a topic that aligns with one of these four domains. At the end of each chapter is a section entitled **EQuip Yourself**, which includes strategies, applications, and exercises designed to further your development and growth.

These four domains of emotional intelligence do not stand alone, independent of one another. Rather, they are interdependent, fitting together like puzzle pieces to present a complete portrait of what an emotionally intelligent person looks like. Emotional intelligence is therefore a comprehensive model that is used to understand how cognitions and emotions affect both personal and interpersonal behaviors. The development of emotional intelligence requires an integration of the competencies and behaviors that make up each domain of this model (see Figure 1-2). As you read this book, many of the examples and illustrations will demonstrate how the integration of all four domains is necessary to achieve an emotionally intelligent whole.

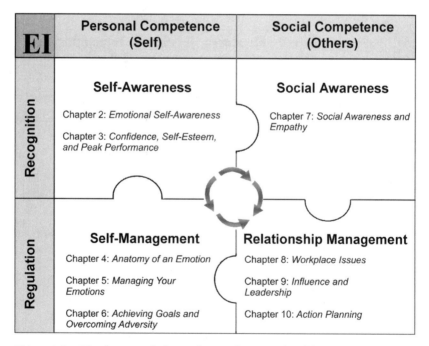

Figure 1-2. The framework for understanding emotional intelligence.
Self-awareness affects self-management and social awareness; self-management and social awareness affect relationship management.

Chapter 2

Emotional Self-Awareness

.... **In this chapter, you will learn** ....

+ how self-awareness forms the foundation of emotional intelligence
+ a definition of emotional self-awareness
+ how to move from self-awareness to self-management
+ first steps toward enhancing your emotional self-awareness
+ how to *EQuip Yourself* for self-awareness.

Self-awareness is the foundational skill of emotional intelligence. It is the base from which all other EI competencies arise. Self-awareness means tuning in to what's going on with you emotionally: recognizing and acknowledging your emotional state. Without an awareness of your emotions, you cannot begin to harness their power toward your hoped-for outcome in any situation. Without an awareness of your emotions, your EI is nonexistent.

As mentioned in the Preface, throughout this text, occasionally we are going to be inviting you into our classroom experience as trainers of EI,

Guiding Principle

Self-awareness is the foundational skill of emotional intelligence. Without an awareness of your emotions, your EI is nonexistent.

allowing you to live vicariously through those who have joined us for training in this content. Imagine yourself sitting there with us, exploring this material with a group of other interested participants and consider how the discussion of these EI discoveries unfolds.

A Glimpse into the Classroom: Self-Awareness

"So, how are you feeling today?" We ask this of the group of participants gathered in the classroom. A simple question and yet they stare back at us blankly. They're not used to this question, often posed so superficially, being asked with the expectation of an actual thoughtful response. We anticipated this and have come prepared. We refer them to a chart of funny faces, each expressing a different emotion. "Find the face that best captures your emotional state at this moment and put a circle around it." With some reluctance, the group gets busy tuning in to their emotional self-awareness.

Two or so minutes tick by and the participants are starting to share their responses. Marjorie says that she feels hopeful. "Great! What are you hopeful about?" She's hopeful that this course will offer some meaning and value to her, that it will help her assess her EI skills. Bill shares that he's feeling a little anxious today. "Anxious, huh? How come?" He paints a picture of the pile of work he needs to get done in preparation for an important presentation at the end of the week. James raises a somewhat reluctant hand and tells us all that he's feeling a little suspicious this morning. "Suspicious?" we respond. "That's an interesting one. Tell us more." He talks about the email he received last week from his boss telling him, without further explanation, that he had been registered for this course. He says he's not sure why he's here. Perhaps a little more work in self-awareness will help James connect with why his boss wanted him to attend our course.

So how are *you* feeling?

Go on, answer the question for yourself right now. How are you feeling at this moment as you sit with your nose in this book? What emotional state would you describe for yourself?

Notice that in the Glimpse into the Classroom exercise on self-awareness, we asked not only what people were feeling but also why they were feeling it. The second part of this question is very important. It's not enough to simply label your emotional state and then go about your business. Recognizing what you feel is just the starting point of self-awareness. This recognition is only useful when you take it to deeper levels where you are

- ◆ seeking to understand your emotions
- ◆ identifying where your emotions are coming from
- ◆ uncovering the drivers of your emotions
- ◆ recognizing the effect your emotions are having on your performance.

For some people, self-awareness comes easily. There are those who just seem to have a natural connection with their emotional selves and are tuned in to the ever-shifting emotional currents that run through their bodies. Then there are those who truly struggle to connect with their emotional states. They have to focus significant energy to uncover the emotions that lie within. Which way does it tend to be for you?

Whether you are someone who struggles with tuning in to your own emotional state or someone who does so naturally and finds it difficult to understand why everyone around you seems so disconnected, bear in mind that true self-awareness is not an easy thing to pull off. We live in a culture that values outward action (often in the form of reaction) but places little emphasis on the reflection required for self-attunement. The speed of our lives rarely allows for introspection. Even when we happen on quiet moments, we are often too exhausted from maintaining our frenetic pace to put them to good, self-reflective use.

Consider This

Jeff's father-in-law, who serves as an executive in a large federal agency, seems to carve out some self-reflective time while mowing circles on his riding lawnmower. For years his family has encouraged him to let the grass grow into a meadow to save all the time associated with mowing. His reluctance to do so seems to stem less from his love of a finely manicured lawn than from the value he derives from some time to simply be inside his own head. Where are the self-reflective opportunities in your life? Perhaps you think in the shower, while driving, during your fitness routine, while drinking your early-morning coffee. How do you make these times sacred and maximize the introspective opportunity they present?

DEFINING SELF-AWARENESS

Psychologists John Mayer and Peter Salovey are often credited with coining the term "emotional intelligence" (Salovey & Mayer, 1990). In a series of articles written in the early 1990s, Mayer and Salovey defined self-awareness as an understanding of both your moods and your thoughts about your moods. In addition, they emphasized that this awareness contributes not only to better decision making but also relates to your ability to understand and interact effectively with others.

Mayer and Salovey's work was built on and popularized by Daniel Goleman in his book *Emotional Intelligence: Why It Can Matter More Than IQ* (1995). Goleman supports Mayer and Salovey's core definition of self-awareness, but he also broadens the definition to include accurate self-assessment and self-confidence. Goleman's definition of self-awareness therefore includes three basic competencies:

1. *Emotional self-awareness*: Reading one's own emotions and recognizing the potential impact of those emotions upon individual performance.

2. *Accurate self-assessment:* Knowing one's individual strengths and limits.

3. *Self-confidence:* A sound sense of one's self-worth and capabilities.

In the next chapter, where we explore self-esteem and confidence, we will highlight those aspects of self-awareness that connect with Goleman's competencies of accurate self-assessment and self-confidence. But for our purposes here, we are defining self-awareness in its simplest form, remaining true to the core of self-awareness as defined by Mayer and Salovey, Goleman, and others.

Emotional Self-Awareness

Emotional self-awareness requires that you recognize and tune in to your emotional state and go beyond mere recognition of your emotions to a deeper exploration of why you are experiencing that emotion.

FROM SELF-AWARENESS TO SELF-MANAGEMENT

This definition of self-awareness clarifies the importance of going beyond mere recognition of your emotions to a deeper exploration of why the emotion is present. It is this analysis that offers the true value of being self-aware. Recognition coupled with understanding leads to choice. You cannot manage emotions you are not aware of or do not fully understand. When you understand your emotions, a pathway begins to develop that leads from self-awareness to self-management. There are four stepping-stones along this pathway: attunement, understanding, acceptance, and attending.

Attunement: Your ability to tune in to your emotional state at any given moment. This would be like having a Doppler radar view of your inner weather systems.

Understanding: Your ability to unearth the root of a recognized emotional state, to come to know objectively why you are feeling the way you are.

Acceptance: Your willingness to accept whatever emotions—good, bad, or ugly—you discover within yourself. These emotions arose for one reason or another; denying or repressing them is not going to serve you.

Attending: Your ability and willingness to give your emotions a voice, to express them in an appropriate way. This ability falls under the realm of emotional self-management, which we will explore in greater depth a bit later.

SELF-AWARENESS AND PERFORMANCE

American Express Financial Advisors is often touted as one of the early adopters of emotional intelligence training as a performance tool. In the early 1990s, just as researchers were beginning to look into and publish articles about EI, AmEx discovered that they had a problem getting their financial advisors to sell life insurance policies successfully, even to those clients whose financial plans clearly called for it. Now, life insurance is one of those issues fraught with emotion to begin with, but AmEx's challenge lay not in overcoming the emotions expressed by their clients, but rather with the emotions the AmEx financial advisors were experiencing themselves.

When the issue of sluggish sales of life insurance policies reached the desk of a high-level executive at American Express's insurance arm, he commissioned a team to look into the root cause. It turns out that client emotions did play a role in the sluggish sale of life insurance policies, but not in the way one might think. This was a classic case of Freudian countertransference! Heightened client emotions caused by the thought of purchasing life insurance policies transferred to sympathetic emotional responses among American Express's financial advisors. These emotional responses in turn made it difficult for advisors to sell policies. Advisors reported feeling shameful, guilty, untruthful, and at times, unethical when they encouraged clients to purchase policies from them. These emotions, often lurking beneath the surface during client interactions, compromised the financial advisors' effectiveness in selling life insurance.

But not all financial advisors at AmEx were experiencing difficulties in selling life insurance. A small cadre of advisors seemed to be consistently successful in closing sales. Why were these financial advisors effective when so many of their colleagues were not? In the end, it all came down to self-awareness. Interviews with these successful advisors revealed that they had developed strategies for being aware of and managing the potentially derailing internal emotions that may emerge during a client interaction. Armed with this insight, AmEx launched a series of experimental training, some of the first corporate training targeting the development of emotional competencies. This training focused primarily on competencies related to self-awareness and self-management skills. At the end of the first round of training, 90 percent of the participants reported a significant improvement in sales performance.

Consider This

Both authors are fans of the popular 1990s sitcom *Seinfeld*. If you're familiar with the show, you'll recall that the character named George is something of a loser. A self-described short, stocky, bald man who is often unemployed and lives with his parents, things just never quite go his way. In one episode, George comes to the realization that every decision he has made has been wrong, every instinct he has leads to failure. In this depressing but shining moment of self-awareness, George commits to doing the opposite of whatever it is he would normally do. Suddenly things begin to turn around for George—he gets a pretty girl, he lands his dream job with the New York Yankees, he finds a plum apartment. His new-found success is the direct result of having tuned in to his self-awareness, recognizing a behavioral pattern that was getting in his way (in his case, following his own self-defeating instincts), and committing to make a change. If it can work for George, it can work for you as well. What behavioral pattern do you need to become more aware of and perhaps seek to change?

Guiding Principle

Building self-awareness begins with the commitment to do so.

FIRST STEPS TOWARD SELF-AWARENESS

Think of all that you do that is affected by your emotional state: your decision-making, your actions, and your interactions. Indeed, as pointed out with the AmEx experience, your overall performance and often your very success are outcomes of your emotional responses and your ability to manage them effectively. This, of course, highlights the point we're trying to make here: Emotional self-awareness is critical to your capacity for seeking successful, joyful, fulfilled lives.

So what do you do if you come to realize that you're not very good at this self-awareness thing? If you recognize that self-awareness is an area in which you need to grow, a skill you need to develop more fully, how exactly do you do that?

The first step to building self-awareness, as is the case with any challenging journey, is to make a commitment. Understand that self-awareness is not easy. Taking a good, hard, honest look inside can be scary and sometimes downright painful. There may be a lot of self-denial to overcome, a lot of excuses to wade through, before you reach your true, rock-bottom self. And of course, once there, when in touch with your unfiltered self, if you find something you know needs to change, well, then there's only more hard work ahead. We believe it's an important and worthwhile journey despite these challenges. Ultimately, the decision to make this effort rests with you, and the commitment to doing so is yours alone to make.

Consider This

I have two lights in my bathroom at home. One is a vanity light—a row of bright bulbs located directly above the mirror over the sink. The other, dimmer and a bit amber from the tint of the glass in the fixture, is positioned on the ceiling more toward the middle of the room. When I evaluate my appearance in the bathroom mirror, I can see different results based on which light I turn on. I like the view I get with the ceiling-mounted fixture. Its dimmer, amber light shining from behind me fails to reveal certain details of my appearance that I often prefer to overlook . . . a middle-aged spreading of my body, some lines starting to form on my face, a slightly receding hairline, and so forth. In this light, I look slimmer, more fit, and the amber tint creates the illusion of a glow I associate with being healthy. When I want to see what I really look like, I turn to the bright, harsh truth of the vanity light and brace myself for a dose of reality.

How honest is the light you shine on yourself?

People in our courses often suggest that there is no time for self-awareness in their lives. They say they'd like to do it and they understand the importance of it, but they just can't fit it in. That's a bit of a cop out, especially given that self-awareness doesn't really require all that much time. No one spends hours sitting around being self-aware. It's one of those things that can be built into the small, spare moments of your busy day.

EQuip Yourself
with Self-Awareness

If you are committed to deepening your self-awareness, here are some techniques to try.

Set an awareness trigger.

- Set a watch alarm or use your email program to send yourself a note a handful of times through the day. When the alarm goes off, or when the email chimes in your in-box, it's time to check in with your self-awareness.

+ Ask yourself two simple questions: How am I feeling? Why am I feeling it?

+ Tune in to your emotion in the moment and decide if it's serving you well. Choose what to do with it, if anything.

+ Build awareness into the free moments in your day, between the day's events. Use the time you spend commuting. Take a quick stroll following lunch. (One of the authors has a coaching client who has created some self-reflective time by spending an extra minute or two sitting in the stall after using the bathroom. At least it's relatively safe from interruption!)

Reflect on behaviors instead of emotions.

+ Connect with your emotions through the back door of your external behaviors. Some people really struggle to connect with what's going on with them emotionally, so digging around inside of themselves may not work so well at first. Because behaviors are driven by emotions, you can practice connecting with your emotions by reflecting on your behaviors.

+ Imagine being followed around by someone with a video camera who is capturing on tape all of your actions and interactions through the day. Now imagine that at the end of each day, you get to sit and watch the tape. You'd be observing your own behaviors through the course of the day's events, and in the viewing, you'd be able to reconnect with the emotion you were experiencing at each point along the way.

+ Rewind the mental video you have of yourself and your interactions through the day and reflect on that. Use your calendar and computer to remind you of the meetings you had, the phone calls you made, the emails you sent.

+ Notice emotional patterns or identify events or people that trigger certain emotional responses in you. Even the simple act of connecting to your emotions, albeit in the past tense, provides you practice in doing so, practice that eventually will allow you to become more emotionally self-aware in the moment.

Keep a self-awareness log.

+ Chart your emotions using a notebook, your computer, or perhaps on a large, wall-mounted calendar. Not only does this technique push you to tune in and connect with your emotions at least once a day, but it also provides you with a map or historical reference of your emotional journeys, a record that could offer interesting insight over time.
+ Ask yourself: What mood do you awake with? How does it change through the day? What causes it to change?

Go to the balcony.

+ See yourself as if looking down from a balcony over a stage. From this vantage point, you are able to be a momentary observer of what is happening both around you and within you.
+ Use a few quick questions to help you connect, tune in, and choose appropriate action: "What's the situation down there?" "What am I feeling about that situation?" "How are those feelings supporting or getting in the way of what I want in this situation?"

Develop your feeling vocabulary.

+ Use the list of feelings in Table 2-1 to help you identify and describe what you are feeling.
+ Rate the intensity of your feeling. The feeling words on the table are ordered in intensity from lowest to highest.
+ Exercise precision in describing your emotional state to help fine-tune your emotional self-awareness.

Table 2-1. Words that Express Feelings

Mad:	Sad:	Glad:	Afraid:	Confused:	Ashamed:
Bothered	Down	At ease	Uneasy	Curious	Uncomfort-
Ruffled	Blue	Secure	Apprehensive	Uncertain	able
Irritated	Somber	Comfortable	Careful	Ambivalent	Awkward
Displeased	Low	Relaxed	Cautious	Doubtful	Clumsy
Annoyed	Glum	Contented	Hesitant	Unsettled	Self-conscious
Steamed	Lonely	Optimistic	Tense	Hesitant	Disconcerted
Irked	Disappointed	Satisfied	Anxious	Perplexed	Chagrinned
Perturbed	Worn out	Refreshed	Nervous	Puzzled	Abashed
Frustrated	Melancholy	Stimulated	Edgy	Muddled	Embarrassed
Angry	Down-	Pleased	Distressed	Distracted	Flustered
Fed up	hearted	Warm	Scared	Flustered	Sorry
Disgusted	Unhappy	Snug	Frightened	Jumbled	Apologetic
Indignant	Dissatisfied	Happy	Repulsed	Unfocused	Ashamed
Ticked off	Gloomy	Encouraged	Agitated	Fragmented	Regretful
Bristling	Mournful	Tickled	Afraid	Dismayed	Remorseful
Fuming	Grieved	Proud	Shocked	Insecure	Guilty
Explosive	Depressed	Cheerful	Alarmed	Dazed	Disgusted
Enraged	Lousy	Thrilled	Overwhelmed	Bewildered	Belittled
Irate	Crushed	Delighted	Frantic	Lost	Humiliated
Incensed	Defeated	Joyful	Panic stricken	Stunned	Violated
Burned up	Dejected	Elated	Horrified	Chaotic	Dirty
Outraged	Empty	Exhilarated	Petrified	Torn	Mortified
Furious	Wretched	Overjoyed	Terrified	Baffled	Defiled
Blind rage	Despairing	Ecstatic	Numb	Dumb-	Devastated
	Devastated			founded	Degraded

Chapter 3

Confidence, Self-Esteem, and Peak Performance

.... **In this chapter, you will learn** ....

- ◆ how self-awareness relates to confidence and self-esteem
- ◆ how to live above and beyond your job description
- ◆ how to develop your self-awareness using the Johari Window
- ◆ the importance of feedback in developing your self-esteem
- ◆ how to *EQuip Yourself* to develop your confidence and self-esteem.

Last chapter's discussion on self-awareness focused on the importance of understanding your emotions and the impact that your emotions can have on your behaviors. There is, however, a deeper, existential level of self-awareness that has to do with the discovery of the very purpose, meaning, and value of your life. The emotions of confidence, self-esteem, capability, efficacy, and potentiality continually well up and flow from this deepest level of self-awareness. Let's begin our exploration into this level of self-awareness by visiting the classroom and answering a simple little riddle.

◆

A Glimpse into the Classroom: Confidence

What is it?

When it is present I tend to move forward.

When it is lacking I tend to move backward.

What is it?

The first slide in our PowerPoint presentation asks the audience for a one-word answer. Several participants respond with "desire," "motivation," "skills," even "love." All of these answers are possible, but we are looking for a different answer. Finally someone responds with the word we are fishing for: "Confidence."

◆

Confidence can be defined as an inner belief in one's purpose, ability, and self-worth. People who are confident are convinced that their lives count for something and that they have something of tremendous value and significance to offer the world. Confidence is one of the most important benefits of self-awareness. The self-aware ask questions such as:

Who am I?

What are my gifts?

Why am I here?

Where am I going?

What gives my life purpose and significance?

What are my values?

What values and behaviors do I want to intentionally express in the world I live in?

Confidence is the by-product of discovering the answers to these questions. This is because confidence flows *naturally* through people who have discovered that there is a reason for getting out of bed in the morning that goes above and beyond their job descriptions.

HOW TO LIVE ABOVE AND BEYOND YOUR JOB DESCRIPTION

"What is your name and what is your role is in the company?" The question that begins introductions for the seminar draws the usual responses: "I'm Joe. I'm a programmer with the ECLD department." "I'm Tesa. I'm with R & D over in the DCP Division." Of course we have no idea what they are talking about. We can only assume that this means something to all of the participants who by now have been thoroughly indoctrinated into the acronyms of their company. The truth is, none of this actually *means* anything, until it is Susan's turn to share. "I'm Susan, and I sell hips for a living." Happy that she was speaking our language (and perhaps lucky that she did not mean H.I.P.S.), one of us curiously replies: "You sell hips?"

"Yes."

"So on Monday morning you wake up, come into work, call on some doctors and hospitals, and sell hips."

"Yes."

"And on Tuesday, you wake up come to work and sell hips again?"

"Yes."

"And Wednesday?"

"Hips!" Susan replied amusingly, and then she added: "But that is not what I really do. What I really do is improve the quality of people's lives, and make it possible for people to walk around the lake or enjoy a bike ride again. If it weren't for people doing what I do, then people like Bo Jackson wouldn't even be able to walk."

Thoughts drift for a moment to Major League Baseball All-Star and former National Football League running-back sensation Bo Jackson. In 1991 he suffered a hip injury that not only ended the career of one of the youngest and most gifted athletes to ever play professional sports, but also would have left him crippled for life had he not been able to receive hip-replacement surgery. It was a salient example of the significance of Susan's work, but the lesson was not lost in it. Susan not only helps people to walk again, she has learned one of life's very important secrets. She has developed a philosophy about her job, and this philosophy gives her an emotionally compelling reason to wake up every morning and go to work with joy, enthusiasm, and confidence.

People who live life with great emotional energy often do so because they are inspired. Their lives are characterized by a clear sense of meaning, direction, and significance. When they wake up in the morning they enter the new day purposefully, with an emotional drive that is called inspiration.

THE TOLL BOOTH STORY AND RELATIONAL THINKING

Dr. Charles Garfield (*Chicken Soup for the Soul*; Canfield and Hansen, 1993) tells a colorful story about a young man who managed to maintain a healthy level of confidence and self-esteem while working for eight hours a day in a toll booth. Most of us would not consider a toll booth the ideal place to develop inspiration and enthusiasm. In fact, most toll-booth operators have been replaced by machines.

What made things different for this young man was that he had discovered a way to *relate* the particulars of his job to those things that he valued the most, to those things that gave his life a sense of meaning, value, and purpose. Every day when he strolled into his toll booth, he mentally and physically filled it with music and dance. Physically, he actually practiced dancing, while fulfilling his responsibilities as gatekeeper on the Oakland–San Francisco Bay Bridge. Mentally, he developed a perspective that added several layers of meaning to an otherwise mundane job.

We call this aspect of self-awareness *relational thinking*. Relational thinking occurs whenever you relate the particulars of your job to something that gives you an ultimate sense of meaning and purpose. In comments to Dr. Garfield, this young man summarized his relational thoughts: "I don't understand why anybody would think my job is boring. I have a corner office, glass on all sides. I can see the Golden Gate, San Francisco, the Berkeley hills; half the Western world vacations here . . . and I just stroll in every day and practice dancing."

28

If emotional intelligence is all about learning how to use your emotions *intelligently*, then Susan and our toll-booth dancer are great examples of emotionally intelligent living. Both of them are using self-awareness to discover the true meaning of their lives and thereby tap into a supply of emotional energy that can only be described as inspiration.

Consider This

We are infusing daily activity with emotional energy whenever we are

- saving people's lives
- providing for our loved ones
- making the world a better place
- making a difference in someone's life
- living with integrity and in accordance with our values in everything we do
- saving the environment
- protecting animals
- inventing a solution to some problem or a cure to some disease
- spreading good cheer and smiles
- pursuing random acts of kindness
- spreading good news
- encouraging the faint-hearted
- believing in a team member
- making someone laugh.

Such energy is at the core of confidence and self-esteem. How does your job description read when you infuse it with meaning?

DEVELOPING YOUR SELF-CONCEPT: THE JOHARI WINDOW

The big idea here is that few things help us through life and prepare us for its challenges like insight into who we are and what we can do. People tend to suffer distress when they have no clear conception of who they are, why they are here, or where they are going. Conversely, a healthy self-concept produces confidence and self-esteem in all of us. So how do we develop this kind of insight? Psychologists Joseph Luft (Jo) and Harrington Ingham (Hari) have developed the Johari Window model to help us understand the importance of both self-disclosure and feedback in developing our self-concept.

The Johari Window is based on the idea that when it comes to self-knowledge there are four kinds of information:

Quadrant 1: There is information known to self that is known to others.

Quadrant 2: There is information known to self that is not known to others.

Quadrant 3: There is information known to others that is not known to self.

Quadrant 4: There is information that is not yet known to self or to others.

The Johari Window displays this information in a four-quadrant model (see Figure 3-1).

	Known to Self	**Not Known to Self**
Known to Others	Open	Blind
Not Known to Others	Hidden	Unknown

Figure 3-1. The Johari Window.

The area of *openness* in Quadrant 1 is very special. This is the area in which our awareness of our personal strengths and limitations is shared by others. Referring back to Daniel Goleman's list of competencies under self-awareness, we might call this quadrant Accurate Self-Assessment. This area of openness is where we feel the most free to explore our human potential, because we are working from a foundation of acceptance and understanding.

As a simple example, consider a 10-month-old infant taking her first steps. Her concept of self that she can walk is actually better known to her parents than it is to her. They give her feedback in the form of encouragement: "You can do it!" She trusts them and takes her first steps. They provide the requisite celebration of her newfound skill, and "I can walk" soon becomes a permanent part of her self-concept. This experience as well as many others forms an area of openness between parent and child that becomes the foundation of all future growth.

The Johari Window reminds us that our self-esteem, confidence, and potential are maximized when we increase the area in Quadrant 1. This is where we discover our significance, our greatness, our challenges, and our limitations. This is where we learn to laugh at ourselves and at each other, because we realize that we are all works in progress. There are three ways to increase this area of openness:

1. *Through Self-Disclosure:* when we are willing to be vulnerable and share hidden aspects of ourselves with people, we are inviting them into our hidden world to encourage us, to coach us, to support us, and to help develop us into what we are capable of becoming.

2. *Through Feedback:* when we are open to feedback, other people can reveal blind spots to us that either reinforce strengths and abilities that we did not even know we had, or redirect us to work on areas of development.

3. *Through Discovery:* Emerson said: "Ideas are in the air." Life is a journey, and discovery keeps us hopeful and excited about the future. Who knows what will be revealed to us in the future?

Grandma Moses picked up a paintbrush and started painting when she was 76! We all have hidden talents that we are not aware of yet.

Notice that no one is perfect according to the Johari Window. Growth is possible only when we learn how to accept ourselves and each other with all of our strengths and limitations. According to this model, growth is hindered whenever we hide too much from others and thus deny them of an opportunity to offer support. Growth is also hindered when other people refuse to give us the kind of honest feedback that can help us to manage our lives more effectively. In the end our potential is unlocked by forming honest and trusting relationships with people who accept us enough that we can disclose our flaws, and care about us enough to give us the insight we need to be the best we can be.

EQuip Yourself
with Confidence and Self-Esteem

Approach people daily with a spirit of benevolence.

+ When you are happy with yourself and have discovered what gives your life inspiration and significance, then you are free to approach other people in a spirit of good will, enthusiasm, and genuine interest in their well-being.
+ The more you approach other people with a spirit of benevolence, the happier you will be with yourself, and the more you will discover what gives your life inspiration and significance.

Increase the feeling that you are making a difference by challenging yourself and seeking feedback.

+ Seek out challenging opportunities that you know are critical for a project's success.
+ Occasionally ask team members, colleagues, customers, or supervisors to give you feedback about the importance

and significance of your contributions. Even open-ended questions like "What is it that you value the most about my contributions?" can yield encouraging and confidence-lifting results.

♦ Seek feedback from people who are positive and happy and know how to provide encouraging and constructive feedback.

♦ Avoid feedback from people who are unhappy and negative because such feedback is often counterproductive and can actually tear you down.

♦ Engender this constructive and positive feedback by providing it to others first. Make sure you let your team members know how important their work is to you and how your collaborative projects would not be successful without their inputs.

Proactively and intentionally live out your values at work.

♦ List some of the core values you recognize as being a part of how you define yourself.

♦ Reflect on how these values play out in terms of your at-work style. What does it look like when you are truly living and modeling these values at work?

♦ Think of a time when your at-work actions fell out of alignment with one or more of your values and your vision for living and modeling your values.

♦ Brainstorm three things you could do to more fully represent your values in the workplace.

Develop your sense of mission and purpose. Confidence, self-esteem, and peak performance occur whenever your individual genius and productivity are motivated by a spiritual mission or an all-consuming purpose greater than yourself—be it God, the environment, religious faith, humanitarian concerns, political ideals, or some other ideal to which you would like to dedicate your energy. The key is to find a way to relate your individual efforts to your greater sense of purpose:

- Seek opportunities to model your value in the workplace in whatever ways you can. For example, you may have a difficult time seeing a connection between completing a task like data entry and fulfilling your sense of calling to preserve the environment, but you could promote and practice recycling in your office.
- Keep in mind that the workplace is only one venue for you to live out your sense of purpose. You may need to give financial support, offer your services, or volunteer your time in other ways outside of the workplace to fulfill more completely your sense of mission and purpose.

Learn how to trust your intuition. Hunches, gut feelings, extra-sensory perceptions—we're essentially talking about intuition here, a sort of inner knowing. Intuition is part of the unconscious mind, not actually our gut, which helps guide us toward making good choices. We might think of it as tapping into a forgotten pool of wisdom we hold, a pool formed drop by drop through the experiences of our lives. The more life experience we have, the deeper the pool of wisdom becomes. To harness the power of your intuition:

- Use your analytical skills to understand the pros and cons the next time you have an important decision to make.
- After you have completed your due diligence, use your self-awareness to unlock the gate and wade into the pool of your unconscious wisdom.
- Seek out the guidance of your intuition and then *trust* it as the mediating force that leads you to your final decision.

Your confidence will actually increase when you realize that you can tap into this pool of wisdom as needed. Your intuition, like an oracle or a sage that you carry around with you, is always accessible as long as you are using your self-awareness to listen to it. The key is to trust that your intuition is there to support you. You need only to seek its guidance.

Chapter 4

Anatomy of an Emotion

.... **In this chapter, you will learn** ....

- ♦ where emotions come from and why they are so powerful
- ♦ to recognize emotions as signals to take action
- ♦ the physiology of the human brain and its role in managing your emotions
- ♦ the link between disruptive emotions and reactive behaviors
- ♦ how to *EQuip Yourself* for better emotional understanding.

Seeking to understand your emotions—where they come from and why they are so powerful in certain situations—is to delve into the hardwiring of your human brain, rediscover forgotten and sometimes painful memories from your past, and unearth some deep-seated beliefs and ways of thinking that you may not have been consciously aware you were holding. In other words, it is to dig deeply into your self. Although such a journey is often not an easy one, it is an important one for each of us to take, one that carries us further down the path to emotional intelligence.

As we've done previously, let's begin this exploration with a visit to our EI classroom for a little storytelling about when our emotions have gotten in our way.

A Glimpse into the Classroom: Confronting Emotion

"In your group, share a story of a time when your emotions got the best of you, when you had an emotional response to a situation that led to behaviors that undermined your intended outcome for that situation." This is one of those exercises some participants were afraid might come up in a course on EI—an activity in which they have to reveal themselves to the other participants, making themselves somewhat vulnerable by relating an embarrassing story. Around the room, people are looking at each other uneasily, unsure how to start, and then, just like in every other EI class we've ever facilitated, someone breaks the ice and starts telling his tale.

We include this exercise in our EI course not to embarrass people but rather to help them feel more comfortable. Hearing such stories from others helps us realize that though we may feel somewhat embarrassed by those times when our emotions got the best of us and we behaved in a way we wish we hadn't, everyone has had similar experiences. The storytelling normalizes the experience of an emotional override, those times when our emotional selves wrested control of our behaviors from our rational thinking selves. Potentially embarrassing? Sure. Perfectly human? Absolutely.

As the storytelling unfolds during the group work, we, as facilitators, wander around and eavesdrop just a bit. From one class to the next, the stories maintain certain parallels. There's the unintended-angry-outburst-at-a-spouse story. There's the tale of trepidation at being called in to see the boss. The road-rage saga almost always presents itself. The details of an escalating conflict with a colleague at a business-unit meeting usually are recounted. These parallels exist because these are our collective stories. They belong to all of us. They are part of our human experience, a manifestation of being emotional creatures. And now, with a richness of stories to base our exploration on, we can dig into how these emotional responses play out within us, and indeed, why we even have emotions at all.

WHY AM I SO EMOTIONAL?

It is often said that our emotions reside in our hearts. When we refer to how we feel about something, we often indicate that feeling as emanating from the chest. To fully understand our emotions, though, we need to first understand that emotion truly is all in our head.

Your emotions are initiated in your brain. Yes, your brain, the one that you often think about as being computer-like. What we sometimes describe as the rational, logical, problem-solving brain does exist, at least in part. And most of the time, you are operating within this rational, thinking part of your brain. You are aware of what's going on around you, you are choosing and directing your behaviors in a conscious and rational way, you are thinking through challenges and tapping into previous experience and wisdom to seek solutions to those challenges. This is the human brain with which you likely are most familiar. But there are other aspects of the brain too, more primitive than what was just described, and they hold great power, which is revealed when activated by certain situations.

To better understand these more primitive functional areas of the brain, let's take a journey back in time to visit our primitive ancestors. Imagine our prehistoric forebears living in the wilderness. It was a hard and hostile world, presenting true physical dangers on a nearly daily basis. Picture one of these early humans, a youngster perhaps, out on a hunt for some small game. Focused on stalking a hare, the young hunter doesn't yet notice that danger lurks near. A low growl comes in through the ear and is processed by the brain. With extraordinary speed and no real conscious thought, an alarmed response blasts through the hunter's body. Breathing

> **Guiding Principle**
>
> *Essentially all emotions are signals to take action.*

becomes rapid and shallow, heart rate accelerates, adrenaline is released into the bloodstream, and muscles tighten, ready for action. This instinctive physiologic response, designed to support survival in the face of danger, is, of course, known as fight or flight.

Fight or flight is an emotional response triggered by your brain to move you toward taking action. That's essentially what all emotions are—signals to take action. Humans are hardwired with this sort of emotionally activated circuitry as a mechanism for supporting survival. Fight or flight as an emotional response in the face of a physical threat moves you toward protecting yourself from whatever that danger may be. These protective behaviors usually take the form of either preparing to do battle or preparing to move quickly out of harm's way. Emotions may also move you closer to some things that your brain interprets as supporting your survival—finding a mate, bonding with other humans in the community, taking part in activities that bring you joy. The behaviors you exhibit that support these activities are responses to emotional signals as well.

The fight-or-flight response, in the scenario just described, serves our young hunter well. The large cat, the source of the low growl initially heard, moved in for an assault. The first stone thrown by our hunter caught the cat on the side of the head and gave it pause. The second stone, landing squarely on the bridge of the cat's nose, sent it into retreat. The hunter backed away slowly, watchfully, before fully accelerating in the opposite direction.

WHEN THE SABER-TOOTHED TIGER IS REALLY A KITTY CAT

Fight or flight is a classic case study of how emotions influence behavior. Fear is one of the most primal and powerful of the emotions. When activated, the fear response drives you to action toward protecting yourself from danger, real or imagined. Consider that if the growl experienced by our young hunter had turned out not to be a large cat at all but instead a friend playing a prank, the initial emotional response, activated by the quick-acting emotional center of the brain, would have been the same.

Only when the rational-thinking part of the hunter's brain had caught up with what the situation really was would the emotion have quieted.

For all of us, as humans living in our present-day world, this is an important point. We are still hardwired with the same emotional physiology that supported the survival of our primitive ancestors in their dangerous and hostile world. Granted, and sadly so, our modern world has its true dangers as well, and fight or flight still strives to support us when we encounter such dramatic and unfortunate circumstances. But fight or flight also threatens to undermine us when the danger we encounter is not actually one that is truly life or death but merely feels that way in the moment. After all, when was the last time you crossed paths with a large, hungry cat roaming the corridors of your offices? Many of the perceived dangers we experience today are just that, perceived. The degree of true danger is therefore open to interpretation.

EMOTIONAL OVERRIDE AND THE HUMAN BRAIN

To understand how human potential can be undermined by your emotional responses, you need to get to know your brain a little better. As previously suggested, you are probably already familiar with the rational-thinking part of the human brain. The *neocortex*, which consists of all the convoluted gray matter at the top of the brain, manages the higher brain functions of awareness, reasoning, voluntary movement and action, conscious thought, and language skills. Again, most people spend the majority of their time operating out of this part of the brain.

In the case of the young hunter being confronted by the threat of the fierce cat, we introduced a more primitive part of the brain, one that evolved long before the neocortex. All vertebrates have a mass of cells situated at the top of the spinal cord that comprise the *brainstem*. The cells of the brainstem coordinate most of our involuntary functions—the cardiopulmonary apparatus, for example—and govern our most animalistic instincts, including fight or flight. Sometimes referred to as the *reptilian brain*, this primitive brain has the power to override the rational-thinking functions of the neocortex and take control of our actions when it perceives a threat.

That covers the upper and lower parts of the brain. Now, let's explore the middle. Tucked beneath the neocortex and wrapping around the brainstem in something of a horseshoe configuration is a series of structures comprising the *limbic* area of the brain. It is from here that emotions originate. The limbic area, sometimes called the *mammalian brain*, stores emotionally linked memories. It is this area of the brain that triggers learned emotional responses to particular circumstances.

The reference to mammals with regard to this part of the brain has to do with the learning capacity of the limbic system. Take a dog, for example. Let's call him Rover. One day, Rover, just a pup for the purposes of our story, goes to the park with his human. Rover's human brings a ball along, intending to teach Rover how to fetch. At the park, Rover's human waves the ball around above Rover's head and then with a mighty toss throws the ball across the grass. Rover tears after the ball, skidding to a halt where the ball landed. Rover sniffs the ball a few times and then hearing his human call for him, comes racing back, leaving the ball where it lay. Not exactly what Rover's human was hoping for, but that's what learning is all about. After several more tries and several more walks to retrieve the ball, Rover finally catches on. The human throws the ball. Rover chases it down, scoops it up, and brings it back to the start. What does the human do now that Rover has successfully completed the trick? Of course! Rover gets treats, ear scratches, and "Good Boy!" acknowledgments all around.

Now, here is the important part—in this shining moment of triumph and reward, Rover's mammalian brain is making note of this experience. His brain is recording that the behavior he just exhibited, which we'll call fetch, is *"Good for me!"*—that is, good for him in that it bonds him to the human who looks after him, thus supporting his survival. This emotionally charged message is now stored in Rover's brain, and he will remember and act on it for the rest of his doggy life. This emotional-message-encoding mechanism also works the other way. If Rover were ever to do something that his human preferred he not do, say pee on a new pair of shoes, for example, a different message would be sent and learned—*"Not good for me!"* This message carries power too.

Just like Rover, we humans learn *"Good for me!"* and *"Not good for me!"* lessons throughout our lives. Being around people who care about us—*"Good for me!"* Getting called into Dad's study, the principal's office, or the shareholder's meeting to explain our actions—*"Not good for me!"*

Over the course of your life's experience, you have accumulated and stored literally thousands of emotional memories in your mammalian brain. These memories comprise the total of your life's emotional experiences and serve as activation points for emotional responses when you encounter current-day situations that are reminiscent of events from the past. New situations that link to *"Good for me!"* memories within the brain activate emotional responses and trigger behaviors that encourage us to fully engage. Events that link to *"Not good for me!"* memories activate emotional responses and trigger behaviors that seek to steer us away or protect us from such things.

Take public speaking, for example. If you are someone who received a standing ovation from your seventh-grade classmates at your first try as a speechmaker, you will log that experience in your emotional brain as being one that is good for you. It brought you joy, made you feel liked and respected by your peers, and acknowledged your effectiveness as a public speaker with important things to say. In the future, opportunities that come your way to present yourself and your thoughts in a public forum will be exciting for you. They'll be viewed as an opportunity to shine, to gain more respect and accolades. Your emotional brain will drive you to seek out and embrace situations that link back to the *"Good for me!"* message you retain concerning public speaking.

On the other hand, if you're like most of us, that first speech in the seventh grade didn't go so well. Feeling nauseated, shaking violently, and losing one of your notecards were bad enough, but the silence and dumbfounded looks that greeted you upon your conclusion are forever burned into your emotional memory. Based on this clearly *"Not good for me!"* experience, how do you think your emotional brain will react when you receive an assignment to address the assembly at the next division meeting? Don't worry though, it's not truly life and death, it just feels that way!

Just like Rover, you remember and act on these emotional lessons for the rest of your life.

THE EMOTIONAL GATEKEEPER

With the understanding of how emotional responses are learned and how these messages reside in our mammalian or limbic brain, we now can introduce what might be considered the gatekeeper of the system—the *amygdala*. The amygdala is an almond-shaped mass of cells situated at the base of the limbic horseshoe. As sensory stimuli from a person's surroundings enter the brain, the amygdala is monitoring them closely. At the first sign of a situation that links to a powerful emotional memory, the amygdala leaps to action, directing the person's behavior based on previously learned emotional responses: a fearful recoil, an angry outburst, a joyous whoop, or a round of bust-a-gut laughter.

Dr. Joseph LeDoux (1996), a neuroscientist at New York University, has studied the amygdala and its role in our emotional responses. He describes the amygdala as being quiet most of the time, but always alert for the need to sound the emotional alarm and trigger what is deemed to be appropriate action. Through his research, LeDoux discovered that an emotionally linked stimulus enters via the human senses and simultaneously travels two pathways in the brain, what he calls the high road and the low road. The high road leads up into the neocortex, where the stimulus and all of its data-rich associations can be analyzed in a rational and conscious way. At the same time, the same stimulus, in a more roughly defined, less data-rich stream, is transmitted via the low road to the amygdala, which, as is its nature, sounds the alarm. The key difference between the high and low roads is the time it takes a stimulus to travel them and activate a response. As you've likely guessed, the low road is the faster route. Whereas the amygdala leaps to action in a fraction of a second, the folks at 6 Seconds EI Network draw the name of their organization from the notion that the conscious thought process or high road takes a full six seconds to process what's going on. The speed at which information travels the low road is both a blessing and a curse. When a speeding car is bearing down on you, the amygdala's quick response system may save your life. When a colleague challenges you in a meeting, the same quick response, if not managed and filtered, may get you into trouble.

MY AMYGDALA MADE ME DO IT!

Although it's true that your emotional brain has the power to influence your behaviors long before your rational brain knows what's going on, this does not give you permission to play victim to your amygdala. When an emotional override results in an inappropriate outburst at a staff meeting, you do not get to say, "Wait a minute. I took a course on emotional intelligence and according to the instructor, my amygdala made me do it!" That, of course, is not what this journey into EI is all about. Emotional intelligence has to do with learning how to use all of this emotional energy *intelligently*. The importance of delving into the mechanism by which your brain activates emotional responses that guide your behaviors is rooted in the ability that understanding provides toward beginning to manage emotional responses *with your rational-thinking brain*.

Granted, there are times when the amygdala sounds the alarm launching you into action so passionately that you are almost powerless to choose a different course. But most of the time, life's events are not so dramatic. In these more common and nuanced cases, your emotions bubble up more slowly within you, not so much an alarm but more a flashing yellow light urging caution. It is in these times that your responses are guided by a combination of emotionally charged memory and rational thought, two behavioral guidance systems opposing one another in a tug of war for control of your actions. This is where emotions get really interesting.

THE EMOTIONAL TUG OF WAR

Imagine a staff meeting in which a team member interrupts you while you are sharing an idea you are passionate about. The team momentum suddenly shifts in the direction of the interruption, and soon the opportunity to present the idea is lost in the shuffle. You are, of course, feeling a variety of emotions about this, but the one that threatens to send you into an explosive reaction is anger. Your initial response to this situation is being directed by your amygdala. What you perceive to be a disrespectful interruption is one of those *"Not good for me!"* situations you learned about long ago, and now your amygdala is going to come to your rescue. Fulfilling its duties as gatekeeper of emotional response to situations you encounter, your amygdala will sound the alarm and begin the process of activating any number of reactive behaviors. You might fire off an angry tirade at your co-worker. You might embarrass yourself by ridiculing him or by sniping at him.

All of these reactive behaviors represent one side of the tug of war that is being waged between your emotionally charged brain and your rational brain. You might call this *reactive* side of the tug of war *emotional un-intelligence*, because you are allowing your emotional impulses to manage your behaviors instead of using your rational intelligence to manage both your emotions and your behaviors. Indeed, if you are able to delay your emotional reaction long enough to engage your rational brain, you will discover a new list of behavioral options that could lead you to handle the situation in a more intelligent and successful way. This *proactive* side of the tug of war represents *emotional intelligence*—the idea that all human beings are responsible for using rational-thought processes to both understand and manage emotional impulses.

DISRUPTIVE EMOTIONS AND REACTIVE BEHAVIOR

To be fair, not all emotionally reactive behaviors will create problems for you. For example, there is usually no need for concern about emotional override when your spontaneous behaviors are driven by emotions like love, happiness, enthusiasm, warmth, or kindness. When you feel compassion for a homeless person and spontaneously reach into your pocket and offer a charitable gift, you are not really committing an emotional foul. Indeed, if you think about the emotion of kindness too much, then you may end up in your own little mental struggle: "On the one hand, I could give him the money, but am I then enabling him to remain in a homeless pattern and not seek a better life? On the other hand, if I don't give him the money, then he may not be able to meet some of the basic needs required to even begin to get back on his feet." In the end you will probably be okay no matter how you handle this interaction.

There are, of course, times when spontaneous enthusiasm can get you into trouble. Early in the 2004 presidential primaries, Democratic front-runner, Howard Dean, learned this lesson the hard way when his enthusiastic speech ending "Yeehah!" was parodied over and over again by the media.

These examples of reactive behavior should not concern you nearly as much as the examples of emotional override that may result from the intrusion of disruptive emotions:

- anger or defensiveness
- fear or anxiety
- guilt or shame
- feeling "down"
- insecurity
- embarrassment.

This is the lexicon of emotions that tend to get the best of you in certain situations. We call these emotions *disruptive* because they so often threaten to override rational thoughts and take *disruptive* control of behaviors. When you are aware of these emotions and take personal responsibility for managing them, you can maintain a sense of control, or perhaps a better way to say this is you can maintain a sense of composure. When you lack awareness and avoid personal responsibility, then you often lose composure and end up looking foolish. All of these disruptive emotions have the power to trigger the amygdala and produce a variety of reactive behaviors that are inappropriate in many human interactions. You lose your temper, you intimidate others, you surrender under pressure, you sulk and complain because you didn't get what you wanted, and so on. Such behaviors risk sabotaging personal and professional success. But this does not mean that these disruptive emotions are bad or even negative. When well managed, these emotions can provide you with tremendous amounts of information and energy to help you navigate through difficult situations and choose the right response proactively. Table 4-1 highlights the difference between managing and not managing our disruptive emotions.

Table 4-1. Proactive and Reactive Ways to Manage Unpleasant, Disruptive Emotions

	Six Unpleasant Emotions	
Disruptive Emotion	List of Reactive Behaviors *When the amygdala is in control of the emotion and directing behaviors*	List of Proactive Behaviors *When the rational mind is managing the emotion and directing behaviors*
Anger/Defensiveness	Yell; threaten; become demanding; escalate; curse; argue and get loud; use physical outbursts; direct your anger at the wrong object or person; vandalize, turn to violence; harm people or harm yourself; turn to passive-aggressive self-defeating behaviors.	Use calm, assertive communication; practice conflict resolution; provide people with feedback; increase your understanding and practice reflective listening; connect with the hurt, fear, or concern that is beneath the anger; take a walk and try to figure out what the anger is telling you to do; take a time out; calm yourself down; find a safe cathartic activity.
Anxiety/Fear	Freeze; regress; panic; make irrational decisions; flee, hide, and avoid; lose composure; worry and obsess; become overly controlling and hypervigilant; micromanage; unwilling to take appropriate risks and move outside of your comfort zone; phobias; agoraphobia.	Slow down; exercise appropriate care and caution; prepare and practice; assess the situation and use problem-solving skills; get more training and develop your skills; ensure your safety; purchase insurance; develop confident and assertive behaviors; call 911.

Table 4-1. *(continued)*

Six Unpleasant Emotions

Disruptive Emotion	List of Reactive Behaviors *When the amygdala is in control of the emotion and directing behaviors*	List of Proactive Behaviors *When the rational mind is managing the emotion and directing behaviors*
Guilt/Shame	Become overly critical and blaming of self and/or others; become self-condemning instead of learning from bad choices or mistakes; become overly responsible and easily manipulated by other people's emotions, issues, and concerns; develop poor boundaries; become addicted to approval; regress into feelings of worthlessness, inferiority, and shame; hide, lie, and cover up; become a caretaker and enabler; turn to addictive behaviors to feel better; avoid all risk in order to avoid making a mistake and feeling guilty.	Apologize; make amends; take responsibility, show remorse, and take steps to repair the situation; learn from bad choices and mistakes; ask for forgiveness; accurately assess responsibility and set better boundaries; make decisions that you will not later regret; develop your appreciation for rules, systems, and procedures that are tried and true; develop your intuition and wisdom and use it to guide your decision-making process.
Feeling "Down"	Lose energy and motivation; feel powerless; regress to self-pity; whine and complain; become a drain on others; fail to take initiative; become indecisive; overeat and turn to addictive behaviors; stay in bed, call in sick, and make irresponsible choices; neglect family and children; lose interest in activities you usually enjoy; feel hopeless; feel despair; turn to suicidal thoughts and behaviors.	Exercise, get plenty of rest, take care of yourself, and eat well; add activities to your life that give you energy; develop your sense of inspiration and purpose; make a change to your daily routine; reach out and help someone else; put life into perspective and try to find the silver lining in your circumstances; grieve and process your losses with a psychologist, counselor, clergy, or a good friend; go to see a psychiatrist or a medical doctor if your depression persists.

(continued)

47

Table 4-1. *(continued)*

	Six Unpleasant Emotions	
Disruptive Emotion	List of Reactive Behaviors *When the amygdala is in control of the emotion and directing behaviors*	List of Proactive Behaviors *When the rational mind is managing the emotion and directing behaviors*
Insecurity	Exhibit critical behaviors, tearing other people down so you can feel better about yourself; exhibit jealous behaviors; overcompensate by yelling at others or acting like you know it all; embellish the truth; misrepresent facts and information and tell stories that are not true; overcompensate by bragging about yourself; avoid challenges and shut down; demonstrate an inability to handle constructive, corrective feedback or reprimands.	Develop supportive, nurturing relationships, and use people you admire as role models to help you develop yourself; be aware of your self-talk and use positive affirmations; challenge yourself to step outside of your comfort zone; surround yourself with positive, secure people; create small successes for yourself; reach out and help other people who are less fortunate.
Embarrassment	Exhibit angry, defensive behaviors; hide the truth from yourself and others; avoid accountability; lash out at others; lie to cover up; shame others; shame yourself; threaten others; exhibit inappropriate parental behaviors such as physical, emotional, or verbal abuse of children; expect children to be perfect and to develop faster than the normal rate; excessively yell at children and blame them for making you "look bad."	Learn how to laugh at yourself and accept your flaws as part of being human; develop an attitude of unconditional positive regard toward others; remember that "to err is human, to forgive is divine"; accept humanity in yourself and in others; learn from your inadequacies, setbacks and failures; admit your flaws to others and ask them to support you with your development plan.

◆

EQuip Yourself
with Emotional Understanding

This process of understanding and managing your emotions is not the same as denying or repressing them. Remember, your emotions are there for a reason. They indicate that something is either *"Good for you"* or *"Not good for you."* And so to deny or repress your emotions when you are interrupted at a staff meeting, for example, is equivalent to denying that the interruption is linked to one of your *"Not good for me!"* memories. Denying the emotion is therefore a form of denying the logic that stands behind the emotion. The goal is not to deny the emotional signal but to be aware of it, to manage it, and then to choose your behavior proactively.

It is helpful to summarize this goal as a three-step process:

1. **Self-Awareness**
   Be aware of what you feel. Awareness includes accurately labeling your emotion as well as understanding why the emotion is there.

2. **Self-Management**
   Manage your emotions so your emotions do not manage you. There are a variety of techniques we will discuss in the next chapter to help us manage emotions.

3. **Use your understanding of emotions to choose an appropriate behavior.**
   Emotions are actually *informative.* Your emotions provide valuable information you can use to choose an appropriate behavior. Use your rational brain to *listen to what your emotions are calling to your attention.* For example:

   ◆ Anger is calling your attention to the idea that something is wrong, an injustice has occurred, or a conflict needs to be resolved.

49

- Anxiety is calling your attention to the idea that more caution and care are needed to manage the situation effectively.
- Feeling "down" is calling your attention to the idea that you need to make some kind of a change so you can manage your energy more effectively.
- Guilt is calling your attention to the idea that you need to apologize, make amends, or learn from a mistake.
- Insecurity is calling your attention to the idea that you need to develop a skill set, find out what makes your life significant, or connect with what you are passionate about.
- Embarrassment is calling your attention to the idea that you need to be more discreet, to learn how to laugh at yourself and accept yourself, or to be less of a perfectionist.

The point of this third step is to ask the behavioral question: *If my amygdala is sounding the alarm about situations that are "Not good for me!" what appropriate behavior will I choose to right the injustice, to resolve the conflict, to handle the danger, to reenergize myself, to deal with wrong behaviors and mistakes, to build my self-esteem, to avoid embarrassment, and so on?*

What is the emotional signal trying to teach me about what I should do?

Chapter 5

Cognitive and Behavioral Strategies for Managing Your Emotions

.... **In this chapter, you will learn** ....

- ♦ the impact of self-awareness on emotional self-management
- ♦ how thoughts and behaviors influence your emotions
- ♦ behavioral strategies for managing your emotions
- ♦ cognitive strategies for managing your emotions
- ♦ how to *EQuip Yourself* for emotional self-management.

W hat is change?

What does it mean to make lasting, individual, behavioral change toward improving performance?

This is an important question to ask in our fast-paced, do-more-with-less, focus-on-productivity workplace environments. Let's face it, in today's

> **Guiding Principle**
>
> *Change happens when you make new choices and make them consistently.*

workplace, putting effort toward continuous growth and personal development sometimes doesn't seem feasible for those who wish to get things done and be rewarded with increasing levels of responsibility, leadership, and pay. Certainly the widespread use of tools such as 360-degree feedback assessments mays provide the insight and awareness needed as a basis for change, but what exactly constitutes *change* itself?

The truth is that anyone can claim to have changed. I have worked with more than 100 couples in counseling settings, and one of the most common occurrences I have observed is for the couple to come into the second session with either husband or wife (whomever is more desperate) proclaiming: "I've changed." This may or may not be accurate. It is often what one wants to hear, but the proof is in the behavior. At the end of the day, real change is measured by whether or not we are able to make new *choices* and to make them consistently. This kind of change is at the heart of self-management.

Daniel was a rising star in his company. During his first six months, he quickly distinguished himself from many of his peers by becoming the number one sales rep in his region. His task-oriented, fast-paced, hardworking style did not go unnoticed, and within two years he was promoted to a supervisory position. As supervisor he managed people in the same way he managed tasks. His pacesetting style worked well with the high-performing, self-starting members of his team, but he became quickly irritated and impatient with his direct reports who worked at a slower pace. The more he pushed them, the more time they seemed to spend analyzing details, processing data, or building consensus, slowing things down even more. His impatience usually revealed itself in a demanding tone of voice—"I don't care what it takes. Just do it!"

A few employees felt so disrespected and intimidated by Daniel's managerial style that they went to Human Resources to discuss the situation. On several occasions Daniel was given feedback about his style, but rather than accepting the feedback, he often became defensive. Daniel was given a tremendous opportunity to develop his self-awareness through feedback and, from this, to make changes through self-management. Instead he made excuses. "That's just the way I am. It is how I

> **Guiding Principle**
>
> *Self-awareness is as fundamental to self-management as a clock is to time management.*

am hard wired. You can't expect me to change who I am." What Daniel was saying in effect was, "This is not what I choose. This is who I am." In the end Daniel lost his job with the company.

Someone has wisely said: "You will never ever change what you do not believe you have chosen." When people attribute their behaviors to disposition, to emotions, to uncontrollable urges and impulses, to external causes, or to external situations, they give up their power to manage those behaviors, and, in doing so, they avoid taking responsibility for them. Some people do not do the hard foundational work of self-awareness and therefore do not gain the insight and feedback necessary to make changes. Table 5-1 illustrates the relationship between self-awareness and self-management.

As the table illustrates, those who lack self-awareness are almost completely untrustworthy when it comes to making new choices and demonstrating the competencies of self-management. Many of us intuitively know not to trust people who lack self-awareness. We may not always speak about this distrust, but at some gut level, there is a realization that without self-awareness, people are doomed to repeat the same mistakes.

Table 5-1. The Impact of Self-Awareness on Self-Management

	Assumes Responsibility for Self-Management	
Degree of Self-Awareness	Yes (%)	No (%)
Strong	49	51
Poor	4	96

$N = 427$, $p < .001$ (Burckle and Boyatzis, 1999).

Self-awareness is as fundamental to self-management as a clock is to time management. Indeed, there is a 96 percent likelihood that those who refuse to do the work of self-awareness will also be deficient in the area of self-management.

Even when people are self-aware, however, it does not always mean that they will make the kinds of adjustments that lead to personal growth and development. Only half of those who are self-aware actually take responsibility for the insight that awareness provides and make new choices around how they will manage their emotions and behaviors.

At times there is a tendency to confuse self-awareness with growth. Many people who are self-aware are knowledgeable about their problems, but they do not move toward a solution. They are willing to look at themselves in the mirror, but are unmoved by what they see, or lack the commitment to make the necessary adjustments. The path of least resistance is paved with good intentions. Self-awareness certainly does not equal change, but it is foundational to change. The goal is always to move from self-awareness: "here is what is going on" to self-management: "therefore this is what I need to do."

SELF-MANAGEMENT AND YOUR EMOTIONS

Let's assume that we all struggle with one or more of the disruptive emotions outlined in chapter 4. We are all aware of the disruptive emotions inside of our bodies, and we know from past experience that these disruptive emotions have the potential to get the best of us in certain situations. Some of us will be especially vulnerable to anger, some to anxiety, some to guilt, some to feeling "down." We all want to respond appropriately when the emotion is triggered, but to do this we have to manage the disruptive emotion or the emotion will manage us. One way to think about managing emotions is to consider how emotions, thoughts, and behaviors work together holistically in a person's body. The following story will help us to explain how this all works (see Figure 5-1).

Dagwood decides to take a class in emotional intelligence and asks himself the question, "How can I manage my anxiety so that I can begin to

Thoughts

Dagwood secretly thinks that his boss Mr. Dithers is a jerk. Still, over the years, he has willingly accepted increased levels of responsibility, worked long hours, and has successfully performed everything that has been asked of him. All of this increased responsibility has been dutifully fulfilled, without any corresponding increase in salary. Dagwood begins to think that he deserves a raise.

Influence Feelings

Reinforce Thoughts

This entire experience reinforces Dagwood's thinking. Dagwood walks away thinking, "Wow, I was right. Mr. Dithers really is a jerk."

Dagwood's thoughts influence his feelings. On the one hand, Dagwood feels confident that he deserves the raise because of his work. On the other hand, he did get caught sleeping on the job a few times, and experience has taught Dagwood that Mr. Dithers is a very difficult person to approach. His feelings of confidence are suddenly overwhelmed by feelings of anxiety as he considers going into Dithers' office to request the salary increase.

Influence Behaviors

Dagwood's feelings influence his behaviors. As Dagwood approaches his boss he is timid: "Is this a good time to talk?" Dithers is impatient. He bluntly responds, "What is it? Can't you see that I'm busy?" Dagwood quickly backs out of the situation with an apologetic remark.

Figure 5-1. Managing your emotions.
BLONDIE © KING FEATURES SYNDICATE.

approach Mr. Dithers with more confidence?" (With respect to emotional intelligence, this really becomes two questions: How do I manage my anxiety? How do I generate the emotion of confidence?) Dagwood learns that most experts in the field of psychology consider themselves to be cognitive/behavioral in their approach to managing emotions. This means that Dagwood can learn how to manage his emotions by either managing his behaviors or managing his thoughts. Let's take a glimpse into Dagwood's classroom and discover the power that our behaviors have in managing emotions.

BEHAVIORAL STRATEGIES FOR MANAGING YOUR EMOTIONS

---◆---

A Glimpse into the Classroom: Behavior and Emotion

"Everybody stand up!" In moments 23 men and women stand up to participate in an experiment that is especially designed to connect with those participants who favor a kinesthetic, tactile learning style. "Pretend you are Mr. Snuffleupagus from Sesame Street." Modeling the physiological behaviors of the woolly mammoth from Sesame Street, all the participants are now standing with shoulders drooped and arms dangling forward to mimic an elephant's trunk. With the mopiest of voices, each participant repeats out loud "I am soooo happy. You would not believe how happy I am. I can't wait until tomorrow." The participants quickly realize that it is difficult to feel an emotion like happiness when their behavior is lethargic.

---◆---

There are two behavioral rules at work here that will help us to understand the behavioral strategies for managing our emotions.

Rule #1: The brain does not want to feel an emotion that is inconsistent with the physiology of the body.

Rule #2: When you are feeling a disruptive emotion, ask yourself what emotion you want to feel and then behave consistently with that emotion.

Consider the following examples:

Problem: You feel lazy and want to feel energetic.

> **Guiding Principle**
>
> *When it comes to managing your emotions, what you think about what happens to you is more important than what actually happens to you.*

Behavioral Solution: Start exercising and eventually your feelings will catch up with the active behavior.

Problem: You feel anxious about initiating a conversation with your supervisor.

Behavioral Solution: The emotion you want to feel is confidence, so you ask yourself the question: "What does confidence look like (behaviorally)?"—Use these behaviors as you approach your supervisor—keep your head up, maintain eye contact, square your shoulders, wear professional attire, walk with a slight skip in your step, use a firm handshake and an assertive voice. The confidence will follow.

Problem: You feel angry and you are afraid that you will say the wrong thing if you do not get your anger under control.

Behavioral Solution: Do something that makes you feel good, like taking a walk around the lake.

Problem: You and your spouse feel love for each other, but you really want to rekindle some of the romantic feelings that you used to have for each other.

Behavioral Solution: Ask yourself the question: "What does romantic love look like (behaviorally)?" Start using those behaviors—write love poems, send flowers, call each other up to go out on a date, surprise each other, have romantic candle-lit dinners, and so on.

Problem: You are feeling *down* and *dull* and you want to feel *happy*.

Behavioral Solution: Happy people do happy things. What activities in your life make you feel happy? Start doing these activities and you will bring happy feelings into your life.

> **Guiding Principle**
>
> *Think about how you want to feel and then act in ways that are consistent with that emotion.*

COGNITIVE STRATEGIES FOR MANAGING YOUR EMOTIONS

It is early Monday morning, and Susan is in her office thinking about the project she has just been assigned to lead and all of the related work that needs to be completed by the end of the week. With so much difficult and time-sensitive work to be accomplished, she begins to think about the challenge of delegating this work to her staff. "I'm really going to have to depend on Josephine and Harold," she muses, considering her two best and most dependable team members. She relies heavily on these two and hopes she's not overworking them.

At 9:00 she meets briefly with each of them and delegates the expectations and responsibilities for the coming week. Both assure her that they will do everything they can to meet the suspense dates, and as the meeting ends, Susan feels confident and hopeful that the project will be successful.

Later in the morning, Harold runs into Peter by the coffee maker. They chit chat for a moment, and then Harold says, "Can you believe all of the work she is piling on top of me? That woman is just trying to make my life miserable!" Peter listens and empathizes with Harold's situation. Although Harold appreciates the chance to vent to a colleague, he returns to his work area still feeling frustrated and irritable.

Later that evening, Josephine meets her husband at a local restaurant for dinner. He asks her about her day, and she tells him about the project. "Can you believe all of the work that she is giving me?" she exclaims. "You know, I think she must really trust me and believe in me to give me so much responsibility. It's a good sign, don't you think?" Josephine is feeling confident and secure about her work performance.

There is very little difference between Josephine and Harold. Both are good workers, both are dependable, both have a very busy work week ahead of them, delegated to them by the same person. The only real difference between these two people is how they are thinking and feeling.

Harold thinks, "She is trying to make my life miserable" and feels irritable. Josephine thinks, "She is showing me how much she trusts me" and feels confident. Josephine's response to her workload represents one of the most important truths about managing disruptive emotions: What you *think* about what happens to you is more important than what actually happens to you. In other words, what is important is not what is happening *to you* but what is happening *in you*.

THE ABCs OF LIFE

Dr. Albert Ellis is a cognitive-behavioral psychologist known throughout the world as the father of Rational Emotive Therapy. He introduced the world to the idea that all of our disruptive emotions can be effectively managed if we simply take the time to analyze our thoughts and use our rational brain to think more accurately and realistically about the circumstances that surround our thoughts, feelings, and behaviors. His simple thesis was this:

> Your feelings follow your beliefs. What you believe about your world determines how you feel.

Dr. Ellis's Rational Emotive model of understanding and managing disruptive emotions is called: **The ABCs of Life**. **A** refers to the *activating events* of life. These are the circumstances, events, and experiences that precipitate our thoughts, feelings, and behaviors. **C** refers to our *consequential emotions and behaviors*. Our tendency in life is to blame our feelings and behaviors on activating events, without realizing that there is always something in between **A** and **C**—**B**, our *beliefs about the activating event*. The ABC model says that our feelings are determined by **B** and not by **A**. It is our *beliefs* about activating events that determine how we feel, *not the events themselves*.

We can apply the ABC model to the example above about Susan and her project task delegation.

A—Activating Event
Susan delegates work to Josephine and Harold.

B—Belief about Activating Event

There are actually many beliefs that Josephine or Harold could have:

1. My supervisor believes in me and thinks I am a good, hard worker.

2. My supervisor has it in for me and is trying to make my life miserable.

3. My supervisor knows that I am stressed out and doesn't care.

4. My supervisor doesn't understand my limits and is just trying to get all of the help she can.

5. My supervisor is ruining my life.

6. No, really, I'm just fine. It's no big deal that I have to work 80 hours this week.

C—Consequential Emotional Response

The emotional response completely varies depending on what is going on in the belief system.

This example shows how different ways of viewing the same event can lead to different emotional reactions. We can therefore manage our emotions by adding a **D** to our model. **D** refers to the idea that we can *dispute our thinking and replace self-defeating, irrational beliefs with rational, logical beliefs.*

SELF-DEFEATING BELIEFS

It requires a lot of effort to dispute the way you are thinking in every single situation. The cognitive approach is most effective when you realize that what you tell yourself in specific situations depends on the general beliefs you hold. To illustrate, let's have some fun with the authors of this book. Pretend that I hold to a general belief that says, *"People should know what I am thinking and feeling without me having to tell them."* Now, suppose I feel angry because my co-author, Jeff, did not call me to wish me a happy birthday.

The activating event is:

A—Jeff did not wish me a happy birthday.

The belief in this situation is:

B—Jeff should have known better.

Jeff knows how important my birthday is to me.

Jeff should have called me.

Jeff should call me now and apologize.

The consequential emotions are:

C—Anger, disappointment, hurt, resentment, revenge, and so on.

Notice that what I tell myself in the situation is dependent on my general belief. If I had a different general belief such as: "It is not rational to expect people to be mind-readers. If I want people to understand me, then I need to let them know how I feel, and even then they have the freedom to ignore my feelings," then I would tell myself something much different in the situation. When an activating event **A** triggers off a train of thought **B**, what we consciously think in the moment is both supported and determined by a set of general beliefs that we apply to the event.

What this means is that the best way to manage your emotions cognitively is to examine and dispute your underlying beliefs to make sure they serve you well. Many of your general beliefs are rational and logical and do serve you well, but some of your beliefs may be rigid and inflexible, even irrational and self-defeating. The above example that *"people should know what I am thinking and feeling without me telling them"* is an example of a self-defeating belief. It is self-defeating because *it is ontologically not true*. If you believe something that is not true, then you are setting yourself up for disappointment. It is just a matter of time before someone comes along and fails to understand you, and then you are going to be upset because of the belief.

Another example of a self-defeating belief is: *"To be worthwhile, I must be successful at everything I do."* Because this belief is a generalization, it will apply to all of your performance-based activities, and since this belief is self-defeating, it will eventually lead to dysfunctional emotional and behavioral responses. At work you take on a project-management role and several mistakes later you are looking at a failed project. Because of your self-defeating belief you conclude that you are not worthwhile, and then you "act out" your conclusion. You may get depressed or anxious, you may get angry and start blaming people, or you may feel shame and avoid taking future risks. At best you get defensive, make some excuse, and try to avoid looking like the failure was your fault. You may save face in the situation, but all of this leaves the self-defeating belief untouched, and so it is there to trip you up whenever some future failure triggers it off. To be successful, you must challenge any self-defeating beliefs that you hold.

Consider This

Most self-defeating beliefs are a variation of one or another of the 12 self-defeating beliefs' listed in Table 5-2. Take a look at this list now. Which ones do you identify with? Which are the ones that guide your reactions? Which ones do you need to dispute and change to more effectively manage your emotions and behaviors?

Table 5-2.   12 Self-Defeating Beliefs vs. 12 Rational Beliefs

12 Self-Defeating Beliefs	12 Rational Beliefs
1. I need love and approval from those significant to me—and I must avoid disapproval from any source.	1. Love and approval are good things to have, and I'll seek them when I can. But they are not necessities—I can survive (even though uncomfortably) without them.
2. To be worthwhile as a person I must achieve, succeed at whatever I do, and make no mistakes.	2. I'll always seek to achieve as much as I can, but unfailing success and omnipotence are unrealistic. Better I just accept myself as a person, separate from my performance.
3. People should always do the right thing. When they behave obnoxiously, unfairly, or selfishly they must be blamed and punished.	3. It's unfortunate that people sometimes do bad things. But humans are not yet perfect—and upsetting myself won't change that reality.
4. Things must be the way I want them to be—otherwise life will be intolerable.	4. There is no law that says things have to be the way I want them. It's disappointing, but I can stand it—especially if I avoid making events into catastrophes.
5. My unhappiness is caused by things that are outside of my control, so there is little I can do to feel any better.	5. Many external factors are outside my control. But it is my thoughts (not the externals) that cause my feelings. And I can learn to control my thoughts.
6. I must worry about things that could be dangerous, unpleasant, or frightening—otherwise they might happen.	6. Worrying about things that might go wrong won't stop them from happening. It will, though, ensure that I get upset and disturbed right now!
7. I can be happier by avoiding life's difficulties, unpleasantness, and responsibilities.	7. Avoiding problems is only easier in the short term—putting things off can make them worse later on. It also gives me more time to worry about them!

63

Table 5-2. *(continued)*

12 Self-Defeating Beliefs	12 Rational Beliefs
8. Everyone needs to depend on someone stronger than himself or herself.	8. Relying on someone else can lead to dependent behavior. It is OK to seek help—as long as I learn to trust myself and my own judgment.
9. Events in my past are the cause of my problems and they continue to influence my feelings and behaviors now.	9. The past can't influence me now. My current beliefs cause my reactions. I may have learned these beliefs in the past, but I can choose to analyze and change them in the present.
10. I should become upset when other people have problems and feel unhappy when they're sad.	10. I can't change other people's problems and bad feelings by getting myself upset.
11. I should not have to feel discomfort and pain—I can't stand them and must avoid them at all costs.	11. Why should I in particular not feel discomfort and pain? I don't like them, but I can stand it. Also, my life would be very restricted if I always avoided discomfort.
12. Every problem should have an ideal solution, and it is intolerable when one can't be found.	12. Problems usually have many possible solutions. It is better to stop waiting for the perfect answer and get on with the best one available. I can live with less than the ideal.

◆

EQuip Yourself

Manage Anger

- ◆ **Practice postponing your anger response for small increments of time**—Eventually, you will be able to postpone indefinitely and choose your response.
- ◆ **Find the triggers**—Identify the situations and circumstances that tend to trigger your anger response and manage those situations.

- **Mix pleasantness with anger**—Just as oil doesn't mix with water, anger doesn't mix with feelings of pleasantness. This is a behavioral strategy. To manage your anger, do something that makes you feel good—like taking a walk around a lake.

- **Reframe your anger**—Anger is often a signal to ask yourself the question: What is actually beneath my anger? The primary emotions that tend to drive anger are fear, deep concern, worry, guilt, and hurt. When you use your self-awareness to connect with your primary emotions, you are actually managing your anger by *reframing* it as one of these primary emotions. For example: instead of feeling angry at someone, you are feeling undervalued and misunderstood. These emotions will help you to handle the conflict-resolution dialogue more effectively, as we shall address in chapter 8.

- **Realign your expectations**—Anger often occurs because we feel an injustice has taken place. Sometimes there are injustices that we need to get angry about, such as groups like MADD being angry at intoxicated drivers. But other injustices are really violations of rules that exist in our minds that are not necessarily universally accepted social, legal, or ethical principles. In other words, sometimes when people fall short of our expectations, we get angry as if an injustice has occurred, when actually our expectation is unrealistic given the differences that exist between people. The solution is to adjust your expectations and bring them into greater alignment with reality.

- **Choose your battles carefully**—There are things in life that are worth spending your anger energy on, but you have to separate them from the things that are trivial. When you feel angry, your amygdala is not always drawing a clear distinction between a real injustice and a trivial offense. To help you make that distinction:

  - Take a step back, breathe, and ask yourself if the situation is worthy of a battle.

- Remind yourself that you don't have enough anger energy to make everything a battle, so you are committed to choosing your battles very carefully.
- Ask yourself if this situation is going to matter in 10 years. If your answer is no, then the situation is not worthy of your anger. Save it for something more important.

Manage Anxiety

- **Ask anxiety inventory questions**—Anxiety is an emotion that will tend to narrow your field of perception by making it difficult for you to see what is going on and what your choices are. We often get paralyzed by anxiety because we can't come up with a good answer to a question like: *"What do I do?"* Instead, we can ask:

  - What is going on here?
  - What's the worst thing that could happen?
  - How likely is that?
  - Is it in or out of my control?
  - Is there anything I can do?

- **Recognize the irrationality of worry**—Much of the time we spend worrying is unproductive, because worrying does not actually accomplish anything. It has been estimated that all but 10 percent of what we spend our energy worrying about is actually within our control. Focus your worry energy on the things that you can control that are actually important. Then you can move more quickly from worry to problem solving and use your time more efficiently.
- **Go ahead and worry, but with a purpose**—When you are worried, you can't manage the feeling by telling yourself to just stop worrying. After all, you probably have a reason for being anxious. One way to manage this anxiety is to give yourself permission to be anxious, but give it clear boundaries:

- Try to set worry times. Decide to spend 20 minutes worrying about an issue or a concern and create a list of *what if?* scenarios. *What if this happens? What if that happens?*
- Next, honestly confront the possibility that these things could happen by turning worry into anticipation: *If such and such happens . . .*
- Finally, turn anticipation into action: *Then I will . . .*

This particular strategy is designed to relieve your anxiety by helping you to see that even if what you fear does happen, you can handle it!

- **Resist using worry as a tool to manipulate others**—Worry can be used as a way to get other people to do what you want them to do. Parents do this all the time with children. A child is expected not to climb a tree because the parent is worried about the potential for an injury. The child complies, not because of understanding the safety issues, but because the child does not want the parent to worry. In effect, the child is managing the parent's worry *for the parent.* The desired behavior in the child actually reinforces the worrying behavior of the parent. The parent is unwittingly teaching the child to be manipulated by emotion instead of teaching the child how to think about what is or isn't responsible behavior. If you recognize that worry *can at times* be used as a tool to manipulate others, then you can manage it by reminding yourself that it is wrong to use your emotions to manipulate people.
- **Carpe Diem!**—See your present moments as times to live, rather than obsess about the future.

Manage Shame and Guilt

- **Be willing to face your feelings of guilt**—Guilt is often an emotional signal that is telling you that your behaviors are not in alignment with your core values, that you have actually done something wrong or irresponsible. Have you *really* done something wrong, or are you feeling guilty about establishing boundaries and setting limits (such as not watching the grandchildren because you have other plans)? If you have actually done something wrong and you feel guilty, then the best way to manage this kind of guilt is to apologize for the wrong you've committed and offer some suggestion to make the situation right.

♦ **Only take responsibility for your *own* guilt**—If, however, you have not done anything wrong, then perhaps your guilt is a signal telling you that you need to establish better boundaries with people and not expect yourself to take on responsibility for something that someone else is responsible for. Guilt is the emotion of responsibility, and sometimes people can be *overly* responsible for other people. If you are taking on responsibility for someone else's choices, then your guilt signal will actually be *overactive*. You can manage this guilt by recognizing the importance of establishing healthy boundaries with people.

♦ **Understand the difference between guilt and shame**— Many people feel condemned by guilt and live as if their past disqualifies them from having a hopeful future. Their guilt causes them to feel uniquely flawed, imperfect, and inadequate. This kind of guilt is more accurately called shame. Shame is one of the most neutralizing emotions that a person can experience. When people feel shame, they tend to avoid the challenges and opportunities that allow them to grow, learn, and develop into what they are capable of becoming.

♦ **Put guilt in perspective**—The wake that is created by a boat riding across a lake provides a nice metaphor for understanding how to manage guilt. The wake does not drive the boat forward, it simply reveals where the boat has been. Similarly, your past does not determine who you are or where you are going; it simply describes where you have been. It is the past and does not drive the present.

Look at your guilt as a marker along the trail that is signaling you to pause, reflect, and learn what you need to learn to move forward with better judgment and better understanding.

♦ **Try not to let your guilt overwhelm you when you fail or make a mistake**—Your guilt is simply a signal for you to learn. In Hollywood, a mistake is called a *mis-take*. The producer announces a do-over, re-shoots the scene, and then the *mis-take* becomes an *out-take* and is shown to the movie audience at the end of the film. These *bloopers* are sometimes the funniest scenes in the whole movie, with famous Hollywood actors laughing at themselves making mistakes. Learn to see your mistakes as *mis-takes*. They are learning opportunities. They are bloopers that you get to look back on and laugh about.

♦ **Reconsider your cognitive programming**—Perhaps your guilt is not your own but is actually a composite portrait made up of the messages you received while growing up.

♦ **Forgive yourself**—Accept the choices you have made in life, whether they feel good or bad, as where you were in that moment doing the best you could with the information and resources you had on hand.

Manage Feelings of Burnout and Depression

♦ **Listen to your feelings**—If you are feeling lethargic, lacking energy, and uninterested in activities that normally energize you, your feelings are probably telling you that you need to change the way you are organizing the activities of your life:

  ♦ Add an activity that you know will energize you.
  ♦ Subtract an activity that you know is draining you.
  ♦ Adjust the amount of time you are spending on activities that drain you.

- **Stick to the stress-management basics.**
  - Increase your physical activity.
  - Eat well.
  - Get plenty of rest.
  - Take quiet times for yourself.
  - Be true to your core values.

- **Create small successes**—If you are trying to achieve a long-term goal or are involved in a long project, create short-term goals to help you to experience a sense of accomplishment along the way.
- **Practice relational thinking**—As discussed in chapter 3, the more you can relate the details of what you do to an idea that gives your life a sense of meaning and value, the more you will do your work with inspiration, enthusiasm, and energy.
- **Choose strategies based in behavior**—Some of your best strategies for dealing with feelings of burnout and depression are behavioral:

  - Take a vacation.
  - Increase your fun factor.
  - Do activities that you know will bring fun, energy, and happiness into your life.

- **Reexamine your self-talk**—Don't forget your ABCs.
- **Don't hesitate to seek professional help if you need it**—There is a difference between feeling down or lethargic and experiencing clinical depression. If you are susceptible to prolonged periods (two weeks or more) of having a depressed mood most of the day and losing interest in activities that you normally enjoy, and no matter what you try you cannot seem to bring yourself out of your depressed mood, then you may be experiencing a clinical form of depression for which you need to seek out the services of a qualified medical professional such as a psychiatrist, or a qualified mental health professional such as a psychologist.

Chapter 6

Achieving Goals and Overcoming Adversity

.... **In this chapter, you will learn** ....

- ♦ how emotions drive your ability to achieve your goals
- ♦ how to train your brain for success
- ♦ how to be optimistic in the face of a setback.

....

GETTING OUT OF BED
IS AN EMOTIONALLY INTELLIGENT ACT

What is it that drives you toward successfully accomplishing your goals? Achieving lofty goals often requires sacrifice; nothing is gained for free, every threshold you try to cross carries a toll. How do you determine when the prize you seek outweighs the cost of attaining it? This is an emotional determination, and it is from your emotional power that you draw energy as you struggle to achieve what is important to you.

Let's check in on our EI classroom, where a discussion is now unfolding that may shed additional insight onto how your emotions factor into your ability to achieve your goals.

◆

A Glimpse into the Classroom: Sacrifice and Reward

"Who here gets up really early in the morning?" we ask the class. Hands go up. "Anna, what time do you get moving in the morning?" She replies that she gets up at 4:30 a.m. "4:30? Ouch!" we respond with a grimace. "You can't tell us that you actually enjoy getting up that early?" She shares that though she's been arising this early for many years and has grown accustomed to it, she wouldn't claim to like it. "So why do you do it? Aren't there mornings when the alarm goes off that you just want to toss it out the window and keep sleeping?" Anna acknowledges that getting out of bed at 4:30 a.m. is tough some days, but then goes on to describe how awakening so early on weekdays allows her to get on the road ahead of the traffic, get to the office before many of her colleagues arrive so she can have some uninterrupted and very productive work time, and, most important, leave work early enough to be home with her kids in the late afternoon and evening. Heads around the room nod as people see themselves in Anna's story. Anna has made the choice to give up something that she'd like to do—sleep in on certain days—in favor of something that is important to her—spend time with her kids while balancing a demanding career. We are each faced with similar choices every day. Although we may entertain the notion of sleeping in, and would certainly enjoy doing so, we get out of bed each day to get busy on those things that are important to us.

◆

Think of something you once desired and eventually attained—a goal you achieved, a milestone you reached, a triumph you realized—and now think of all that you had to sacrifice, the pain you had to endure, the struggle you faced to attain whatever this desire was. Why did you do it? Weren't you tempted along the way to abandon your quest? Wouldn't it have been easier to just give up? Just as Anna gives up the pleasure of extra sleep to gain something of greater value to her, this accomplishment of yours, and the fact that you actually did accomplish it despite the challenge of doing so, is a glowing testament to your emotional intelligence. Let us explain further.

WHAT DOES A MARSHMALLOW HAVE TO DO WITH SUCCESS?

There's a wonderful story often mentioned in discussions of EI about a research study done at Stanford University back in the 1960s. The study focused on delayed gratification and involved four-year-old children and marshmallows. Researchers would present a marshmallow to a four-year-old; but before giving the marshmallow over to be eaten, they'd offer the child a deal. The researcher claimed to need to step out of the room for a few moments and told the child that she or he could eat the one marshmallow at any time. If, however, the child would wait and not eat the marshmallow until the researcher returned to the room, the child could have two marshmallows. With an assurance that the child understood the game, the researcher got up and left the room. According to the record of this experiment, in some cases, before the door even closed on the researcher's exit, the child gobbled up the marshmallow and the game was over. These kids had given in to what to a four-year-old must have seemed an overwhelming temptation, to enjoy this tasty little puff of sugar as soon as possible. Of course, in doing so, these kids were forfeiting the opportunity for doubling their reward . . . two marshmallows as opposed to just the one.

There were children who tried not to eat the single marshmallow immediately. Some of them hid their eyes as if to make the temptation disappear. Some turned away from the table or occupied themselves in other ways. One child even licked the table around the marshmallow. These kids fought the impulse for immediate gratification, attempting instead to apply energy toward achieving a greater goal. Some of them were actually successful in doing so. Upon the researcher's return, there was the child *and* the uneaten marshmallow; and the child was, as promised, justly rewarded.

The researchers asked two important questions of this experiment:

"What quality was it about these children that allowed them to resist temptation and focus on a grander goal, even at the impulse-driven age of four?"

"What value would this quality bring to these children's lives as they grew older?"

The research study picked up 14 years later. The once four-year-old participants were now 18-year-old high school students. The research team found that the "marshmallow grabbers" suffered low self-esteem and were viewed by others as stubborn, prone to envy, and easily frustrated. Those kids who were able to delay their gratification in the face of the marshmallow temptation had scored better on their college entrance exams, were more successful in achieving goals, were more socially competent and self-assertive, were better equipped to deal with the challenges and uncertainties of life at that age, and had, by most measures of success for a young adult, thrived in their lives.

OF MARSHMALLOWS AND EMOTIONAL INTELLIGENCE

So how does any of this relate to EI?

You have goals you're striving to attain. You are working hard for a promotion or perhaps to finish law school. You're saving for your dream house or putting money away for retirement. You're sweating to shed a few pounds or putting miles underfoot as you work up to running a marathon. To stick with the marshmallow metaphor, you might call such goals your *Grand Marshmallow Goals*. You can imagine how it will feel to realize your goals, how these achievements will benefit your life. You can imagine how wonderful it will be to take a big puffy bite out of the *Grand Marshmallow*.

Whatever achievements you seek to realize though, there are temptations along the way that try to lure you off the path. Distractions, diversions, doubts . . . these are the small marshmallows you must resist in pursuit of your Grand Marshmallow. The small marshmallows certainly taste good, and it is tempting to eat just one or two. But deep inside, you know that the satisfaction they would bring would be fleeting and that giving in to these small marshmallow temptations ultimately undermines the pursuit of your grander goal.

> **Guiding Principle**
>
> *The ability to stay focused on an important goal is rooted in your emotions.*

The ability to turn away from temptation and stay focused on an important goal is rooted in your emotions. You are attempting to overcome the emotional lure of small marshmallow temptations and at the same time to move passionately and enthusiastically toward your goal. Success actually requires two acts of emotional self-management:

1. You need to develop an emotional attachment (passion, enthusiasm, excitement, desire) to the goal you are trying to achieve.

2. You need to use the strength of this attachment to overcome any challenges (temptations, emotional lures) you encounter along the path to goal fulfillment.

The researchers at Stanford who worked with the "Marshmallow Kids" all those years ago termed this behavior Goal-Directed Self-Imposed Delay of Gratification. We simply call it emotional intelligence.

All of this begs the question: *"How do I create emotional attachments to my goals that are stronger than the desires I already have to give in to my temptations?"*

TRAINING YOUR BRAIN

In the pursuit of your goals, your brain can be either friend or foe. At its baseline root as a behavioral guidance system, the human brain works to maximize pleasure and minimize pain. This is an offshoot of the *"Good for me!"* versus *"Not good for me!"* behavioral protocol housed within the emotional center of the mammalian brain discussed in chapter 4. This level of the brain is not "aware" of the long-term goals you've set or choices you've made about priorities in life. The emotional brain is disconnected from your desire to lose weight, for example, and may lead you down the path to temptation when the dessert tray comes around. Seeking to maximize pleasure and minimize pain, this impulse-based aspect of your brain determines that, indeed, your immediate pleasure (*Good for me!*) would be to partake of some dessert, and recognizes, in fact, that it is painful (*Not good for me!*)

> **Guiding Principle**
>
> *Training your brain means teaching your emotional brain what is truly important to you. It requires the creation of an emotional connection with the goals you've set for yourself.*

to deny yourself such a treat. The desire to enjoy some dessert in this case is an amygdala-triggered emotional reaction and therefore often hard to resist. Resisting is hard but not impossible to do.

Training your brain literally means teaching this emotional aspect of your brain what is truly important to you. It requires the creation of an emotional connection with the goals you've set for yourself, a connection powerful enough to override your brain's immediate-gratification protocol, which initially attempts to influence your behavior. In this effort, you are striving to bring your emotional brain into your long-term, goal-driven vision. This requires reversing the wiring on what your brain understands as *"Good for me!"* and *"Not good for me!"* in terms of this particular goal. You would be teaching your emotional brain that cheating on your weight-loss plan, even just this once, is to actually experience the pain of failure in realizing a goal you desire and that true pleasure lies in achieving this goal on which you've placed such a high degree of importance. Through this process, the pain of failure becomes more painful than the pain of resisting temptation, *and* the desire to experience the future thrill of success becomes stronger than the desire to give in to the dessert.

SUCCESS BEGINS WITH SELF-AWARENESS

Once again self-awareness plays a critical role when it comes to controlling impulses, delaying gratification, and training your brain toward the achievement of challenging goals. Activating your self-awareness in this regard means being clear about what your goal is and why you want it. If you hold only a vague notion or a fuzzy picture of a goal, it won't seem real or solid enough to you. You're striving to establish a powerful emotional connection to your desired outcome and you need something for those emotions to latch on to. Gain clarity by following these two steps:

1. Create a clear picture of what it is you desire. What does success look like? What will it feel like when you have achieved this goal? Vividly imagine the joy and pride contained in the experience of attaining your goal.

2. Establish clarity as to your motivation for achieving this goal. Why do you want it? What value will its attainment bring to

your life? It is from this clarity around your motivating driver for achieving this goal that your effort gains its emotional energy. If this energy is powerful enough for you, temptation doesn't stand a chance.

CREATE A CLEAR PICTURE OF WHAT IT IS YOU DESIRE

Vision is the powerful tool you use to bond emotionally with your goals. As the term implies, vision allows you to "see" your goal achieved, first in your mind and then in reality. You must be able to close your eyes and envision yourself having attained your goal, to imagine every aspect of the experience, to feel what it is like to have accomplished this outcome you've worked so hard to realize. Your mind cannot distinguish between what is real and what is vividly imagined. To vividly imagine a desired outcome generates an emotional response in your body—you literally experience what it will feel like to have succeeded. This experience, activated by your emotional brain in response to a vision held in your mind, connects you even more fully to what it is you seek to achieve. This is the basis for leveraging the power of your emotions toward realizing your goals.

ESTABLISH CLARITY AS TO YOUR MOTIVATION FOR ACHIEVING THIS GOAL

Connecting with your motivations for achieving whatever your goal may be locks in your emotional connection to that goal all the more. *Why do I want this? What will it bring to my life?* For someone who has struggled to quit smoking, the birth of a grandchild and the incredible desire to be a part of that child's life as he or she grows up can be an emotionally powerful driver to stop smoking and thereby remain healthy. The pride, sense of self-satisfaction, and measure of individual success that will be yours on attaining a long-sought professional position is a driver rooted in emotion. All motivating drivers get their power from an emotional connection to the outcome they are driving you toward. A goal lacking an emotional connection is a goal to which you are unlikely to commit the energy required to attain it.

OPTIMISM: EI FOR OVERCOMING LIFE'S SETBACKS

Not all desired achievements come easily. In fact, no matter how emotionally connected to them you may be and how hard you work to realize them, some never materialize at all. Sometimes you just fail. What does EI have to say about that?

In Goleman's model of EI, he includes the competency of optimism as being part of the EI domain of self-management. Optimism? Is he referring to the bright, sunny attitude that the glass is always half full and that behind every gray cloud there gleams a silver lining? Not at all. This is not the Pollyanna School of Optimism. This is the Seligman School of Optimism.

Dr. Martin Seligman is a professor of psychology at the University of Pennsylvania and author of *Learned Optimism* (1991) among other books. Seligman describes optimism as being based in how we make sense of the setbacks we experience in life. This is what he calls our *explanatory style*, having to do with how we *explain* to ourselves psychologically what went awry when life throws a challenge or setback our way and, more important, what we can do about that challenge or setback.

Two salespeople are giving a presentation to an important client. It doesn't go well. The optimist of the two will evaluate what went wrong, acknowledge the individual actions that contributed to the outcome, set in place a plan for improvement, and fully believe in the possibility of success the next time around. We might view this as a positive or optimistic explanatory style. The optimist follows a specific explanatory path in the face of setback. He or she:

- does his or her best to assess the situation objectively
- owns the outcome
- commits to a course of action for change
- holds a powerful belief in the possibility for implementing that change successfully.

The other salesperson, lacking the optimism of his partner, may find himself in a downward spiral of negative thinking and self-doubt, feeling powerless to do anything different toward a more successful outcome in the future. This person obviously holds a different set of beliefs and operates under a more pessimistic explanatory style.

Consider This

What is your typical explanatory style when things don't quite go your way? Consider the last time you experienced a setback of some significance and reflect back on your self-talk and subsequent behavior in response to that circumstance. Rate your response in this situation on a scale from 1-5 with 5 representing a highly optimistic response and 1 representing a low optimistic response. How reflective is this score of your usual level of optimism in the face of a setback? How might you strengthen your optimistic viewpoint in preparation for future challenges you may face?

None of us experience a life free from setbacks. We all have known times when life has simply not gone our way. It is our EI that allows us to be resilient in the face of these setbacks, to pick ourselves up, dust ourselves off, gather our wits, and press ever onward. Our EI competencies concerning self-awareness and self-management—the abilities to understand our emotions and leverage them toward appropriate behavioral performance without letting these emotional responses in the face of life's challenges undermine our intentions—are what we draw on in times of struggle. Our EI forms the basis of our explanatory style, determining our optimistic or pessimistic outlook. Optimism, as a component of self-management, may then be defined as

> the ability to recover from setbacks, to learn from mistakes and less-than-positive outcomes, and to have faith in our abilities to implement change toward eventual success.

EQuip Yourself
for Optimistic Goal Achievement

Empower your success with the energy of your emotions. Practice training your brain as to what's truly important to you, create emotional bonds to the visions you hold, and harness your sense of optimism to overcome life's challenges. Follow these strategies for success:

Keep Your Eye on the Grand Marshmallow

1. Think of a goal you would like to commit yourself to— something that holds significant meaning in your life. There are, no doubt, things that you'll have to give up to attain this goal, sacrifices to be made, temptations to overcome.

2. Generate a list of the temptations that hold the potential to lure you off the path of fulfilling your desired goal. Of these temptations, which is most enticing to you? How will you avoid or overcome this temptation when it crosses your path?

3. Clarify a list of strategies you'll employ to stay focused on your goal and empower you to disregard the temptations that threaten your success.

Practice Your ABCs for Optimism

In chapter 5, we introduced you to the ABCs: activating event, belief, and consequential response. This simple but powerful tool is the key to maintaining an optimistic outlook in the face of setback:

1. Start applying the label "activating event" to the daily challenges you face.

2. Designate a little alarm sound that goes off inside your head whenever you notice such an event coming your way. Recognizing the challenges of life as activating events will trigger an awareness of your ABCs. You'll recall that you have the power to choose your beliefs and thus your response to any challenge that confronts you.

3. Choose optimism by enacting the attitude that each challenge you face offers learning and growth. There is no such thing as failure except failure to learn.

Chapter 7

Social Awareness

.... **In this chapter, you will learn** ....

- why empathy is so important to success in your relationships
- the difference between empathy and agreement
- how to communicate your empathy to others
- why empathy works
- how to avoid behaviors that destroy empathy.

The motion picture industry has presented us with some of the best examples of how body language conveys meaning. In *The Godfather, Part II*, when Al Pacino sends a furtive glance to his personal bodyguard and *caporegime*, Al Neri, the viewer is immediately drawn into the underworld of organized crime, where the emotional intelligence skill of social awareness is needed to understand the scene. This is because facial expression, not words, is used to convey the awful truth that Michael Corleone has just put out a hit on his brother Fredo. We begin our discussion on social awareness with a classroom exercise on how to read the emotional messages that people communicate using body language.

◆

A Glimpse into the Classroom: Social Awareness

"What emotions are being expressed in this video clip?" A scene from the movie *Titanic* is playing with the sound muted. Participants have been asked to pick up on the nonverbal cues of the actors in the scene and identify the emotions they represent. The emotional messages transmitted through the body language of the actors are easily converted into an emotional vocabulary: fear, shock, surprise, confusion, anxiety, and seriousness. A participant named Emily is particularly astute as she observes "resignation." Emily is picking up on the very subtle nuances of expression on the face of the actress Kate Winslet, who is at the same time both shocked at and accepting of the fate of the ship that was originally thought to be unsinkable—her thoughts and facial expressions alternately shift from surprise and bewilderment: "How could this be happening?" to acceptance and resignation: "What are we going to do?" By tuning in to these subtleties of nonverbal communication, Emily is demonstrating a high degree of the emotional intelligence competence of social awareness.

◆

Why is it important to sense what other people feel without their verbal messages? The answer is that people are not always authentic in telling you exactly what they think and feel. Consider the following examples:

- A team leader closes the meeting thinking he has buy-in on an idea. He fails to realize that the team is gathering again in the parking lot outside. This second team meeting, undermining the first, could have been avoided if the leader had noticed Carla's downcast face and Jones and Smith rolling their eyes at each other as he failed to take another of Carla's ideas seriously.
- A salesperson is trying to win over a potential customer with enthusiasm, not realizing that the customer has sent several nonverbal cues requesting time alone to process the information internally.

- A waiter, upset about a 10 percent tip, fails to realize that the tip would have been the usual 20 percent if he had picked up on the nonverbal signals that requested attention at one point during the meal, and a desire for privacy at another point.
- An interviewer decides against hiring someone who not only claimed to be very interested in the job but also claimed to have several years of experience. There was just something about the lack of alertness, the scrutinizing looks, the fidgety hands, the lack of eye contact, and the glance at the watch that made the interviewer distrust the interviewee's answers.
- An employee walks into her supervisor's office and notices immediately his annoyed sigh, the tension in his neck, and the "What now?" look. Sensing that he is very focused and feels interrupted, she says, "You're really hard at it, sir. I'm sorry to interrupt you. Is there a time later on this afternoon or tomorrow when we can discuss the Johnson proposal?"
- A mother asks her eight-year-old son, Andrew, if something is bothering him. The boy says, "No, it's nothing." His downcast facial expression and the tone of his voice tell a different story though. His mother knows not to push. Instead they bond over a competitive game of basketball. After the game they pour two ice-cold glasses of juice. At the perfect moment Mom asks: "Now tell me what's wrong." Andrew shares his story.

All of these examples demonstrate how social awareness can make the difference between success or failure in social interactions. When we are attentive to emotional cues and listen well to others, we reduce unproductive conflicts and increase the likelihood of mutually beneficial outcomes.

EMPATHY: THE HEART OF COMMUNICATION

Some people would call empathy the art of communication. It's true. The more you can develop your empathic skills, the more effective you will be at communication. But empathy is defined as taking an *active interest* in other people's concerns. Therefore, it is more than just an art.

Empathy is an attitude. It is a way of being. *To be active* requires conscious effortful behavior. *Interest* requires a genuine heartfelt respect for what another person has to offer. To engage ourselves in the active pursuit of understanding another human being, we need to be convinced completely in our hearts that all people have equal dignity and worth and therefore deserve the respect of being listened to.

This is why we call empathy the *heart* of communication. Best-selling author and leadership expert John Maxwell (1993, p. 117) says it this way, "People do not care how much you know until they know how much you care." There is no quicker path to demonstrating that you care about another person than to communicate to that person with empathy. If you want someone to care about what you think, you have to care about what he or she thinks. In your heart of hearts you need to believe that:

- ◆ understanding is as important as being understood
- ◆ listening is as important as being listened to
- ◆ caring is as important as being cared about
- ◆ other people's ideas are as important as your ideas
- ◆ giving respect is as important as receiving it.

BUILDING BRIDGES

Imagine two people standing across a wide expanse from one another, each with his or her own set of intentions, perspectives, ideas, interests, positions, feelings, and concerns. They would like to have a conversation that resolves a problem they share, but the conversation is difficult because the expanse represents a large gap in their understanding of one another. The only way that they can solve the problem in mutually beneficial ways is to build a *bridge of understanding* across this gap separating them. Intellectually, they both have taken enough training in communication to know that the sender and receiver are two different operating systems, and that real communication doesn't happen unless they can, together, create an area of shared understanding. Theory and practice are often two separate entities, however, and in the case of communication, our heads often imagine what our ears fail to hear.

The difference between theory and practice is often the difference between thoughtful, effortful communication and default communication. When two people in a communication exchange disagree with one another, each person will often experience the other person's posi-

tion as an attack. We have already explored what the brain does when it senses an attack. The amygdala immediately sends both sender and receiver into defense mode, and both parties default to a style of communication that is characterized by debating and defending their individual positions. Using our analogy, this means that the sender begins to build the bridge of understanding from *her side* of the ravine. The receiver, in response, senses his position as being under attack, and so he begins to build the bridge of understanding from *his side* of the ravine. The result, of course, is that instead of understanding taking place, you end up with a debate in which each person is trying to get the other to come over to his or her side.

CHARLIE: Sally, I thought we decided that we were going to roll out the product by the end of the month.

SALLY: No, Charlie, we don't have a firm date, because Quality hasn't come back with their final results.

CHARLIE: Quality needs to work with our timeline. If we let them set the timeline, we'll be here until next year.

SALLY: Quality is moving as fast as they can and they aren't going to compromise their results.

CHARLIE: Look, my salespeople are already taking orders and promising delivery. There are a lot of people who are depending on an end-of-month suspense date.

SALLY: Look, Charlie, your sales team is putting the cart before the horse. I can't make that promise.

When two people try to persuade each other with compelling reasons, they rarely are able to persuade each other's emotional states. The more

Guiding Principle

If you want to influence people, you need to understand empathically the power of their point of view and to feel the emotional force with which they believe it.

Charlie *feels* his timeline slipping away, the more emotional he will get defending his side of the conversation. The more Sally *feels* the concerns of Quality are not being respected, the more emotional she will get about defending her position. Sally and Charlie's conversation will keep going back and forth in a stalemate, until one of them changes *the rules of engagement*. Clearly, these rules of engagement should not be determined by the amygdala. It requires effort and thoughtfulness, but this conversation will be much more productive if either Charlie or Sally *begins to build the bridge of understanding from the other person's side of the ravine*. The principle is simply this: To influence people, you must understand their point of view and feel the emotional force of their belief.

This means that the best way to get people to enter into your frame of reference is to first enter into theirs. This is Stephen Covey's (1989) fifth habit: *Seek first to understand, and then to be understood*. This is the essence of empathy. Empathy is a communication tool that builds a bridge of understanding between two people by starting on the other person's side of the ravine. It is a way to communicate your understanding so that the other person will feel more of the compassion that you have for him or her.

One reason why empathy bridges the communication gap is because it "reaps what it sows." When one person is willing to get close to another person's world of meaning and feeling, it engenders the same behavior in return. The good news is that empathy is completely within the control of the person who chooses to apply it. You cannot control how other people think and feel, but you can control the degree to which you will enter into that world of thinking and feeling. Through empathy, you make the kind of connection that allows you to then draw other people into your world of meaning and feeling.

EMPATHY DOES NOT EQUAL AGREEMENT

One important distinction needs to be made here. Empathy does not equal agreement. Some people unfortunately confuse empathy with identification. They use phrases like:

"I know just what you mean."

"Boy, you got that right! I know exactly how you feel."

"I'd feel the same way if that happened to me."

"Oh, you poor dear. I'm so sorry this happened to you."

These kinds of phrases actually join two people together in an emotional alliance. There can be comfort and sympathy in knowing that another person feels or thinks the same way that you do, but this is not what we mean by empathy. The confusion actually causes some people to avoid practicing empathy because they are concerned that understanding implies agreement, and they are not willing to send a signal to the other speaker that they agree. Empathy, when done correctly, does not establish an agreement. What empathy does is create a common ground that makes it easier for two or more people to explore a mutually beneficial agreement. Consider what the conversation between Charlie and Sally would look like if either person decided to change the rules of engagement by using empathy and building the bridge from the other side of the ravine:

CHARLIE:	Sally, I thought we decided that we were going to roll out the product by the end of the month.
SALLY:	No, Charlie, we don't have a firm date, because Quality hasn't come back with their final results.
CHARLIE:	(Coming over to Sally's side of the ravine.) You mean that safety may be an issue that holds up the roll-out date?

SALLY: Yes. Apparently there are some inconsistencies in the test results, and Quality needs to do some additional tests.

CHARLIE: (Still on Sally's side) How serious are the inconsistencies?

SALLY: It is hard to tell. We're moving as fast as we can to get you what you need without compromising our research.

CHARLIE: (Still on Sally's side.) Well, I certainly appreciate the effort. The last thing I want is for your people to compromise their research. Do you understand our sense of urgency?

SALLY: Not really. What's up?

(Now Charlie gets to build the bridge back to his side of the ravine.)

CHARLIE: Well, there is so much buzz going around, my sales team is already taking orders and customers are expecting delivery. There are a lot of people who are depending on an end-of-month suspense date.

SALLY: You're already getting customer response and you're hoping we will all be able to meet an end-of-the-month deadline? (Now Sally is on Charlie's side of the ravine.)

CHARLIE: Well, it would sure make everyone happy.

SALLY: I can't make a promise, Charlie, without the final results, but now that we understand each other's concerns, let's communicate them to our teams. I'll make sure my people understand the sense of urgency.

CHARLIE: Thanks, Sally. I'll make sure that the sales team respects the quality issues.

WALKING THROUGH THE SKILL OF EMPATHIC LISTENING

One of the best ways to demonstrate your empathy for another person is to listen to that person with reflective, empathic listening responses. Empathic listening is a way to communicate your understanding so that the other person will feel more of the respect that you have for him or her. As you respond to people, it is useful to listen for material they may be sharing in the form of:

Thoughts they are considering

Feelings they have

Behaviors that are a part of them

Experiences they are having or have had.

Your empathic response should reflect an understanding of and a willing-ness to get close to those aspects of the other person's world. It can be helpful to organize your thinking by considering that *people have feelings* in response to *events* that occur. The most basic way to organize your understanding is to use the following format:

"You feel (feelings) because (the event: a thought, feeling, behavior, or experience)."

The event may be any of the four types of material listed previously. For example, sometimes we have feelings because of emotions we are having—"I feel guilty because I've been angry."

In addition to the most basic, "You feel _____ because _____," you may find yourself using the following variations:

Multiple feelings expressed
"You feel ____ because ____ and you also feel ____ because ____."

Mixed feelings expressed
"On the one hand you feel _____ because _____, but on the other hand, you feel _____ because _____."

In the event that an important component is missing or you are unclear about it, you may find yourself asking questions or requesting more information:

Event Missing

"It sounds like you're feeling _____, but I'm not sure what's going on to make you feel that way."

Feeling Missing

"So these issues (summary of event) are going on, but I'm not sure how you feel about it."

Empathic listening includes being curious, asking good questions, and inviting more information:

"Tell me more about that."

"What are some of the details?"

"How did that happen?"

"What is important to you about that?"

"How did that make you feel?"

"What are some of your ideas about this?"

"What can I do to help/support you?"

"What do you want?"

"What is your intention?"

"What would things look like if they were better?"

"Do you mind if I ask you some questions about that?"

When you are using these empathic listening skills with another person, try to avoid beginning your questions with the word "why." "Why" questions are often perceived to be a challenge or a threat to what the person is thinking, and this invites defensiveness. The goal is to make people feel your curiosity and the interest you have in them. *"Why would you think that the customer is unhappy?"* is not nearly as effective as, *"What do you think is going on that is making the customer unhappy?"*

WHY EMPATHIC LISTENING WORKS

Why do we place so much importance on reflective, empathic listening responses? The simple answer is because they work. They are especially helpful when the speaker is under stress, when someone has a problem or an important need, when the speaker is very passionate about something, when two or more people are negotiating, or when teams are building consensus and brainstorming for ideas. Empathic listening then becomes the tool that allows people to explore their issues and concerns in a way that usually leads to creative and effective problem solving.

Unfortunately, when people are first introduced to these listening skills, they are often resistant and hesitate to use them. They feel as if any attempt at structuring communication is too mechanical and not *natural* enough. We believe that *all* communication is structured (or at least should be!) and that structure, in and of itself, does not prevent the expression of individual style. The only reason why these empathic listening skills do not feel natural is they have not been *practiced* enough. Once they have been sufficiently practiced they will become a very natural part of the communicator's repertoire. Indeed, we have never met a counselor, social worker, teacher, or some other trained listener who uses reflective listening skills on a regular basis, complain that the skills are too wooden and mechanical. In fact, most experts in this area of communication will agree that reflective listening, when used properly and daily, is the most effective tool one can use to overcome the difficulties of human communication.

Author and communication expert Dr. Robert Bolton (1979) describes six *peculiarities* of communication that hinder effective communication but can be avoided easily through empathic communication. Four of these problems are common to speakers, two to listeners. When one realizes how common these six peculiarities are, the incentive to use empathic listening techniques increases. Indeed, our listening skills not only help us to communicate warmth and genuine concern for people, but they also provide us with the checks for accuracy that eliminate many of these communication difficulties:

1. Words have different meanings for different people.

2. People often "code" their messages so that their real meaning is masked.

3. People frequently talk about "presenting problems" when another issue is of greater concern to them.

4. Speakers may be blind to their emotions or blinded by them.

5. Listeners are often easily distracted.

6. Listeners hear through "filters" or "mental models" that distort much of what is being said.

Words have different meanings for different people.

Consider what parents mean when they say: *"I can't trust you"* and what teenagers mean when they say: *"You don't trust me."* Both are using the same word, "trust," but with different meanings. Parents are usually talking about obedience and responsibility, *"I don't trust that you will make the right decision."* Teenagers are usually talking about freedom, *"You don't trust me enough to give me independence on this issue, either the freedom to make the right choice, or the freedom to make the wrong choice and learn from it."* Empathy allows us to clarify these different meanings of the same word.

People often "code" their messages so that their real meaning is masked.

The children's game of hide and seek is played more often by adults than we realize. We are often ambivalent about exposing what we really think and feel to others. On the one hand we want to be known and understood; on the other hand we want to stay in hiding. When it comes to communication, our favorite hiding place is behind *coded* messages. That is, we express ourselves *indirectly* on many topics and feelings. Consider these examples:

> At bedtime a child asks his parents, "Could you read me a bedtime story?" The parents agree, and after the story is read the child says, "Read me another one." The child proceeds to ask 20 questions of

a story he practically has memorized because he has heard it so often. His empathetic parents realize that *"Read me another one"* is code for *"I'd like you to stay here with me a while longer."*

A manager says to a direct report: "Thanks for putting together that spreadsheet. I am going to use it in my presentation at our next board meeting." Behind this message are several possible meanings that may or may not be what the manager thinks or feels. *What do you think the message behind the message is?*

In both of these examples it becomes the listener's job to *decode* the message behind the message. Empathy, including carefully observing the body language and using reflective listening skills, makes the decoding possible. In the second example, the direct report notices his manager perusing the figures on the spreadsheet with a look of concern on his face. There is no eye contact. The direct report decides that the manager is concerned about accuracy and that the real message is: "I hope you double-checked your figures because I don't want to look like a fool." The direct report uses his reflective listening skills to confirm this, "You're welcome! I'm honored that you are using my work. Do you have any concerns about those figures?"

Imagine this same example playing out in a different way. The manager makes direct eye contact and gives the thumbs-up sign. The direct report decides that the manager is concerned about giving credit where credit is due, and so the real message is: "I hope you know how valuable you are to this organization. I am very pleased with your work." Again, empathic listening skills can be used to confirm this, "You are welcome. I'm glad the spreadsheet is helpful. It feels good to know I have your vote of confidence."

The process of getting at real meaning in these communication examples involves moving from what is directly observable to what is hidden. The directly observable includes the body language, the tone of voice, and the content of a person's message. Thoughts and feelings, however, are often hidden. We use empathy to tune into the facial expressions and the nonverbal cues, and we use empathic listening responses to clarify the content. By focusing our empathy and our empathic listening skills on what is directly observable, what is hidden will often rise to the surface.

People frequently talk about "presenting problems" when another issue is of greater concern to them.

Suppose you are mentoring a colleague, and this person comes to you with a presenting problem: "I really would like to have a better relationship with my supervisor." You probe for more information and this person says: "I never seem to know where I stand with my supervisor because s/he never gives me feedback on my performance." If you do not use empathy to continue to explore this statement, then you are likely to respond with whatever theory comes to your mind:

"I've always gone by the principle that no news is good news."

"It helps to realize that feedback is a rare occurrence around here because everyone is so busy."

"Maybe you need to get your feedback from other sources, like your peers or your customers."

"You know supervisors are required to respond to requests for 360-feedback evaluation. If you send our 360-feedback survey to five of your co-workers and to your supervisor, then s/he will be required to fill it out for you."

All of these theories address the presenting problem, and some of them may even be helpful. But what if the presenting problem is not the *real* problem? What if the real problem has to do with something that is much more vulnerable and much more difficult for this person you are mentoring to connect with, much less reveal? It is much easier for one to complain about someone else's behavior than it is to get to the core of what one needs to change. Empathy creates the communication environment that makes it safe for people to explore their root issues. In this case a more important concern might be something like: "I really have a hard time just walking up to a supervisor and asking for feedback. I always want the supervisor to initiate it, and when she doesn't, I don't know how to go about getting it." This deeper concern is only revealed through the use of empathy.

Speakers may be blind to their emotions or blinded by them.

Trying to figure out how to solve a problem when you are emotional is like trying to understand an impressionist painting when you are standing too close to it. Distance and perspective are often needed to figure out what is going on. Emotions, especially anxiety, have the power to narrow a person's field of perception, thus making it difficult to solve problems. When this happens, it is often helpful to process thoughts out loud with a good friend who is willing to listen.

The listening friend rarely has to do anything more than provide reflective, empathic responses to what is being said. The empathic responses operate in much the same way that a mirror operates when it is reflecting back to you information about how you look. The mirror doesn't actually solve the problem. That is, the mirror will not actually pull out a comb and fix your hair for you. You make the necessary adjustment. The mirror simply reflects back the information that is needed to make that adjustment. This works well as long as you are not standing too close to the mirror. In the same way, most of us are pretty good problem solvers, as long as we are not standing too close to the emotions that surround our problems. Empathic listening is the mirror that gives us perspective on our problems. It doesn't actually solve our problems, but it provides us with the perspective needed to make the necessary adjustments.

Listeners are often easily distracted.

One of the reasons for poor listening is that people can think much faster than they can talk. We speak 125 words per minute, but we are able to listen to 500 words per minute. Many of us grow bored with the slow pace of conversation. The extra 375 words per minute of space in our brain is easily distracted. We find ourselves filling this space with our own agendas, with our clever arguments, with our plans for the weekend, or with something else that is stimulating our brain. Empathic listening can keep us focused on the speaker, because it allows us to capitalize on this thought speed by filling the extra thinking time with our reflective responses.

Listeners hear through "filters" or "mental models" that distort what is being said.

One mode of thinking people use when they are listening is called automatic processing. Imagine if every time you communicated with someone you had to mentally process every thought that was presented.

"We are going to hold our annual Fall Conference this year in New Orleans."

You could easily spend a half an hour of your time looking up *Fall Conference* in the employee manual and Googling *New Orleans*. This is 30 minutes of mental energy that can be conserved, *as long as you possess the cognitive skill to process this information automatically.*

Thankfully, people do possess this skill and are able to make automatic, quick judgment decisions by using their mental models.

Mental models are the filters or lenses that people use to see and interpret the world.

We can think of our brains as operating like Rolodexes, those now-outdated storage systems we used for keeping track of names, addresses, phone numbers, and other such information. Our mental Rolodex works like this: When an idea or concept enters our mind, we mentally search our Rolodex for whatever information we have related to that idea or concept. Our information may be extensive or somewhat limited. One of the functions of the mental Rolodex is to organize this information into themes or categories that are relevant for reducing ambiguity and uncertainty. Such organization allows for quick judgment decisions.

This means that when you hear someone say "New Orleans," your mind immediately flashes through the thoughts and images you associate with this city. What you hear then is dependent on your filter, and it may be very different from what the other person is saying. Your mental models help to make communication efficient, but they can also distort what you hear. When you are aware of your mental models, you can use your empathic listening skills to have open conversations in which mental models may be exposed and shared.

FEELING BLOCKERS: THE OPPOSITE OF EMPATHY

One final way to understand empathy is to understand the behaviors that are the opposite of empathy. If empathy involves entering into and understanding another person's world of thoughts, feelings, and ideas, then the opposite of empathy is any behavior that breaks down the flow of communication and increases the emotional distance between people. We call these behaviors communication spoilers or feeling blockers.

> **Feeling Blockers**—Any behaviors that reduce the likelihood that the speaker will constructively explore or express his or her true thoughts and feelings.

Dr. Robert Bolton (1979) has outlined the 12 most common feeling blockers. It has been estimated that these behaviors are used over 90 percent of the time when one or both parties to a conversation have a problem to be dealt with or a need to be fulfilled. Unfortunately, we often interject feeling blockers into conversations without realizing it. The unintended effect is the exact opposite of empathy. Feeling blockers trigger defensiveness, resistance, resentment, withdrawal, and feelings of defeat or of inadequacy. They also decrease the likelihood that the person feeling blocked will find a solution to his or her problem.

As you look through the list, take a moment to reflect on any behaviors you see that may be getting in the way of developing your social awareness. We all use these behaviors from time to time, and the result is not always negative. Sometimes we will use these behaviors with little or no effect on emotional closeness. When people are under stress or have difficult problems to solve, however, the likelihood that these behaviors will damage the relationship increases greatly. A good rule to follow is to avoid all feeling blockers whenever you or another person is under stress.

> **Guiding Principle**
>
> *Whenever you or another person are under stress avoid all feeling blockers.*

The Twelve Feeling Blockers

Judging Responses

Criticizing: Making a negative evaluation of the other person. "You brought it on yourself; you've got nobody else to blame for the mess you are in."

Name-Calling: "Putting down" or stereotyping the other person. "What a dope!" "Just like a woman. . . . " "Egghead." "You hardhats are all alike." "You are just another insensitive male."

Diagnosing: Analyzing why a person is behaving as he or she is; playing amateur psychologist. "I can read you like a book—you are just doing that to irritate me." "Just because you went to college, you think you are better than me."

Praising Evaluatively: Making a positive judgment of the other person's actions, or attitudes. "Now that is a great-looking haircut." Teacher to teenage student: "You are a great poet." (Many people find it difficult to believe that praise can be a feeling blocker. When you praise *evaluatively*, you are actually sending a subtle message that says, "You are not acceptable unless you are doing the behaviors that I am praising." The repeated use of evaluative praise will eventually be experienced as judgmental behavior. People resist being judged and evaluated and will shut down when they do not feel as if they are unconditionally accepted.)

Sending Solutions

Ordering: Commanding the other person to do what you want to have done. "Do your homework right now." "Why?! Because I said so. . . . "

Threatening: Trying to control the other's actions by warning of negative consequences that you will instigate. "You'll do it or else . . . " "Stop that noise right now or I will keep the whole class after school."

Moralizing: Telling others what they should do or "preaching" at them. "You shouldn't get a divorce; think of what will happen to the children." "You ought to tell him you are sorry."

Excessive/Inappropriate Questioning: Closed-ended questions are often barriers in a relationship; these are questions that can usually be answered in a few words—often with a simple yes or no. "When did it happen?" "Are you sorry that you did it?"

Advising: Giving people solutions to their problems. "If I were you, I'd complain to the manager." "That's an easy one to solve. First . . . "

Invalidating Responses

Diverting: Pushing the other's problems aside through distraction. "Don't dwell on it. Let's talk about something more pleasant." Or: "Think you've got it bad? Let me tell you what happened to me."

Logical Argument: Attempting to convince the other with an appeal to facts or logic, usually without consideration of the emotional factors involved. "Look at the facts. If you hadn't bought that new car, we could have made the down payment on a house."

Reassuring: Trying to stop the other person from feeling the negative emotions he or she is experiencing. "Don't worry, it is always darkest before the dawn." "It will all work out OK in the end."

EQuip Yourself
for Social Awareness

Practice, practice, practice your empathic listening skills.

- Begin with people who naturally come to you to talk about or process their concerns. These people may include close family members, friends, customers who come to you with complaints, and perhaps some of your co-workers.
- Make it a habit to never respond to these people with advice, solutions, policies, or alternative perspectives *until* you have listened to them empathically and asked them

transitional questions like: *"Have I understood you correctly?" "Did I connect with your core concern?" "Tell me more about that." "How can I help you or support you in this?" "Would you like to hear my thoughts about that?" "Do you want my advice or do you just need me to listen?" "What do you think you need to do?" "What is your intuition or your gut feeling telling you that you should do?"*

Reflect on the results of your interaction. After you have empathically listened to your friend, family member, or colleague, take a moment by yourself to reflect on the actual results of the interaction. Ask yourself:

+ How did your listening skills help the other person to work through his or her concerns?
+ How did empathic listening keep a tense situation from escalating?
+ How did it create a natural bond between you and the other person?
+ What other benefits have you experienced from offering empathic listening as a way to demonstrate your awareness and understanding of other people?

Value your listening skills. The more you discover the benefits of empathic listening, the more you will use the skill. You will also become better at *paraphrasing,* and you will become adept at recognizing the difference between those situations in which empathic listening is not necessary and those in which it is critical for success.

Chapter 8

EI and Workplace Issues

.... **In this chapter, you will learn** ....

How emotional intelligence relates to relationship management in the following areas:

- ♦ moving through and leading change
- ♦ managing interpersonal conflict
- ♦ enhancing effective teamwork.

....

RELATIONSHIP MANAGEMENT

Imagine lying on a white sandy beach, feeling warm rays of sunlight and a gentle ocean breeze. You are listening to the soft sounds of the waves splashing against the rocks. The laughter of children at play brings a smile as you recall fond memories from your own childhood. You are feeling a meditative peace, a oneness, pleasantness, and the joy of solitude. In this wonderfully calm and relaxed state, the challenges of your day-to-day life seem far away. In this place, there is no need to manage disruptive, intrusive emotions, no need to practice empathy with others who are troubled; even the need to be creative and resilient fades away.

But don't be fooled—although escape, real or imagined, is always a gift, you will no doubt eventually have to leave this place of solitude and go back into the real world. It is this real world where you will have to manage stressful change, work with a difficult team member, resolve an emotional situation, or deal with some other unwanted tension or conflict. The real world is a matrix of relationships and all of the challenges that relationships bring. It is here, in the relational real world, that your emotional intelligence is perhaps most important.

The EI domain of relationship management is where theory is tested and principles are practiced. This is where the *rubber meets the road*. At the end of the day, it is in the context of your interpersonal relationships where you will find the perfect opportunity to apply, practice, and develop all of the skills and competencies you have learned in your exploration of self-awareness, self-management, and social awareness. In this chapter, we're going to explore the application of these EI skills and competencies to three common and sometimes challenging workplace issues: change, conflict, and teamwork. All involve the establishment and management of good working relationships with colleagues, bosses, direct reports, customers, and other stakeholders in the workplace. With regard to being effective in these relationships in the challenging arenas of change, conflict, and teamwork, your day at the beach is over and it's time to put your EI back to work.

EI AND CHANGE

It goes without saying that change is pervasive in the workplace. Driven by rapidly advancing technologies, the need to stay competitive in the marketplace, and in some cases, by our own need to seek constant improvement, change is one of the greatest forces acting on us in the world today. The pace, power, and potential for disruption brought about by change, coupled with the notion that people often find themselves resisting change they haven't themselves chosen, make the process of change and all that accompanies it, a wonderful practice field for EI.

To understand fully how to apply EI to change, a careful distinction must be made between two terms that are often used interchangeably: *change* and *transition*. *Change* itself is something external to you—it is a decision or choice made or natural event that takes place that affects your environment, situation, or context. This is not to say that change doesn't affect you internally. Of course it does, and in some cases, it does so significantly. But it is helpful to separate the internal impact of change from the external event.

The label we apply to this internal aspect of change—the human journey through change—is *transition*. Transition is the internal human process of adapting to change. It is the psychological reorientation you undergo in the face of a change event. When people say that change is difficult, they're not actually talking about change itself. Change is what happens *around* you. It is the *way* things are going to be different. Transition is what happens *within* you. It is *how* you adapt to make the change work. External change can force all kinds of internal changes, such as:

- the need to adapt to different circumstances
- the need to implement different behaviors
- the need to establish new relationships
- in some cases, the need to alter the very way you view yourself and your place in the world.

It is often not the change itself that people resist, but rather the transitional journey required by the change that makes them uncomfortable. And so it is with regard to navigating this transitional journey that you need to apply your EI.

Consider This

The ABC model we introduced in chapter 5 provides you with another way to think about the difference between *change* and *transition*. *Change* can be thought of as an *activating event (A)*. *Transition* includes both your *beliefs (B)* about the activating change event, as well as your *consequential* emotional and behavioral responses (C). You handle the activating change event (A) with emotional intelligence by managing the transition—your beliefs, insights, and attitudes (B) and your consequential emotions and behaviors (C).

Consider a change you have experienced and reflect on how the ABC model fits that event.

Navigating the Transitional Journey

William Bridges (1980) is something of a guru on the subject of organizational change and transition. He describes change as seeking a new beginning, a new way. Now that sounds pleasant enough, but here's the rub: you can never achieve a new beginning without first experiencing an ending.

This immutable rule is the source of much of the emotional angst around change and transition—people typically don't like endings. Endings are always characterized by loss, and loss always forces you to let go of something. You can't begin to journey toward a new beginning unless you first let go of how things are at present. Simply put, the question that always begins the journey of transition is: "What do I need to let go of?" And the process of letting go carries all sorts of emotional baggage with it.

Complicating things even further is that the journey toward your new beginning requires you to pass through the *neutral zone*, or what William Bridges sometimes refers to as the wilderness. The neutral zone is the place in between the old way and the new. It is a lonely place, a place where the past is gone and the future is uncertain, leaving you feeling off balance, lost, and confused. In this in-between state, you often lack a clear sense of who you are, what you're doing, or where you are going. At best, the new beginning may

Guiding Principle

You can never achieve a new beginning without first experiencing an ending. Endings are always emotional.

seem like a shining beacon in the far-off distance, but the darkness of the neutral zone makes it impossible for you to really know what the "new way" is going to be like until you arrive at its threshold. Because of the discomfort and uncertainty associated with the neutral zone, you are inclined to find a way out of it as quickly as possible. Sometimes it seems that the quickest way out is to simply go back to where you came from. This often leads to clinging to the past to a certain degree.

Author Marilyn Ferguson said it well,

> It is not so much that we are afraid of change or so in love with the old ways, but it's that place in between that we fear. . . . It's like being caught between trapezes. It's Linus when his blanket is in the dryer. There's nothing to hold on to.

Consider This

- ◆ Consider a change you have experienced in your life. Choose something significant, something dramatic, perhaps even something traumatic. Reflect on your journey through that change.
- ◆ What event or decision brought the change about?
- ◆ What did you have to let go of or allow to end to move forward?
- ◆ How long did the journey take before you arrived at some sense of a new beginning?
- ◆ What was it like when you were in the middle, having let go of the old way but not yet arrived at the new?
- ◆ What emotions did you experience along the way, and how did your EI come into play?

As you've likely guessed, self-awareness figures significantly in leveraging your skills of EI toward supporting you in navigating a transitional journey brought about by a change event. Tapping into your self-awareness around a change in your life requires you to go back to that very basic, two-part question we raised in chapter 2: *"How am I feeling (about this change) and why am I feeling it?"* Until you get a grasp on your emotional state with regard to your changing circumstance, you will not be effective in making the journey through change successfully.

If change brings loss, then one way to connect with the emotions you may be experiencing during a transition is to think of transition as a kind of grieving process. The emotional rollercoaster we all experience as change unfolds in our lives is often compared to the grieving process we experience when we realize we are about to lose someone or something important to us. Elisabeth Kübler-Ross framed the five stages of this process—denial, anger, bargaining, depression, and acceptance—in her book, *On Death and Dying* (1969). Ask yourself if you are experiencing any of the emotions associated with these five stages of grief. You may, of course, experience variations of these emotions or perhaps still different emotions when confronted with your own change circumstance. As described in chapter 2, the key is to identify the emotions you are feeling and apply the four steps that carry you from self-awareness to self-management:

- Attunement—Acknowledge your emotional state regarding the change.
- Understanding—Explore why you feel the way you do about the change.
- Acceptance—Own the emotions you feel and seek their signal to action.
- Attending—Express your emotions appropriately, applying strategies for effective emotional self-management.

Relationship Management and Leading Change

Leading others through change is a true relationship management issue. If navigating change individually is difficult, you can only imagine the challenge associated with guiding others through the uncertainty of change and its associated transitional journey. We have sometimes described it as akin to the process of herding cats.

In the workplace, the process of change and transition often creates a human drama with the players acting out two different roles. One role is played by those who are initiating or driving the change. These initiators of change are often perceived as being seated at the higher levels of authority within the organization. The other role is played by those driven into transition by the change. The people in this role are expected to be good followers of change, good *transitioners* if you will, but they often feel victim to decisions made from on high. It has been said that people do not resist change, people resist *being changed*. Those who wish to lead change will quickly learn that it is not easy to move others into transition.

> **Guiding Principle**
>
> *To be successful as an agent of change, you will need to leverage many of the EI competencies that link to the social awareness and relational skills domains, but you will also need to manage your own emotions first.*

This is not to say that leading change can't be done successfully. Indeed, there are many fine examples of leaders doing an exemplary job of it. The challenges, real or imagined, faced by individuals traversing the wilderness of transition are not to be taken lightly, however. Successful change agents will leverage many of the EI competencies that link to the social awareness and relational skills domains, but they will also need to *manage their own emotions first*. This means that while you are leading the way through change, you are often also engaged in your own individual journey, shifting from something familiar and comfortable to something new and uncertain. You will likely have your own emotions to deal with along the way, thus, you have the added responsibility of modeling emotional self-management, knowing that others are watching and looking for cues as to how they should act in the face of change.

Leveraging your EI to maximize your effectiveness as a leader of change requires you to:

♦ Model appropriate emotional expression and behavior with regard to your own individual journey through the change. Resonate with the emotional challenges and demonstrate your own sense of optimism for a positive outcome. (Learn more about resonant leadership in chapter 9.)

- Realize that your emotional journey is not the same as the emotional journey of those you are leading. The people you are working with will transition through their own emotional journeys at their own pace. One of your biggest challenges will be to empathize with their pace and not expect them to automatically operate at your pace. You cannot be 10 steps in front of them or they will not follow.

- Understand the emotional journey people experience as they move through transition. Figure 8-1 illustrates some of these various emotions. This figure also illustrates that there is a period of time between the *ending* and the *new beginning* during which there is *usually* a very real dip in performance, productivity, and morale. People do not usually like to experience a dip in *their*

The Transitional Journey

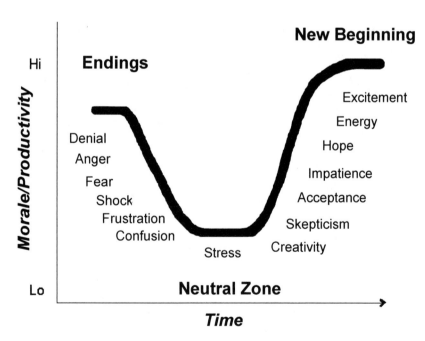

Figure 8-1. The emotional stages and learning curve associated with the transitional journey.

own productivity and morale. Those who are leading change will need to create an environment in which it is okay for individuals to temporarily contribute less and learn more. It is a time for moving up the learning curve and evaluating individuals based on growth and not contribution. Change leaders who are most effective both *expect* and *accept* this temporary dip in productivity.

♦ Having accepted the concept of the learning curve, apply a heavy dose of empathy. Each individual affected by the change is going to respond differently, with individual concerns, emotions, and needs. Empathy is your tool for building the bridge from where your people are to where they need to go. As each individual affected by the change responds with different concerns, emotions, and needs, these responses will provide you with the information you need to support their transitional journey.

If individuals are feeling:	*Provide them with:*
Confused	Vision and reasons
Anxious	Skills, training, and encouragement
Unmotivated	Incentives
Frustrated	Empathy and resources
Impatient	Action, ideas, and challenges

Understand and leverage the motivations of those with whom you are working. Come to know what drives each individual in your group and tap into this as a means of inspiring performance through a difficult process.

EI AND CONFLICT

People differ.

Because people differ, conflict is inevitable in all relationships.

There are at least three areas in which people differ and conflict occurs.

♦ People differ in their styles, which leads to *personality conflict.*
♦ People differ in their perceptions, which leads to *perceptual conflict.*
♦ People differ in what they want, which leads to a *conflict of interests.*

Although people often shy away from any sort of conflict, in theory, these three types of conflict are not bad; in fact, each presents opportunities for personal growth, team growth, innovation, and creative problem solving. When our social awareness skills are applied effectively to such conflict arenas, we become more understanding and appreciative of our personality differences, more educated by our perceptual differences, and we negotiate creative solutions around our various interests.

There is also a fourth way in which people differ that leads to conflict:

- People differ in terms of what they expect from one another, which leads to *emotional conflict*.

Unfortunately, unlike personality, perceptual, and interest-based conflicts, conflict arising from differing expectations often creates a breeding ground for highly disruptive emotions including anger, anxiety, embarrassment, fear, and guilt. Left unmanaged, these emotions can be especially destructive to workplace relationships.

Effective relationship management requires that we exercise self-awareness, self-management, and social-awareness skills to successfully address this emotional side of conflict.

Emotional Conflict

One of the most common forms of conflict arising between people occurs simply because we do not always live up to our expectations of one another. For example, Bob expects Sarah to work extra hours over the weekend to complete a project. Sarah thinks that weekends were made for fun and family, and she has an expectation that she should never have to work on weekends. In this interaction, someone is bound to become disappointed.

Disappointment is the emotion people experience when their expectations are not met by reality. For some people, disappointment is experienced as a kind of injustice, with anger being the resulting overwhelming emotion. These people tend to treat their expectations as if they were immutable laws of the universe that cannot be broken. Then, when these expectations are inevitably broken, these people become angry as if some great injustice has been perpetrated on them. The problem with this kind of anger is that it can become very explosive, and such explosions tend to hurt people or make them feel defensive instead of resolving the conflict.

> **Guiding Principle**
>
> *Anger invites defensiveness. When two people are defending their own positions, they are not resolving conflict.*

At the other end of the spectrum, there are people for whom disappointments tend to build on one another, creating an accumulation of unfulfilled expectations that slowly chip away at all of the positive emotional energy of the relationship. When this happens, feelings like joy, happiness, enthusiasm, interest, connectedness, love, friendship, excitement, passion, anticipation, and optimism become depressed and are finally replaced with resentment. Unfortunately, resentment makes conflict irrelevant, because when you resent someone, your heart becomes hard and cold toward that person, and you find yourself losing all interest in working with that person.

Resolving Emotional Conflict

When the emotions of disappointment, resentment, and anger begin to disrupt your relationships, you need to leverage emotional self-awareness, emotional self-management, and empathy to effectively manage the conflict.

Tuning in to Emotional Self-Awareness. The first rule for managing conflict is to remember that the person who is emotionally upset is the person who needs to initiate conflict resolution.

Unfortunately, emotional conflicts often remain unresolved because the person

> **Guiding Principle**
>
> *Resentment poisons the heart. Resentment takes away your interest in connecting with the person you resent. It is hard to resolve conflicts when you don't even care to try.*

who is agitated and upset often expects the sensitivity, empathy, and apology to come from the other side.

Consider this example mentioned earlier:

Bob is upset because Sarah refuses to work on Saturday; or rather, Bob is upset because Sarah's refusal to work on Saturday directly violates his expectation that she should work on Saturday to keep the project on track. This perceived violation of his expectation makes Bob angry. Given his emotional state, it is likely that Bob's agitation may keep him awake for half the night. Meanwhile, Sarah is enjoying her work–life balance and sleeping like a baby.

Now, not only is Bob upset, he is actually going to *increase* his discomfort by expecting Sarah to be both aware of and sensitive to his feelings and to make some kind of an effort to resolve the conflict. Certainly if Sarah's empathy skills are acute enough to connect with Bob's distress, she could come to him with sensitivity and concern and try to resolve the issue. There is a problem, however, with Bob *expecting* Sarah to exercise empathy and concern.

The skill of empathy is not the same as mind-reading.

It is unfair for Bob to use *sensitivity* as a code word that really means "read my mind."

The key to defusing this conflict resides in the recognition of who carries the emotional distress. In this case, the disruptive emotions are inside of Bob's body, not Sarah's. Because the emotions belong to Bob, he is responsible for being aware of the emotions and then for managing them.

Guiding Principle

The person who is emotionally upset is the person who needs to initiate conflict resolution.

Emotional self-awareness, then, is the starting point for managing conflict:

♦ Tune in to the emotions you feel concerning the people you work with, the people you serve, and the people you most care about.

- Are you feeling disappointment, anger, or resentment toward any of these people? Do not expect the other person to be sensitive. The emotion is your responsibility to listen to and to manage.

- Be careful about how much you minimize and then ignore your feelings of disappointment. It is annoying to make every disappointment you experience in life an issue that you need to raise, but at the same time you don't want to ignore an issue for so long that you become resentful. Use your self-awareness to find patterns of behavior that disappoint you. Pattern behavior is significant and should be addressed.

- The good news about resentment is that it tends to grow slowly, giving you plenty of time to address its cause. The bad news is that because it tends to grow slowly, resentment is sometimes easy to ignore. Recognize the signs of growing resentment such as a tendency to become more withdrawn, a loss of enthusiasm and interest, feelings of distaste, feelings of dislike, and even feelings of relief on days when you don't have to be around the person you resent. This will help you to recognize and address your feelings of resentment before they grow so strong that you no longer care to address them.

- Remember that your disappointment, anger, and resentment are signals inside of *your* body telling you that *you* need to initiate conflict resolution.

Exercising Emotional Self-Management. The second rule for managing conflict is for you to realize that you need to manage your anger first and then manage the conflict.

Recall that our working definition of emotional intelligence includes the idea that you are to use your emotions *intelligently* to achieve interpersonal effectiveness with others. With respect to conflict, this means that you need to reflect on the usefulness or effectiveness of anger in leading people to a peaceful, agreeable resolution. Although anger is a normal and healthy emotion, a strong expression of anger will usually invite resistance instead of resolution.

> **Guiding Principle**
>
> *Manage your anger first and then manage the conflict.*

113

For this reason, anger is not the best emotion for you to focus on when it comes to resolving conflict.

> Focus instead on the disappointment, hurt, concern, and loss that are driving the anger.

Anger is considered to be a *secondary* emotion. This means that whenever you feel anger, there is always some emotion that is occurring beneath the anger that is more *primary* to the situation. In our earlier example, Bob is angry that Sarah is not willing to work on Saturday, but he is also concerned that the project will not get completed on time. Bob's anger is actually secondary to his concern. In fact, if he wasn't concerned and didn't care so much about the outcome of the project, he wouldn't be angry. Bob's anger is very real, but his concern is what he really needs to discuss with Sarah.

Notice here that emotional intelligence never asks you to resolve conflict by denying or suppressing your anger. Instead, it suggests that you use your self-awareness to manage your anger by answering the question:

> What is beneath my anger? What are the primary emotions that are driving my anger?

Connecting with your primary emotions supplies you with the emotional information you need to resolve conflict effectively.

Applying Social Awareness. Equipped with self-awareness, and your anger properly managed, you are now ready to initiate conflict resolution. The third rule for managing conflict is to remember that it takes cooperation to resolve conflict.

Any approach that is used to initiate conflict resolution needs to invite the other side to cooperate. The social awareness skill of empathy is what tells you whether or not you have created an environment of cooperation. Your success depends on having an attitude that respects, understands, and appreciates the other side's view of the situation.

Guiding Principle

It takes cooperation to resolve conflict.

It is also advisable to consider what you want to say *before* you say it. Although this approach may lack spontaneity and even seem somewhat calculated, scripting what you want to say will not only help keep you calm, but it will also allow you to communicate in a way that invites cooperation instead of defensiveness.

We would like to call this scripted approach *empathic assertiveness*.

- *Empathic assertiveness* is an attitude that continually respects and affirms that the needs and interests of all people involved in the conflict are equally important.
- *Empathic assertiveness* is also a communication skill that involves stating personal concerns, interests, and needs, as well as asserting that other parties involved do the same: "Here is what I want and what I need." "What is it that you want and need?"

A script that seems to work well for most people includes the following three elements:

1. It contains a simple descriptive statement about what has happened without attacking the other person. It is best to make this statement an "I" statement.

2. The script includes a statement about your primary feelings or your primary concern. In the workplace, it is best to keep this statement focused on your concern about how the situation is affecting the business result, the team, the customer, you, or the person with whom you are trying to resolve the conflict.

3. The script has a statement about how you would like to resolve the conflict.

Once you have scripted a statement that reflects these three elements and then communicated your script to the other person, you will need to use your empathy skills to keep the other person involved. Using the previous example, Bob's scripted conversation with Sarah might look something like this:

BOB: When you refused to work this weekend, I got angry because you put our whole project deadline in jeopardy. And now you are going to have to work extra hard to keep us on track.

No, that sounds too judgmental and accusatory. Sarah is likely to get defensive. Let's try it again.

BOB: I decided to go ahead and do some work on Saturday, because I was concerned that we might not meet our requirements on time. I'm not certain how valid this concern is, so I would like to talk with you about our timeline and how we are going to meet our requirements.

SARAH: Sure, Bob, let's talk.

Social awareness can also help Sarah to handle this conflict with emotional intelligence. By developing her social awareness skills, Sarah will respond to Bob with empathy first, and then with her understanding of the situation.

SARAH: Gee, Bob, I didn't realize that you spent Saturday working because you were so concerned with the timeline. Why don't we look at our priority reports together and that way we can make sure that we are on track to fulfill the project requirements?

BOB: That sounds great.

EI AND TEAMWORK

A colleague of ours has been known to describe collaboration as "an unnatural act between nonconsenting adults." Now although this comment is clearly being expressed with tongue-in-cheek, he makes a valid point. Working with others can be challenging, and we are not always willing to put forth the effort required to realize the full value of collaborative partnerships. Yet working in teams is pervasive in our workplaces. Few of us work solo any longer. Partnering with others in teams to get things done is the culture of the workplace these days, and that doesn't seem likely to change any time soon. Therefore, to truly be effective in our workplace roles, we are required to establish effective working relationships with others. Emotional intelligence figures largely in our ability to build, run, and maintain effective teams and other forms of collaborative partnerships.

Tuning in to Team Process

It happens so often it is predictable. Another episode of Donald Trump's *Apprentice* reality television show demonstrates yet again how amateurs under pressure fail to produce impressive results when teamwork and collaboration are required. The premise is simple enough. Team A and Team B compete against each other in an attempt to win Trump's favor and avoid a visit to the dreaded boardroom where someone is going to get "fired." Each team supposedly represents the *cream of the crop* of young up-and-coming entrepreneurs. Yet all of this skill and talent gathered together in one place tends to make good TV precisely *because they are so bad at demonstrating teamwork*. More often than not, the teams involved break the most fundamental rule of teamwork—they fail to balance the *formula* of thinking, organizing, defining roles, planning, and designing with the *solution* of implementing, producing, and achieving their intended results. In short, they fail to balance process with product.

Every endeavor you undertake includes two components: product and process. The product is the outcome; the process is how you arrive at that outcome. It is our experience that organizations and teams often focus heavily on product, sometimes not paying much attention at all to process. Inevitably, this causes trouble. There is a cost to bear for ignoring process. It may not come due immediately, but it always catches up with you in the end.

Process lurks in the background of your group work. It is akin to the operating system on your computer: When it's running smoothly, you hardly notice it; but when it breaks down, everything comes to a screeching halt. Team process includes things such as a clear sense of common vision, a solid communication structure, effective facilitation and leadership, trust, acceptance of diversity of working style, and many other elements working in sync to enable the successful completion of the team's mission. Emotional intelligence is a component of the process as well. Team members who are not fully using their EI skills are not able to contribute fully to the team and may cause a bottleneck in the work flow. Teams as a whole also exhibit an overall, composite EI. When the entity that is the team is not fully applying its capabilities around awareness and management, the process breaks down and effectiveness suffers.

Consider This

Reflect back on a team you worked with that really performed at a high level. It could be a workplace team (we hope you've had at least one high-performing workplace team!) or perhaps it was a sports team, musical group, or a community group of some kind.

- How would you describe this team experience and what it was like to be a part of it?
- What were some of the things about this team that made it so effective?
- How would you describe the mood of this team as your work together progressed toward its successful outcome?
- Contrast this high-performance team experience with a team you worked with that didn't do so well. What was present in the high-performance team that was missing from this other team experience?

This reflection should highlight for you some of the key pieces of the team effectiveness puzzle. Some of these pieces may seem hard to pin down at first, a little intangible perhaps, but with some thought, all can be traced back to things the team did, consciously or unconsciously, to establish and maintain an effective team process that included, if not actually featured, the components of EI.

Enhancing Team Performance Through Emotional Intelligence

The application of EI with regard to teamwork must be explored at two levels: the degree to which you, as an individual member of the team, are effective in applying your own capacity for EI in your team interactions, and the degree to which the team exhibits solid EI practices overall.

Individual EI naturally comes into play in managing your interpersonal relationships within the team. As with any interpersonal interaction, the tools necessary for self-awareness and self-management are important to maximizing your own personal and interpersonal team performance. Social awareness and appropriate application of empathy are also critical to being able to connect effectively with your team colleagues. Do an honest assessment of how fully you are applying your capacity for EI in your team interactions and make strides for improvement where necessary based on some of the individual EI content we explored in earlier chapters.

Overall team emotional intelligence refers to what Goleman and his colleagues (2002) in *Primal Leadership* call the *emotional reality* of the team. This exploration may begin with your own self-assessment of how effective your team really is. Ask yourself: "How do I feel when I'm about to enter one of our team meetings?" Are you eager and filled with positive energy, or are you anxious and find yourself looking for a way out? This simple "feeling test" reveals a lot about your team. If you feel positive about the team experience, it's likely that many of the other members of the team feel the same. This would indicate that you all share a common sense of direction and purpose, and in general feel that your work together is progressing well, and you have established a good foundation for your interactive team relationships with one another—all signs of strong EI at the team level. However, if you dread attending team gatherings, then obviously things are not going so well and it's likely that you are not the only one who feels this way. In this case, the team needs to do an emotional reality check and assess both what is required and the level of commitment needed to implement the requirements that will get the team back on a more effective track.

If all is well with your team, then your approach should be to identify and acknowledge the things that you're doing well, celebrate them, and strive to maintain them. Apply your emotional intelligence to stay attuned to the "currents" within the team, watching for shifts in the energy. Teamwork has its challenges, and issues may arise even on the most high-functioning teams. Addressing any budding issues early on is critical. Implement self-management and relational management measures as appropriate to stay on course. Just as we discussed taking self-awareness timeouts in chapter 2, teams occasionally need to take process timeouts to check in on how they're doing and recognize necessary adjustments. Process doesn't just happen; it needs to be nurtured and tended to as the team's work unfolds.

If all is not so well with your team, it is important to identify and understand the root causes underlying the difficulty. Just as you would apply your self-awareness to delve into and seek an understanding of a potentially disruptive emotion within yourself, you can do the same with the team's process. You may choose to do this individually at first, seeing if you can reach your own conclusions about what the team needs to get back on a more effective track. You would then share your thoughts with the team overall or with the team leadership specifically. More effective than the individual approach, however, is a process by which the team as a whole explores its issues. This full-team, self-reflective approach requires a fair degree of trust and good will among team members as well as some strong facilitation. It is sometimes helpful to bring in an outside facilitator to help design and guide this sort of interaction.

EQuip Yourself

Navigating Change

Given the heightened emotions often associated with change, change offers ample opportunity to apply the self-management techniques we highlighted earlier in this text.

- **Be aware of your brain.** Observe your emotional brain sending the *"Not good for me!"* signal regarding the change event. Know that you can quiet this voice and lean on your higher thinking brain for a different perspective.
- **Apply your ABCs.** Consider change an activating event. Remember that you have a range of possible beliefs to choose from that will determine your consequential

emotional/behavioral response. Dispute your own thinking, as necessary.

+ **Seek your own motivation for change.** Ask *"What's in this for me?"* and create a clear vision of yourself engaged successfully in a new way of being after the change has taken place.
+ **Tap into your sense of optimism.** Know that you are resilient enough to bounce back from the challenges of change.

Leading Change

+ **Model emotional intelligence in your own journey through change.** Your co-workers will take some of their behavioral cues from you.
+ **Use your social awareness to support others in navigating change.** Empathize with the challenges they face.
+ **Tailor your strategies for inspiring performance to each individual.** Discover what gets those around you out of bed in the morning and tap into that motivator to drive the change behavior.

Resolving Conflict

+ Remember that the person who is emotionally upset is the person who needs to initiate conflict resolution.
+ Manage your anger and distress and then manage the conflict.
+ Remember that it takes respect and cooperation to resolve conflict.

Building Effective Teams

+ **Begin with yourself.** Team effectiveness is derived from each individual team member doing his or her part to contribute and add value to the whole. If you are not fulfilled with your team experience, look at yourself. Use your self-awareness to identify some things that you might do differently, both to add greater value as an individual contributor to the team and to facilitate the full potential of your teammates.

- **Tune in to the overall emotional tone of the team.** If energy is lacking, perhaps the motivation for team participation is not clear to all members. Perhaps team members need to connect with a more powerful sense of vision to understand their individual role in bringing this vision into reality.

- **Examine team optimism.** To what degree does a sense of optimism exist within the team? Recall that optimism is derived from your explanatory style in the face of challenge and setback. How does the team "talk to itself" about the challenges of the work you collectively have before you? How could you generate a more empowered, optimistic outlook within the team?

- **Keep in mind that team membership is not just about giving to the team; it's also about getting something back.** All team members are looking for something in return for the contributions they bring to the whole. Inspiring team-member performance is achieved through these various agendas, needs, and interests in balance with the needs and interests of the team as a whole. Apply your social awareness and empathy to gain an understanding of what each of your team colleagues is looking for from the team experience.

- **Encourage your team members to understand and appreciate one another.** Use work-style assessments and other tools that can help you to discover the strengths that exist within your team's diversity.

- **Observe your team's process.** Psychologically remove yourself from the team and momentarily become an "audience member" to the drama that is the team's interaction to gain valuable insight. Use this insight to make sure that your team is maintaining a healthy balance between process and product, and that all team members are being treated with equal value and respect.

Chapter 9

Emotional Intelligence and Influence

.... **In this chapter, you will learn** ....

- ◆ the difference between resonant and dissonant influence
- ◆ how to use EI to develop resonance in your leadership style
- ◆ how to leverage vision to inspire and influence others
- ◆ how to *EQuip Yourself* to be a more influential leader.

LEADERSHIP IS INFLUENCE

An old Afghan proverb reads: "If you think you are leading and no one is following you, then you are only taking a walk."

Leadership is influence, and emotional intelligence has a lot to say about influence. People tend to follow the influence of others because of an entire range of leadership qualities that emotionally inspire and elevate them to greatness:

> *Vision, Values, Honor, Loyalty, Love, Trust, Friendship, Truth, Wisdom, Heroism, Faith*

When you set out to influence someone to do something, no matter how great or small, your success will largely depend on your ability to inspire, motivate, amuse, create enthusiasm, generate authentic commitment, or engender a spirit of willing cooperation. Success has a lot to do with the mood you create around the task at hand. In short, your success is all about your ability to *moodivate* others.

Emotional intelligence provides you not only with the skills you need to arouse the passions and commitments of others, but also the social awareness that you need to recognize whether or not true influence is happening. Leadership is influence, but not all influence is leadership.

A TOXIC LEADERSHIP STORY

On April 28, 1789, a mutiny aboard the Royal Navy ship, *The HMAV Bounty*, was led against the ship's captain, Lieutenant William Bligh. The change of command left Bligh confined to his cabin, with no real authority to make any demands. In other words, there was no longer any bite to Lieutenant Bligh's bark, but interestingly, he was still able to yield a modicum of influence. Imagine, if you will, the following scenario:

> "Rogers, down on the deck! Give me 50 push-ups." As quickly as the acid-tongued Bligh could bark out his orders, the fearful midshipman dropped to the deck and began pumping out the push-ups. It wasn't until he was on his fifth push-up that he heard the surly laughter of Bligh. Rogers's mind finally caught up with his body, and he rolled over onto his back now feeling slightly foolish as his shipmates broke out into laughter too. It was the third time that the former commander of the *Bounty* was able to pull off the practical joke on an unsuspecting crew member.

When Rogers immediately and unquestioningly surrendered to Bligh's command, he was actually experiencing a form of emotional override with his amygdala, causing him to regress to his default behavior. It wasn't until his rational brain remembered that Bligh was in the brig that he was able to stop himself.

THE DANCE OF THE AMYGDALAS

In chapter 4 we learned that we are programmed to feel our emotions before we process them. This programming serves us well when we encounter severe threat or severe danger, but sometimes we react autonomically to situations that are not threatening at all. Our behaviors become reactive instead of proactive. Proactive behavior is thoughtful, effortful, and conscious, whereas reactive behavior is automatic, lacks effort, and is unconscious.

What happens when two people are reacting to each other at the same time? A kind of emotional dance takes place, a dance that we call the dance of the amygdalas. The best way to describe this dance is to consider a simple example.

Suppose a supervisor walks up to you, looking somewhat stressed and anxious, and in a panicky tone of voice asks: "Can you do something for me?" A reactive response might be: "Sure! What is it?"

How do you know you can help your supervisor? What if the dates and times don't work for you? What if the request is too big or if the request does not align with your value system? In a sense you have agreed to the request without even really *thinking about it*. In fact, you didn't think about it at all, your response was based on what you *felt about it*. The feeling was probably something like guilt, fear, or compassion, and your amygdala directed you into a job-security survival behavior.

In this example, the supervisor's behaviors are also being directed by the amygdala. Feeling stress, anxiety, worry, fear, anger, or frustration, the supervisor has two options. The first option is to count to 10, manage the emotion, and then choose a proactive behavior. The second option is much faster—project the emotional energy onto a direct report with a tonality and body language that says: "You have the power to relieve my emotional distress by doing something for me now."

The dance of the amygdalas occurs because each person is reacting to the other's emotional state. Many people have learned that when faced with aggression or with someone really challenging them, they simply comply. Later, when they have had time to think about their compliance, they may wonder why they gave in so quickly and why they were not more assertive.

DISSONANT INFLUENCE—WHEN THE AMYGDALAS DANCE TO DIFFERENT TUNES

Compliance can actually be thought of as a form of influence. Children comply with parents, students comply with teachers, and subordinates comply with bosses. Many who are in positions of authority will be able to use their authoritative power successfully to get compliance out of others. Compliance can be thought of as influence, but it is certainly not leadership. When all you have is compliance, the influence is actually based on driving a response out of fear, worry, guilt, anxiety, anger, hatred, hurt, concern, or some other disruptive emotion that is being triggered in the amygdala.

If people are responding to you out of this negative range of emotions, your influence will not last over time. This kind of influence is called *dissonant influence*. True influence happens when people's emotions are pushed in the direction of enthusiasm. Dissonant influence occurs when people are thrown off balance and their emotions are driven toward guilt, fear, and anxiety. People will not continue to follow you if they feel intimidated or manipulated into their behaviors. They will make comments behind your back like: "That person rubs me the wrong way." Each successive act of compliance will generate feelings of resentment and apathy, and eventually even numbness. Dissonant influence is not leadership because it doesn't engage people. It doesn't create the kind of emotional environment that allows people to shine. People want to feel inspired, not duped.

Guiding Principle

People do not want to feel intimidated or manipulated into their behaviors.

RESONANT INFLUENCE—WHEN THE AMYGDALAS DANCE TO THE SAME TUNE

Resonance is a term that is often used in acoustic systems. A violinist produces a musical tone by plucking on a string, and the strength as well as the duration of the tone is amplified as the violin chamber reverberates a sympathetic vibration. Stimulus and response are in perfect, synchronistic harmony with each other. We call this music.

There is a kind of mystique to music because one can hear, feel, and experience music, but it is not easy to define. In a sense you can define it through the use of a musical score, but even this needs to be *interpreted* by the musician. Interestingly, as the brass, woodwind, and percussion instruments join the strings creating an entire symphony of sounds, musicians must learn how to interpret not only the music, but each other as well. Carlo Maria Giulini, the former Music Director of the Vienna Symphony Orchestra and the Los Angeles Philharmonic, understood the power of resonance when he observed that the making of great music is dependent on creating synchronicity among musicians.

> My intention always has been to arrive at human contact without enforcing authority. A musician, after all, is not a military officer. What matters most is human contact. The great mystery of music making requires real friendship among those who work together. Every member of the orchestra knows I am with him or her in my heart.

The point here is that human systems, like acoustic systems, can also reverberate with resonance. When someone produces an emotional tone that is sympathetically reflected or echoed back by others, we say that these people are in harmony, or "in sync" with one another. In such interactions among people, a different kind of influence is happening. We call it *resonant influence*. This kind of influence is also cultivated through an emotional dance of the amygdalas, but the dance is experienced by the dancers as positive and engaging. Resonant influence happens when people respond to each other out of feelings of respect, admiration, enthusiasm, warmth, attraction, friendship, inspiration, loyalty, interest, and even fun.

Coaching stories always provide us with great examples of resonant influence. In the early 1920s when famed football coach Knute Rockne encouraged his Notre Dame football team to *"win one for the Gipper,"* he knew that he was plucking on an emotional chord that reverberated throughout the entire team. Inspired by these words, the team actually played with more energy, focus, determination, and emotion. The inspiration came from the desire to win one for their star teammate George "The Gipper" Gipp, who sadly had died from a throat infection.

Daniel Goleman (2002, p. ix) describes resonance as "a reservoir of positivity that frees the best in people." Resonant influence is all about *rubbing people the right way*. We find this kind of influence in people who are positive and energetic about life, who are fun to be with and work with, and whose energy is contagious. These people are self-aware, self-managed, and empathically aware of the emotional force field that either attracts or repels people from one another. In short, these people are emotionally intelligent.

DEVELOPING RESONANCE IN YOUR LEADERSHIP STYLE

Consider for a moment the emotions that you would like the people with whom you work to feel. Your list will probably look something like this:

I would like people to feel . . .

    important, significant
    appreciated, valued
    inspired, motivated
    alive, enthusiastic
    self-determining, authentic
    self-aware, confident
    admired, likable
    competent, smart, capable

Now ask yourself: "What do I need to be like to engender these emotions in others?"

Your answer to this question is one of the most important functions of your job even though it is not in your job description. The primary task of all effective leadership in organizations is to figure out ways to drive other people's emotions in a positive direction. Leaders are *moodivational*, and the way you moodivate others is by developing the emotional competencies in yourself.

There are three competencies that we would like to highlight that are particularly effective in supporting the development of resonance in your leadership style.

> **Guiding Principle**
>
> *You develop resonance in your style by developing your emotional competencies, especially emotional self-management, and empathy.*

1. emotional self-management

2. inspiration and influence

3. empathy

Consider This

Many organizations need to change the way they think about leadership. Leadership is not about positional power or management. There are many leaders who are not managers, and many managers who are not leaders. In fact, Executive VPs, Senior Executives, and CEOs typically score the lowest on EI assessment inventories. Because leadership is more about resonant influence, there are many kinds of leaders at all levels of an organization. This is true because leadership flows primarily from who you are as a person, not from what you can demand from your position.

Emotional Self-Management

"I don't care what it takes. Just do it!" The staff manager shouts out his order, and the admin dutifully responds: "Uh. Okay, sir. I'll get right on it."

"And Jones."

"Oh no, what now?" Jones muses.

"Make sure you have those reports on my desk by three."

"Yes, sir!" Jones walks away feeling both anxious and defeated. Then he remembers something, and a confident smile starts to form on his face. The night before his lottery ticket won the million-dollar lotto. His rational brain informs him that now would be a good time to override the knee-jerk amygdala-driven agreement that he just made with his jerk of a boss. So he turns back toward the tough-talking manager and says:

"Hey, boss."

"What is it?!"

"Make that five."

This amusing commercial for the Minnesota State lottery works because it highlights so brilliantly the burden of working for toxic people, and the joy of feeling free.

Some people, like the boss in this story, use their emotions to master others. The toxic effect of dissonant influence begins with losing control of your emotions around others and then expecting them to manage your emotions for you by responding with the proper behavior. The pattern looks something like this:

> Person A becomes overtly upset about something and starts making demands, instead of managing the emotional distress.
>
> Person B feels anxious, responsible, and maybe even fearful, and quickly calms Person A down by responding to the demand.
>
> Person A gets what he or she needs and feels much calmer and relaxed.
>
> Person B feels immediate relief from the anxiety, guilt, and fear, but has lost a lot of enthusiasm and interest in working with Person A.

This pattern is toxic precisely because Person B is managing Person A's emotions, and Person A is managing Person B's. In a sense, these two people *need* each other. Psychologists call this *co-dependence*. They are *cooperating* in the *dependent* behavior of each other.

A better pattern would be for each person to manage his or her own emotions.

Emotional Contagion

One reason why resonant influence is so dependent on emotional self-management is because of an emotional effect that people can have on

one another called *emotional contagion.*
People give off emotional energy to one
another, and this energy tends to be contagious. The emotional energy that
someone projects will often get reflected
back by other members of a group.
Ghandi once said: "We must be the
change we want to see in the world."
This is especially true with how people
manage their emotional energy.

> **Guiding Principle**
>
> *Resonant leaders mas-
> ter their emotions and
> manage themselves,
> instead of using their
> emotions to master
> others.*

> Smile and the world smiles with you.
> Frown and you frown alone.

Your positive emotional energy can be tremendously infectious, but so
can negative emotional energy. Frown and you just might find a lot of
people frowning back. If emotions are contagious, then we must manage
our emotions in the direction of creating a positive emotional environment for others.

If people want to feel:	Then influential leaders must project:
important	recognition and caring
appreciated	appreciation
inspired	vision and clarity
alive	energy and participation
self-determined	confidence, trust, and freedom
self-aware	openness, curiosity, and acceptance
likable	warmth and friendliness
competent	empowerment and trust

Inspiration and Influence

Nowhere is it more important to project this positive range of emotional
energy than in our communication. Communication is the channel
through which we reveal to people not only the words that we want
them to understand, but also emotional messages that tell them how we
really feel about them. In fact, every time you communicate with someone,
you always send them two messages.

> **Guiding Principle**
>
> *The golden rule of emotional behavior is to project the kind of emotional energy that other people would like to experience.*

1. The content message—This is the actual dictionary meaning of what you want the person to understand.

2. The feeling message—This is the emotional meaning that tells the person how you *really* feel about him or her.

Consider the following simple request:

Joe, can you help me understand how you came up with these results?

How you say this will determine what Joe feels is *your perception of him.* He may feel *accepted* and *appreciated* by you and conclude that you value his input, that you think he is smart, and that you trust his approach. Or, he may feel *judged* and *belittled* by you, and conclude that you do not value his input and in fact think he is incompetent. It turns out that this very simple request is impregnated with meaning depending on *how* you say it. You can be certain that your influence on Joe will be determined by the way you say it.

The influence you have with another person (it works with pets too!) depends largely on how you use the three key elements of communication:

- words
- intonation
- body language

When you use these three elements *congruently*, then they all work together to send the same message to the receiver. "How may I help you?" sounds warm and friendly and as if you genuinely want to help,

> **Guiding Principle**
>
> *To be successful at influencing people, you need to send them positive feeling messages.*

when your tone is melodious, your face is relaxed, and your smile is sincere. But when you use these three elements *incongruently*, then they contradict one another and send the receiver a mixed message. This is why when you raise an eyebrow, add a sigh, and impatiently say:

"How may I help you?" it sounds more like "What do you want now? Can't you see that I'm busy? Hurry up, I haven't got all day."

Albert Moravian did a study at UCLA that determined the significance of these

three elements to actual understanding. He concluded that it all depends on how congruent you are with your message. If you are congruent, then words are tremendously powerful and can account for up to 99 percent of the impact of your message. This is good news for people who want to develop resonance in their leadership style. Simply communicate powerful, positive words of encouragement with sincerity and authenticity in your body language and tone of voice.

Moravian also concluded that when your message is mixed and incongruent, then your audience must determine which message to believe. Only 7 percent of your audience will judge your meaning based on your words. Thirty-eight percent will judge your meaning based on intonation, and 55 percent will base your meaning on your body language. In our previous example, 93 percent of your customers will conclude that you don't really intend to be helpful if you say: "How may I help you?" incongruently.

This portion of the Moravian study is difficult news for people who want to develop resonance in their leadership style. It highlights the importance of managing body language and tone of voice in communication. And now we are back to emotional self-management. The more you manage your disruptive emotions, the more you will manage the effect they can have on your body language and tone of voice when you communicate with others. Time to revisit chapter 5.

Empathy

Assuming that you are managing your emotions well, you are positive and energetic about life, you are doing your best to project the kind of attitude that promotes a healthy emotional environment

Guiding Principle

We don't really manage people; we manage the messages that we send to people.

for others, there is still one more emotional competency that you must master to create resonant influence. Although all of the EI competencies are important for leadership effectiveness, empathy is the most cirtical of all.

How can we say that empathy is the preeminent skill for leaders to develop?

If you want to be successful as a leader of people, you need to be able to read them well. Empathy is like a fine-tuning knob in your brain that helps you to dial in to the often subtle emotional signals that other people are projecting. When you are able to understand the feelings, energy levels, perspectives, and needs of other people, then you have the feedback required to adjust your own approach. One of the biggest challenges all leaders face is the challenge to say the right word at the right time in the right way. Without empathy, your chances of connecting and resonating with people at the right emotional frequency are significantly reduced.

Consider This

Are you the kind of person who can be loud and happy in the morning? Have you ever met someone who is too loud and happy in the morning? There is an amusing proverb that reads: "A loud praise early in the morning will be counted as a curse unto you." Certainly, the ability to wake up with excitement, enthusiasm, and happiness is a sign of healthy emotional self-management. And the desire to sing out loud: "Oh what a beautiful morning!" can be an authentic expression of your emotions. So why can't you influence other people to join you in the (early-morning) fun? Your influence is low because while you are at an emotional 10, shouting for joy, others are at an emotional 3 and find you interpersonally obnoxious. You can't create resonance because you are at different emotional frequencies. So does this mean you must become dull and indiffer-

> ent to connect? Absolutely not. Empathy simply gives you your starting point. It tells you which emotional frequency to tune in to in order to create resonance. So stay positive. Start low. Go slow. Build higher. Then catch fire!

Empathy is the tool that will help you to meet people where they are so that you can lead them to where you want them to go.

Without empathy:

- ◆ You are guessing at what people need.
- ◆ You are expecting that people share your drive and initiative.
- ◆ You are depending on people to tell you when you are off track.
- ◆ You are hoping that you have sincere engagement and not just compliance.

When your empathy skills are strong:

- ◆ You will be able to say and do whatever is appropriate in the moment.
- ◆ You will be able to calm fears, address confusion, communicate compassion, engender trust, and share in a diversity of ideas.
- ◆ You will be able to provide people with the vision and inspiration to lead them where you want them to go.

EI AND VISIONARY LEADERSHIP

Ask someone to rattle off a short list of the characteristics of effective leadership, and vision always appears within the top five items. The archetype of the visionary leader is written into our cultural mythology. From America's founding fathers to Susan B. Anthony, Dr. King, and other advocates of civil equality to Gates, Jobs,

Guiding Principle

Although all of the EI competencies are important for leadership effectiveness, empathy is the most critical of all.

135

> **Guiding Principle**
>
> *If you don't meet peo-
> ple where they are,
> you can't take them
> where you want them
> to go.*

and many more pioneers of our techno-
logical future, leaders promoting a compelling vision have always inspired us.
The ability to conceive and articulate
vision is a critical quality of effective
leadership. If leadership is influence,
vision is one of the primary tools
through which leaders wield that influence. Vision is also the vehicle
through which leaders expand their influence, inspiring the masses to
join them in their visionary quest.

Why is vision so powerful? Why do people so consistently rally around
visionary leaders? To put it quite simply, vision fulfills an emotional need.
People are looking to latch on to a sense of a brighter, more hopeful
future. They desire a sense of direction, a path forward. They seek to be
a part of something bigger than themselves. Vision provides for these
needs. Hope, optimism, direction, connection—these are links to our
emotional selves. It is through the fulfillment of these emotional needs
that visionary leaders achieve their influence.

Consider This

Reflect on leaders you have served with who in their own
way exemplified the power of vision.

+ What five adjectives come to mind when you think
  about how these leaders made you feel as you experienced their expression of vision?
+ In what ways did these leaders connect their vision
  to you personally, making the vision align with who
  you were and what was important to you at that time
  in your life?
+ How did your experience with these visionary leaders
  differ from other experiences you have had with leaders who were not quite so effective at articulating
  vision?

LEVERAGING THE POWER OF VISION

When vision resonates with the members of an organization or community, a powerful emotional attraction is created. The vision itself emits a magnetic force attracting people to move with emotional energy toward the desired outcome. The more a vision resonates with people, the more powerful the magnetic attraction becomes.

What this means for leadership is that people at all levels of an organization can leverage the power of vision as a mechanism for inspiring performance from teammates and colleagues, from those they manage or supervise, and even from their bosses up the hierarchical chain. Indeed, a powerful vision can energize an entire organization. It is therefore necessary for visionary leaders to recognize and accommodate the emotional linkages that need to be established and nurtured for vision to be embraced.

Vision Enrollment

The ultimate goal of any vision broader in scope than a solely individual pursuit is to attract and mobilize others to the same cause. As a leader, you express vision in the hope of enrolling followers. Vision needs to be expressed as something that the target audience will buy into. If that term "buy into" makes vision sound a bit as if it requires a sales job, it often does. Ask any successful salesperson and she or he will tell you that sales is all about establishing an emotional connection between the prospective buyer and the product that buyer is evaluating for purchase. Of course there needs to be a favorable interpersonal connection between the buyer and the salesperson as well. Effective leadership begins with the relationship you as leader have with your people. Effectively enrolling others into your vision requires the establishment of an emotional link between those others and the vision you are promoting. What is the feeling being conveyed by your expression of vision? What is the emotionally attractive force it emits, drawing people to embrace it?

Vision and Values Alignment

Vision is effective when it *speaks* to people at their core. In chapter 6, we described vision as the ability to imagine vividly a desired future outcome. As a leader expressing vision, it is necessary to recognize that this desired future state must be in alignment with the values of those the leader seeks to enroll in the vision. Values operate beneath the surface, guiding behaviors and decisions. A person is naturally and almost unconsciously attracted to a vision that aligns with what he or she believes to be important, one that aligns with the values he or she holds. Conversely, a person is repelled by a vision that he or she does not align with.

Ownership Through Co-Creation of Vision

In *The Fifth Discipline* (1990), Peter Senge explores a concept called *Shared Vision*. Senge discusses five approaches to expressing vision: telling, selling, testing, consulting, and co-creating. Of these, co-creating is most powerful as it provides for the highest degree of active contribution by the members of an organizational community toward the creation of the organizational vision. Co-creation is the least leader-centric of these approaches, allowing and encouraging members of the community to reflect themselves, their needs, interests, ideas, and values in the vision. This level of involvement in the creative process spawns a high degree of ownership, an emotional attachment to what the vision becomes in its finished form, and a deep commitment to seeing the vision's successful implementation.

Vision and Emotional Needs

Vision is often a process brought forward during a time of change, when an organization or other entity is at a crossroads. We discussed change in the previous chapter, and you'll recall how emotional the process of transitioning through change can be. In fact, because vision is a clarification of the future of an organization, sometimes setting a new direction entirely, the vision itself often becomes a vehicle of change. It then becomes important for you as a visionary leader to see yourself as an agent of change. Recognize the need to attend to the emotional experience such change may be bringing about for the people working with you. Inspiring as your vision may be, it is still likely to create an ending of some "old way" and trigger the subsequent grieving process we discussed in chapter 8. Vision may trigger a variety of emotional needs in people, including requirements concerning safety, connection, hope, and achievement. As visionary leader cum change agent, you will find that success depends on your ability to apply your emotional intelligence in support of your people's varied, individual emotional journeys into your hopeful future.

Staying Connected to Vision

It is a common mistake among leaders to call all hands to a meeting, deliver a passionate and compelling expression of a new vision, and then walk away assuming that everyone understood and is on board. It's not that everyone doesn't understand and isn't on board—at that moment, each person may very well be. The issue is more one of how the clarity, connection, and commitment to vision can wane over time if not refueled. As previously stated, the power of vision emanates from its emotional magnetism, and emotions need constant feeding. It's not enough to make a single expression of vision and assume that its energy will be sufficient to keep people on board for the entire ride. Vision must be re-expressed at intervals, its emotional bonds with its implementers reaffirmed and secured.

EQuip Yourself
for Maximum Leadership Influence

To maximize your effectiveness as a leader and exert your leadership influence in a powerful and positive way, remember to:

Manage the mood you create.

- ♦ Ask yourself how you would characterize the mood you create through your interactions with the people with whom you work.
- ♦ Listen and watch for the dance of the amygdalas to ensure that you and those you lead are dancing to the same emotional tune.
- ♦ Change your emotional tune for greater resonance if you recognize that you may be out of sync.

Master the messages you send.

+ Apply your self-awareness to monitor the emotional energy you project via your communication with others.
+ Listen for the feeling messages you are sending.
+ Seek congruence between the words that you choose to convey your meaning and the tone of voice and body language that support that meaning.

Deepen your understanding of resonant leadership.

+ Look for examples of resonant and dissonant leadership all around you in your everyday routine: other leaders, customer service staff at stores you shop in, political leaders on the news, and so on.
+ Watch for examples of resonance and dissonance in movies you watch. Some of our favorite Hollywood examples include: *A Crimson Tide, A Few Good Men, Erin Brockovitch, Hoosiers, Dangerous Minds,* and *The Legend of Bagger Vance.* Observe how the actors in these and other films create resonance and dissonance in their on-screen interactions.

Meet people where they are.

+ Apply the power of empathy as a means of connecting with where your people are emotionally.
+ Revisit chapter 7 for strategies and techniques for empowering your empathetic self.

Create clear and compelling vision.

+ Assess the degree to which you have created and articulated a clear and compelling leadership vision.
+ Ask the people with whom you work for feedback on their understanding of and connection to the vision you have shared.
+ Seek emotional enrollment, values alignment, ownership through co-creation, management of emotional needs, and ongoing connection to vision.

Chapter 10

Putting It All Together—
Your EI Plan of Action

.... **In this chapter, you will learn** ....

 ♦ how to design an action plan for implementing your EI development goals.

....

IS THIS THE END OR JUST THE BEGINNING?

We hope you have enjoyed this exploration into the skills and competencies of emotional intelligence. We hope too that your experience with
this book was not just turning one page after another, but rather that
you took your time, stopping along the way to consider how the concepts
we've discussed had meaning and value for you in both your professional
and personal lives. It is our hope that the theory of EI provided, along
with the exercises and reflections supplied, brought forth both good
insight and good intention for you. Now it's time to convert these insights
and intentions into action.

Back in chapter 1, we made the disclaimer that reading this book, in
and of itself, would not make you more emotionally intelligent. No written

> **Guiding Principle**
>
> *The ultimate goal is to have the skills and attitudes of EI become second nature to you, simply a part of who you are. It's not about* doing *emotional intelligence; it's about striving to* be *emotional intelligence.*

material, training, or coaching alone can accomplish that. The work of growing your emotional intelligence is an everyday commitment. It requires practice, practice, practice. The ultimate goal is to have the skills and attitudes of EI become second nature to you, simply a part of who you are. It's not about *doing* emotional intelligence; it's about striving to *be* emotional intelligence. It's a worthy goal with real benefits for those who make such strides. But as with all worthy goals, it is not so easily attained.

LEVERAGING STRENGTHS AND GROWING IN AREAS THAT NEED DEVELOPMENT

Our challenge to you at the beginning of this book was to:

+ Recognize, acknowledge, and celebrate your strengths with regard to EI. Leverage these gifts to their fullest potential.

+ Identify areas of EI in which you need to grow. Focus some energy on this by putting in place an action plan for development in these areas.

We hope you took us up on this challenge as you worked your way through this content. Did you come to recognize your gifts, those areas for which your emotional intelligence is already strong? And what about the more difficult task of acknowledging aspects of your emotional intelligence in need of growth—did you uncover some EI skills that would benefit from further development? It is common that after participating in a journey like this one you might be filled with good intentions for implementing some of the ideas presented. As you read through the theory and practice of EI framed here, you were likely thinking of how all of this related to your own life, how you might apply these concepts to the people in your life. Perhaps you began considering how to structure more self-awareness timeouts into your busy day or scripting an emotionally intelligent interaction with someone with whom you have an unresolved conflict. We hope you now sit with your head full of such good intentions.

Unfortunately, it is equally common that these good intentions never actually get fulfilled. Just as you close this book and put it on the shelf, your intentions often go with it. Shelving these intentions obviously will not get you where you want to go in terms of this content. Now is the time to capture your intentions, integrate them, and purposefully put them into action. We'd like to provide you with a structure for doing just that.

ACTION PLANNING

Action planning must begin with a clear sense of what it is you need to act on. Although there may be many situations in your life where you can see value in applying your EI to its fullest potential, we're going to suggest that you begin by identifying just one area for starters. Once you achieve success in this first, highest-priority area, you can come back and design an action plan to take on your next development opportunity. Our experience has been that people often fail to achieve their goals simply because they take on too many at once. We encourage you to focus on just one change at a time to maximize your success in this growth process.

Begin by considering these questions:

- What one aspect of your life would gain significant value from applying some of the concepts of emotional intelligence? This would likely be framed as some personal or interpersonal opportunity or challenge currently on your radar for which EI might support a successful outcome.
- What does a successful outcome look like in this situation?
- If this is an interpersonal scenario, who are the players involved?

- Which aspects of EI are critical to your effectiveness in this scenario?
- What specific behavioral action could you take to move closer to your desired outcome here?

Use this needs-analysis table to map all of this information (see Table 10-1). Feel free to modify this format to suit your specific style and/or needs as necessary.

With a target for action now identified and having initiated some thoughts on what effective action may look like, now you are ready to formalize an action plan. Action plans don't need to be fancy; they are simply a

Table 10-1. Putting Emotional Intelligence to Work: A Needs Analysis

Description of Current Challenge or Opportunity:

Key People Involved:

Vision of a Successful Outcome:

EI Competencies to Leverage:

Specific Actions Required to Realize Success:

format to help you clarify and capture your intention and map your progress toward successfully carrying it out. Our suggested action-planning format includes these elements:

- The general area of EI in which the work is going to be done.
- The specific action you are committing to carry out.
- How you intend to measure the successful implementation of the action.
- A time frame within which you will carry out the action, including a date for final evaluation, modification, and reassignment as necessary.
- A clarification of why you want to implement this action, what value the action will bring for you in your life.
- An expression of your degree of commitment to fulfilling this action.

Use this action-planning table to map out your action plan (see Table 10-2).

Note that this action-planning form includes two components that are not always found on such forms: what the effort will achieve and what your commitment level to that achievement is. We feel these pieces are essential to a viable action plan.

Asking yourself what this effort will achieve allows you to clarify for yourself the "What's in this for me?" question. Throughout this book we've suggested many things that could and perhaps should be done with regard to EI to enhance your performance, your relationships, and perhaps even your life overall. But just because we say that these are important things to do doesn't necessarily mean you should do them. The actions you commit to must have meaning for you and add value to your life. You are the only one who can fully determine what those action commitments need to be. Think carefully about the behavioral changes you are about to commit yourself to. What will the achievement of these acts bring to your life? How will they make your life better overall? Are they compelling enough for you to devote the energy and focus required to see them through?

Table 10-2. EI Development Plan of Action

EI Competency	Specific Action Commitment	Measurement	Time Frame

What will this effort achieve? What is my commitment level on this? (1-10)

Our suggestion that you cite a commitment level on a scale of 1-10 stems from the importance of doing a little reality check with regard to goal setting. We have no doubt that your life is quite full, even overflowing perhaps, with things calling for your attention. Through this action-planning process, we are encouraging you to add yet another thing on which to spend your limited focus and energy. How do you prioritize this work in the midst of all else that is calling for your attention? We suggest that you place a value on your degree of commitment toward fulfilling this action, toward making it a part of your everyday routine even if it means that something else gets bumped or otherwise suffers a bit of neglect. Is your commitment level a 9 or is it a 6? In our minds, if you assign anything less than an 8, you may as well forget about it—it's just bound to get lost in the shuffle and there's no sense in even pretending otherwise. Be honest with yourself and your situation. If your commitment level is below an 8, maybe you've chosen the wrong area of focus. Go back to your "What's in it for me question?" and re-evaluate just how important that outcome is for you. Is there an action you could commit to that might bring greater value and warrant a higher degree of commitment?

These two points—what your proposed action will bring to your life and how committed to that action you deem yourself to be—comprise key pieces of the internal support mechanism that you build in support of your desired growth around EI. In clarifying why you want something and how committed you are to getting it, you're establishing an emotional connection with your goal, as discussed in chapter 6. This connection is critical to your success with this development process.

> **Guiding Principle**
>
> *The actions you commit to must have meaning and add value for you. You are the only one who can fully determine what those action commitments need to be.*

But an internal support mechanism alone is not enough; you need to establish an external support mechanism as well. Once you've locked in your own internal commitment and dedication to achieving your development goals, go out and seek others to lend their support to you in this endeavor. Choose people you trust, respect, and who you know care about you, tell them what you intend to work on in terms of your growth and development around EI, and enlist their help as allies in this process. Invite them to keep an eye on you, reinforcing you when you're on track with your intended actions and calling you on it when you slip off course a bit. This is a difficult course to navigate alone regardless of how truly self-aware you may be. Feedback, encouragement, friendly nudges, and positive acknowledgment from others are critical to your success in achieving the growth and development you seek. Who can you invite to join you in this journey?

◆

One Last Glimpse into the Classroom: The Journey

At the very beginning of each of our EI training courses, we go over basic items by referring to a list of "frequently asked questions." We frame these as primary things the participants have on their minds with regard to how our day's exploration of emotional intelligence may go. We humorously suggest that the most frequently asked question among participants is: *What time will we be done today?* This often wins us a chuckle from the group. It is 8:30 a.m., the course has just begun, and people already want to know what time we'll be wrapping up! The next, closely related question is then: *What time is lunch?* We are, of course, establishing some basic expectations for the class. And the third frequently asked question in our course on emotional intelligence: *Will there be a group hug?* Of course, by now, we truly hope that our participants (and you!) realize that group hugs and the like are not what emotional intelligence is all about. Finally we raise the question we all really need to ask of ourselves: *Is Jeff emotionally intelligent? Is Karl emotionally intelligent?* The answer for us, of course, is that we are both on the journey—somewhere between Social Awareness 101 and our PhD in Advanced Empathy Skills. We often teach what we need to learn. Sometimes knowledge is in our heads more than our hearts, our hands, and our feet. C.S. Lewis once wrote: *"My imagination far exceeds my obedience."* That's one thing we can say with certainty. We are all on this journey. Once you understand what the journey is all about, you will begin to recognize and meet other people who are also on the journey. Their place in the journey will rub off on you, and your place in the journey will affect them. Together, we will discover the contagious effect that we can all have on each other's growth. Welcome to the journey!

◆

References

Bolton, R. (1979). *People Skills*. New York: Simon & Schuster.

Boyatzis, R.R., and A. McKee (2005). *Resonant Leadership*. Boston: Harvard Business School Press.

Bridges, W. (1980). *Transitions: Making Sense of Life's Changes*. Philippines: Addison-Wesley.

Burckle, M., and Boyatzis, R. (1999). *Can You Assess Your Own Emotional Intelligence? Evidence Supporting Multi-rater Assessment*. Boston: Hay/McBer Research Report.

Canfield, J., and M.V. Hansen (1993). *Chicken Soup for the Soul*. Deerfield Beach, FL: Health Communications.

Canfield, J., and J. Miller (1996). *Heart at Work: Stories and Strategies for Building Self-Esteem and Reawakening the Soul at Work*. New York: McGraw-Hill.

Covey, S.R. (1989). *The Seven Habits of Highly Effective People*. New York: Simon & Schuster.

Ellis, A. (1988). *How to Stubbornly Refuse to Make Yourself Miserable About Anything*. Secaucus, NJ: Carol Publishing Group.

Ellis, A. (1997). *How to Control Your Anger Before It Controls You*. Secaucus, NJ: Carol Publishing Group.

Goleman D. (1995). *Emotional Intelligence: Why It Can Matter More Than IQ*. New York: Bantam.

Goleman, D. (1998). *Working with Emotional Intelligence*. New York: Bantam.

Goleman, D., R. Boyatzis, and A. McKee (2002). *Primal Leadership: Realizing the Power of Emotional Intelligence*. Boston: Harvard Business School Press.

References

Kübler-Ross, E. (1969). *On Death and Dying*. New York: Macmillan.

LeDoux, J. (1996). *The Emotional Brain: The Mysterious Underpinnings of Emotional Life*. New York: Simon & Schuster.

Maxwell, J.C. (1993). *Developing the Leader within You*. Nashville, TN: Thomas Nelson.

Salovey, P., and J.D. Mayer. (1990). "Emotional Intelligence." *Imagination, Cognition, and Personality*, 9, 185–211.

Seligman, M. (1991). *Learned Optimism: How to Change Your Mind and Your Life*. New York: Alfred A. Knopf.

Senge, Peter P. M. (1990). *The Fifth Discipline: The Art & Practice of the Learning Organization*. New York: Currency Doubleday.

Emotional Intelligence Quick Assessment

This assessment is not intended to replace the more research-based tools we have recommended (see Additional Resources, p. 155). It is, however, designed as a tool for you to use on your own to measure your emotional intelligence. You will be rating yourself on each of the 16 statements below. You should rate yourself using a combination of your own self-awareness as well as feedback you may have received from others. The value of this assessment as a guide for personal development will be maximized if you solicit the feedback of others, especially for those statements that you may be somewhat uncertain about. Therefore, as you rate yourself on each statement, take a moment to reflect on whether or not your rating could benefit from someone else's feedback. Each statement offers a potential opportunity to open up a conversation with someone in order to gain valuable feedback.

In this manner, using both your self-awareness and feedback from others, please rate yourself on each item:

1 = (Almost) Never true about me.
2 = Rarely true about me.
3 = Sometimes true about me.
4 = Often true about me.
5 = (Almost) Always true about me.

1. I recognize situations that arouse strong emotions in me and I am aware of how these emotions affect my behaviors.

2. I acknowledge both strengths and weaknesses about myself and do not get defensive when people offer me feedback about my behavior.

3. I have a self-assured manner and a confident way of presenting myself to others.

4. I control my impulses and stay calm and composed even in stressful situations.

5. I own my behaviors and willingly admit my mistakes to others.

6. I have a willingness to revise my strategies and goals in response to new demands and changing conditions.

7. I set measurable goals and seek ways to improve myself.

8. I look for opportunities and take action to create possibilities.

9. I learn from setbacks, obstacles, frustrations, and failures.

10. I value diversity and connect well with people who are different than myself.

11. I genuinely care about the success of others and seek to provide them with helpful feedback.

12. I inspire others with my words, my stories, or my actions.

13. I take a leadership role in my organization when it comes to accepting and initiating change.

14. I understand how my words, tonality, and body language affect the people with whom I am communicating.

15. I work cooperatively with other people's viewpoints and seek win-win outcomes.

16. I encourage other people to express their viewpoints as much as I assert my own.

SCORING THE EMOTIONAL INTELLIGENCE QUICK ASSESSMENT

Each of the 16 statements relates to one of the emotional competencies of Daniel Goleman's model. If you rated yourself 4 or higher on the statement, then you can consider the corresponding emotional competency to be one of your strengths. If you rated yourself 2 or lower on a statement, then you can consider the corresponding emotional competency an area where you need development.

	Rating	Emotional Competency	Strength or Area for Development?
1.		Emotional Self-awareness	
2.		Accurate Self-assessment	
3.		Self-confidence	
4.		Emotional Self-control	
5.		Transparency	
6.		Adaptability	
7.		Achievement Orientation	
8.		Initiative	
9.		Optimism	
10.		Empathy	
11.		Developing Others	
12.		Inspirational Leadership	
13.		Change Catalyst	
14.		Influence	
15.		Conflict Management	
16.		Teamwork and Collaboration	

List three emotional competence strengths that you would like to leverage:

List three emotional competencies that you would like to focus on for development:

Additional Resources

EI Consortium (The Consortium for Research on Emotional Intelligence in Organizations). www.eiconsortium.org

Comprised of some of the leading researchers in the field of emotional intelligence, the EI Consortium works to aid the advancement of research and practice related to emotional intelligence in organizations. A great source for keeping up with much of the current research in the field, this website offers downloadable research reports, references, and links to other EI-related sites.

Six Seconds, The Emotional Intelligence Network. www.6seconds.org

Drawing its name from research that indicates it takes six seconds for your rational brain to "catch up" with your emotional brain's initial response to an emotional trigger, this nonprofit network aims to help people thrive in the world by maximizing their emotional intelligence. It provides resources, training, and offer an EI assessment instrument.

TalentSmart. www.talentsmart.com

The author of the *Emotional Intelligence Quickbook*, TalentSmart is a training and development firm with a focus on EI. It provides resources for training and assessing emotional intelligence in individuals and organizations.

EMOTIONAL INTELLIGENCE ASSESSMENT INSTRUMENTS

There are many organizations offering assessment instruments for measuring emotional intelligence. Here we highlight three that have been developed by prominent researchers in the field.

EQ-I (Emotional Quotient Inventory). Developed by Reuven Bar-On, this is a self-report instrument in which the score is an outcome of how you respond to the 133 questions comprising the instrument. This assessment measures skills concerning intrapersonal and interpersonal abilities, as well as adaptability, stress management, and general mood areas such as optimism and happiness. The EQ-I is well regarded for selection purposes and career development.

ESCI (Emotional & Social Competence Inventory). Developed by Daniel Goleman and Richard Boyatzis in partnership with the Hay Group, this is a 360-degree assessment instrument compiling responses from a group you invite to offer performance feedback with regard to your degree of emotional intelligence. This instrument aligns with the Goleman model of EI and is designed to assess competencies from the four quadrants of self-awareness, self-management, social awareness, and social skills. The ESCI is well suited to individual and organizational development.

MSCEIT. The name of this instrument is taken from its developers, John Mayer, Peter Salovey, and David Caruso (Mayer, Salovey, Caruso Emotional Intelligence Test). Slightly different from an assessment, this instrument is actually a test, with your score being determined by your choosing the best response to each question. The test measures your abilities in perceiving emotions, applying emotions for facilitating thought, understanding emotions, and managing emotions. The MSCEIT is especially useful in understanding your ability or lack of ability in recognizing emotions in others.

Index

Index

About the Authors

**Jeff Feldman**, President of Eagle's View Enterprises, serves a broad range of clients as a content-based trainer, a group-process facilitator, and a leadership development and personal achievement coach. He applies a background in experiential learning to the design and delivery of meaningful, creative, and high-spirited leadership development and team-building programs. Jeff holds degrees in Education (BS) and Experiential Learning (MS). He founded Eagle's View Enterprises in 1993 after serving five years on the faculty at Penn State University.

Jeff has worked with corporate clients such as 3M, Johnson & Johnson, General Electric, and BASF. He also provides executive-level training to federal employees through the U.S. Office of Personnel Management's management development centers and through direct relationships with a variety of federal agencies. He values his affiliation with training partners, Russell Martin & Associates out of Indianapolis, and RJ Wronski Associates out of Boston. Jeff is co-author, along with Lou Russell, of *IT Leadership Alchemy* (Prentice Hall, 2002).

Jeff can be reached via email at jfeld33@aol.com.

Karl Mulle is a psychotherapist in private practice as well as a popular speaker and trainer with Karl Mulle Productions. With over 24 years of experience in adult education, Karl is recognized for his ability to combine psychological insight with humor and practical application to deliver inspiring messages on human effectiveness. His experience includes work for 3M, Johnson & Johnson, Chevron Corporation, General Electric, and IBM.

Karl is a graduate of Cornell University and holds professional degrees in Divinity and Counseling Psychology. His areas of expertise include developing leaders, building healthy relationships, increasing emotional intelligence, managing stress, developing conflict-negotiation skills, understanding personality differences, developing interpersonal and cross-cultural communication skills, building team unity, and dealing with change and innovation for future growth.

Karl lives in Minneapolis, Minnesota, and can be reached through his Web site, www.karlmulle.com.

Karl and Jeff have been friends and collaborators since an opportunity with 3M brought them together in the mid-1990s. Today they work together on a range of projects, including providing emotional intelligence training to employees of Johnson & Johnson along with training in other areas for the Food and Drug Administration, and Chevron.

100 Questions  About Esophageal Cancer

Pamela Ginex, RN, MPH, OCN
Thoracic Surgery Service,
Memorial Sloan-Kettering Cancer Center

Jacqueline Hanson, RN, BSN, OCN
Thoracic Surgery Service,
Memorial Sloan-Kettering Cancer Center

Bart Frazzitta
President, Esophageal Cancer Education Foundation

Manjit S. Bains, MD
Thoracic Surgery Service,
Memorial Sloan-Kettering Cancer Center

JONES AND BARTLETT PUBLISHERS
Sudbury, Massachusetts
BOSTON   TORONTO   LONDON   SINGAPORE

World Headquarters
Jones and Bartlett
Publishers
40 Tall Pine Drive
Sudbury, MA 01776
info@jbpub.com
www.jbpub.com

Jones and Bartlett
Publishers Canada
2406 Nikanna Road
Mississauga, ON L5C 2W6
CANADA

Jones and Bartlett
Publishers International
Barb House, Barb Mews
London W6 7PA
UK

Copyright © 2005 by Jones and Bartlett Publishers, Inc.

Library of Congress Cataloging-in-Publication Data

Ginex, Pamela.
    100 questions and answers about esophageal cancer / Pamela Ginex, Jacqueline Hanson, Bart L. Frazzitta.—1st ed.
        p. cm.
    Includes bibliographical references and index.
    ISBN 0-7637-4570-7 (pbk. : alk. paper)
    1. Esophagus—Cancer—Popular works.   I. Title: One hundred questions and answers about esophageal cancer.   II. Hanson, Jacqueline.   III. Frazzitta, Bart L.   IV. Title.
    RC280.E8G54 2005
    616.99'432—dc22

                                                                                    2004026189

Production Credits:
Chief Executive Officer: Clayton Jones
Chief Operating Officer: Don W. Jones, Jr.
President, Higher Education and Professional Publishing: Robert W. Holland, Jr.
V.P., Sales and Marketing: William J. Kane
V.P., Design and Production: Anne Spencer
V.P., Manufacturing and Inventory Control: Therese Bräuer
Executive Publisher: Christopher Davis
Special Projects Editor: Elizabeth Platt
Editorial Assistant: Kathy Richardson
Senior Marketing Manager: Alisha Weisman
Marketing Associate: Matthew Payne
Cover Design: Colleen Halloran
Cover Image: © 1999 Photodisc
Printing and Binding: Malloy, Inc.
Cover Printing: Malloy, Inc.

Printed in the United States of America
08 07 06 05 09   10 9 8 7 6 5 4 3 2 1

CONTENTS

From a patient's perspective, it is important to get quality information about such an important topic as cancer in general and esophageal cancer specifically. We certainly have the Internet and all of the information that it can provide, some of which is inaccurate, some of which is outdated, and some of which may be good.

To have a book that specifically addresses esophageal cancer and answers many of the questions one would have about this disease will provide a great comfort to the individual who has been informed that he or she has this disease. As a patient myself, when I first heard that I had esophageal cancer, I decided to not surf the Internet. However, my daughters did that for me and all of the information that was by a consensus accurate or at least seemed to be accurate was information that they shared with me. To have a book about esophageal cancer that was written by leaders in this field at a time when we were gathering information about this disease would have provided a comfort level that would have made the process a lot easier and less tense.

I applaud the publishers and my co-authors of this book for the time and effort they have put into this task, and they should be proud of the product they have placed as a resource before us. From my patient perspective, I cannot help but acknowledge the Memorial Sloan-Kettering doctors and nurses who have allowed me to be here today. Without the expertise and dedication that they bring to the patients in their care, cancer would be as dark a word as it was 10 to 20 years ago.

Through their efforts more of us are living a quality of life that is somewhat comparable to our peers, and with the grace of God they will continue this quest and, hopefully, in our lifetime find a cure for this dreaded disease.

God bless us all.

Bart Frazzitta
June 18, 2004   *v*

The diagnosis of esophageal cancer brings extraordinary emotional, physical, and practical challenges to both patients and those close to them. These challenges can seem overwhelming at times but they are not insurmountable. We believe that knowledge is key to navigating a complex health care system and taking an active role in your care. In this book, *100 Questions & Answers About Esophageal Cancer*, our goal was to provide information that will help you to ask appropriate questions and be an effective patient. Our intention is to answer general questions about the disease, discuss treatment options, identify sources of support, and assist you to manage the side effects of the disease and treatment. Ideally, this information will help you and your loved ones know which questions to ask your doctors to make better informed decisions about your care. We hope that you find this book helpful.

Our inspiration for this book has been our remarkable patients. When faced with this difficult disease, they have shown us the true meaning of strength and courage. We are honored and privileged to care for them and continue to fight to improve treatments and outcomes. For the insight to see the enormous need for this book, we would like to thank Christopher Davis, Executive Publisher for Medicine at Jones and Bartlett Publishers. Esophageal cancer is not a cancer you hear about often, and Chris has the vision to see the need for this book. We also thank Elizabeth Platt for her editorial expertise and her support and patience during the process of writing this book. We would like to thank Randy Lake, our editor at Memorial Sloan-Kettering for his expert assistance and Terry Helms, medical illustrator at Memorial Sloan-Kettering, for her artistic illustrations. Pam would like to thank her husband, Frank, for his love and support.

Pamela Ginex, RN, MPH, OCN
Jacqueline Hanson, RN, BSN, OCN
Manjit S. Bains, MD

We would like to dedicate this book to the men and women with esophageal cancer, along with their families, that we have had the opportunity to care for during their evaluation, treatment, and recovery. We have learned a tremendous amount from their strength and courage. They, along with the thousands of people diagnosed each year with cancer of the esophagus, inspire us and others to work towards improved education, treatment, and support for this disease.

Pamela Ginex, RN, MPH, OCN
Jacqueline Hanson, RN, BSN, OCN
Manjit S. Bains, MD

I would like to dedicate this book to Dominic A. Carone, who, in the short time I knew him, became a friend, a confidant, and a major contributor and partner in the creation of The Esophageal Cancer Education Foundation.

Dominic was instrumental in putting our Web site together, www.fightec.org, and with his passing in October of 2003 I not only lost a good friend, but also lost a crusader who was strong in getting the message to the public that we are hopeful that this book will do.

Bart L. Frazzitta

PART ONE

The Basics

What is the esophagus?

What does the esophagus do?

What is cancer?

What is cancer of the esophagus?

What causes esophageal cancer?

More . . .

1. What is the esophagus?

Esophagus

a portion of the digestive canal, shaped like a hollow tube, which connects the throat to the stomach.

The **esophagus** is a hollow, muscular tube about 10 inches long that connects the throat with the stomach. It lies in front and slightly to the right side of the spine behind the windpipe in the upper part of the chest, and behind the heart in the lower part of the chest.

2. What does the esophagus do?

Gastroesophageal reflux disease (GERD)

a syndrome due to a structural or functional inability of the lower esophageal sphincter to prevent gastric juice from flooding back into the esophagus.

Esophagitis

irritation, inflammation, or damage to the esophagus caused by regurgitation of the acid gastric contents.

Barrett's esophagus

chronic irritation of the lower esophagus that causes the normal lining to be replaced by cells similar to the stomach or intestine, which can tolerate the acid or bile without damage.

There are several layers of muscle in the wall of the esophagus that, by coordinated contractions, help propel food and liquids into the stomach. At the junction where the esophagus meets the stomach, the muscle layers function as a valve to prevent any food from going back (refluxing) into the esophagus. All of us are prone to getting occasional episodes where the stomach contents, including food, acid, or bile, will reflux back into the esophagus. This causes "heartburn." Some people have reflux or heartburn frequently, and this is referred to as **gastroesophageal reflux disease** or GERD (see Question 12). Over time, frequent episodes of the esophageal lining being exposed to stomach acid or bile will cause damage to the normal lining of the esophagus. This damage is called **esophagitis.** Sometimes, after prolonged exposure to acid or bile, the normal lining is replaced by stomach or intestinal lining, which can tolerate the acid or the bile without getting damaged or injured. This change in the lining of the esophagus is referred to as **Barrett's esophagus.** Chances of developing a cancer are significantly higher in the Barrett's esophageal lining than the normal (squamous) lining of the esophagus. Figure 1 is an illustration of the esophagus in relation to other parts of the body.

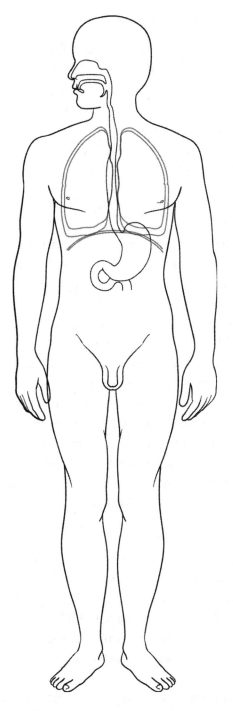

Figure 1. Anatomy of the chest.

3. What is cancer?

Cancer is the word used to describe a group of diseases that affect **cells** in our bodies. There are over 100 types of cancer. In order to understand cancer, it is important to know how our cells normally function and the process that may lead to the development of cancer.

Normal Cells

Our bodies are made up of many different types of cells, with each type uniquely distinguishable from another. For example, a lung cell looks and acts very different from a stomach cell or a pancreatic cell. Each cell has a specific function to help keep us healthy and functioning properly. For example, red blood cells carry oxygen throughout the body and white blood cells help to fight infections. Cells each have a specific "lifespan" and will normally mature over a period of time and then stop growing. Red blood cells normally survive approximately 120 days before they are replaced by new red blood cells. Our bodies are continually at work producing more cells for when we need them. For example, if you have an infected cut on your finger, your body will produce more white blood cells to fight off the infection and then, when the infection is healed, it will stop the extra production of white blood cells.

Damaged Cells

DNA is a substance that helps to direct the activities of a cell. Every cell in our body has DNA. Should this DNA become damaged, a cell will either repair the DNA or it will die. Most often damaged DNA is caused by exposure to something in the environment, such as tobacco smoke. On rare occasions, damaged DNA can be inherited. Sometimes, cells with damaged DNA keep dividing even when new cells are not needed. These extra cells can form a mass that is sometimes called a growth or a **tumor.**

Cell

the smallest unit of living structure capable of independent existence. Cells are highly specialized in structure and function.

DNA (Deoxyribonucleic acid)

a type of nucleic acid found principally in the nuclei of animal and plant cells; considered to be the autoreproducing component of chromosomes and many viruses as well as the repository for hereditary characteristics.

Tumor

any swelling caused by an increased number of abnormal cells.

Tumors

Tumors can be benign or malignant. A **benign tumor** will stop growing and does not invade other tissues. An example of a benign tumor is a lipoma: a soft, fatty tumor that forms under the skin. Tumors classified as **malignant** are composed of cells different from normal cells in several important ways. Malignant, or cancerous, cells lose the ability to stop growing and dividing when they are no longer needed, which means that they keep multiplying. In addition, they also lose the ability to "mature" and do the job they were meant to do. These "immature" cells are often not useful to our body at all. For example, cancerous white blood cells are too immature to fight infection, but they continue to grow and divide even when they are not needed.

Cancerous cells can spread to other organs or parts of the body far from where the cancer originated. When cancerous cells leave their original location and invade other organs, it is a process called **metastasis.** Cancerous cells can invade organs next to where they originated, or they can travel through the body's bloodstream or lymphatic system to reach distant locations. The location where the cancer started is called the **primary tumor.** For example, if a tumor starts in the lung but travels to the liver it is said to be a primary lung cancer that has metastasized to the liver. Both locations have lung cancer cells and are treated by medications that are effective for lung cancer.

4. What is cancer of the esophagus?

Cancer of the esophagus is an abnormal growth of cells occurring within the esophagus. This can occur anywhere along the length of the esophagus. The most common location for cancer to develop is at the

Benign tumor

a growth or mass of abnormal cells that do not invade or destroy adjacent normal tissue.

Malignant tumor

a rapid growth of abnormal cells that replace normal cells, invade other tissues and organs, may recur after attempted removal, and is likely to cause the death of the host if left inadequately treated.

Metastasis

transmission of cancer cells from an original site to one or more sites in the body.

Primary tumor

location where the original tumor began.

The Basics

Gastroesophageal junction
located where the stomach and esophagus meet, also known as the cardia.

gastroesophageal junction, which is located at the bottom of the esophagus where it joins with the stomach.

There are two main cell types of esophageal cancer: squamous cell cancer and adenocarcinoma. Squamous cell cancer arises in the cells that line the esophagus, and adenocarcinoma arises in the glandular cells of the esophagus. Treatment options are the same for both types. The only way to be sure of the type of cancer is to have a biopsy reviewed by an experienced pathologist.

Other types of esophageal cancer are seen less frequently. On rare occasions, sarcoma, lymphoma, small cell carcinoma, mucoepidermoid carcinoma, adenoid cystic carcinoma, and spindle cell carcinoma are diagnosed in the esophagus. It also is possible that cancer starting in another part of the body can occasionally spread to the esophagus.

Bart's comment:

When I was told by my doctor in December of 1999 that I had cancer of the esophagus, it was a total shock. I remember saying to the doctor: "I wasn't aware that you could get cancer of the esophagus." Upon further contemplation of what the doctor had told me, I asked myself: "What information about this type of cancer could I have heeded, or what could I have done to possibly avoid this cancer?" And, in retrospect, there was nothing.

I realized that a person with chronic heartburn over a long period of time could be at risk for this cancer, and that was what I had over the last 15 years. Over-the-counter drugs did their job and the acid reflux would go away. I did not know this could possibly cause cancer, and I believe many people with chronic heartburn are unaware of this possibility. Part of my incentive to be part of this project and other educational information distribution efforts is to let people recognize that this cancer exists and they need to pay attention to this possibility.

5. How common is esophageal cancer?

Cancer of the esophagus is among the 10 most frequent cancers in the world, with over 300,000 new cases each year. One type of esophageal cancer, squamous cell carcinoma, is prevalent in Asia (Turkey, Soviet Union, Iran, Iraq, and China), parts of Africa, and France. Adenocarcinoma of the esophagus has been rising dramatically in the United States and Western Europe, and is the type found in over 80% of patients diagnosed with esophageal cancer. A data analysis from the National Cancer Institute's SEER program found that the number of new cases of adenocarcinoma of the esophagus in white males has doubled from the early 1970s to the late 1980s. The causes for this alarming increase are unclear.

In the United States, approximately 13,000 new cases of esophageal cancer are diagnosed each year. Although cancer of the esophagus is fairly common in some parts of the world, in the United States it accounts for about 1 percent of all cancers.

6. What causes esophageal cancer?

The exact causes of cancer of the esophagus are not known, and researchers and doctors are actively working to identify them. The more they find out about what causes cancer of the esophagus, the better their chances of finding ways to prevent it. Avoiding tobacco entirely and drinking alcohol in moderation are lifestyle factors that may help to prevent the disease. Some factors that may place an individual at risk for the disease have been identified, but a direct cause is not yet known. (Information on risk factors for the disease is included in Part Two.)

Risk and Prevention

What are risk factors?

Is esophageal cancer hereditary?

What are the warning signs of esophageal cancer?

Will taking heartburn medications help
prevent esophageal cancer?

More . . .

7. What are risk factors?

A risk factor is anything that increases an individual's chances of developing a disease. Some risk factors are external, such as the environment (exposure to chemicals) or lifestyle (smoking). We have some control over these external factors and may be able to change our health habits or environment to minimize our risk of disease. Other factors, like inherited genes or traits, are internal factors over which we have no control.

The presence of a risk factor does not mean that an individual will develop the disease.

The presence of a risk factor does not mean that an individual will develop the disease. Also, some individuals develop a disease without having any of the suspected risk factors. In most cases, the disease may be the result of several factors, known and unknown. If you feel you may be at an increased risk for esophageal cancer, it is best to discuss this with your physician. He or she may be able to suggest ways to reduce the risk as well as assess your need for routine check-ups.

8. What are the risk factors for esophageal cancer?

Identifying the factors that place an individual at risk for esophageal cancer is the first step to preventing the disease. The risk factors for esophageal cancer are still being investigated, but some correlation has been found among the following factors.

Individual or Lifestyle Factors:
  Age—The number of cases of esophageal cancer increases with age, with most cases found in individuals over age 55.
  Gender—Cancer of the esophagus is three times more common in men than in women.

Race—Recently, a dramatic increase in new cases of adenocarcinoma of the esophagus has been seen in Caucasians. This is in contrast to squamous cell cancer which is three times as common in African Americans as compared to Caucasians. The reason for this disparity is not clear.

Tobacco use—Individuals who smoke cigarettes or use smokeless tobacco tend to develop esophageal cancer more often than those who do not.

Alcohol use—Excessive use of alcohol can increase an individuals' chance of developing this disease. Individuals who use both alcohol and tobacco have an increased risk of developing esophageal cancer. It is thought that each of these substances increases the harmful effects of the other.

Diet—Esophageal cancer may be associated with poor nutrition. Eating a diet low in fresh fruits and vegetables, and diets lacking in vitamins A, B_1, C or beta-carotene, appears to contribute to the development of esophageal cancer. Researchers are not sure how diet increases the risk of developing esophageal cancer. It is important, however, to eat a well-balanced diet that includes fruits and vegetables. The American Cancer Society recommends eating five or more servings of vegetables and fruits each day, using whole grains such as brown rice and whole wheat instead of refined or processed grains, and limiting red meat.

Medical Conditions:

Reflux—Frequent and repeated reflux results in chronic heartburn, a condition called gastro-esophageal reflux disease (GERD; see Question 2). This chronic reflux can cause changes to the lower esophagus ranging from irritation of the lining (esophagitis), ulceration, scarring or stricture, and change in the lining similar to the stomach or the intestinal lining called "Barrett's" esophagus.

Barrett's esophagus—When cells lining the esophagus are irritated, they can change over time and begin to resemble the cells that line the stomach or the intestines, causing a condition known as Barrett's esophagus. The risk of developing a Barrett's esophagus is 5 to 6 times higher for males than for females, and it is even greater for whites than for blacks. The incidence in Hispanics and Asians is very low. The possibility of cancer developing in the Barrett's esophagus is high and is estimated to be 1% to 2% per year (see Question 13).

Achalasia—A condition where the muscles in the esophagus do not contract as they should. The sphincter at the lower end of the esophagus does not relax normally and the muscular activity in the esophagus is lost, resulting in retention of food in the esophagus. Esophageal cancer is more common in individuals with a history of achalasia.

Irritation of the esophagus—Substances that irritate the esophageal lining, such as swallowing lye or other caustic substances, can lead to significant damage and increase the risk of developing esophageal cancer years later.

Medical history—Individuals who have had cancer of the head and neck have an increased chance of developing a second cancer, including esophageal cancer.

Research is ongoing to identify additional risk factors and possible causes of esophageal cancer. A number of factors are associated with higher incidence of esophageal cancer, but the exact cause and mechanism of development of esophageal cancer is not yet known. The risk factors we discussed may or may not lead to the development of esophageal cancer, and many people who have the disease do not have any risk factors. Lifestyle changes that can be made now to help prevent esophageal cancer include:

1. Quit smoking, do not start smoking, and do not use tobacco in any form.
2. Eat a balanced diet, including fruits, vegetables, and whole grains.
3. Drink alcohol in moderation.

Bart's comment:

A major risk factor in esophageal cancer is chronic heartburn (more than twice a week). If a person has had this condition for 6 months or longer, he should see his gastroenterologist. Smoking and drinking have been linked to esophageal cancer, as has obesity. People who smoke, drink excessively, have GERD, excessive heartburn, or indigestion, and do not maintain a balanced diet are at risk.

9. Is esophageal cancer hereditary?

The vast majority of individuals with esophageal cancer have no family history of esophageal cancer. At this time there are no known genetic links to esophageal cancer, and there is no evidence that it can be passed on to the children of a person who has the disease. However, very rarely, there are families with more than one member who has developed esophageal cancer. Research is ongoing to identify possible causes and risk factors for this disease. If you are concerned about

The vast majority of individuals with esophageal cancer have no family history of esophageal cancer.

the disease, it is best to discuss these concerns with your family physician or a gastroenterologist.

Bart's comment:

Although there is no definite link from a hereditary point of view, some people who have contracted this disease have relatives within their families who have stomach and/or esophageal problems.

Until more information is known it is best to have any symptoms evaluated by a physician.

10. What are the warning signs of esophageal cancer?

Unfortunately, diagnosis of esophageal cancer is usually made in advanced stages of disease when it becomes symptomatic. Diagnosis may be made at the time of an endoscopy for evaluation of symptoms such as heartburn, gastrointestinal bleeding, or surveillance of Barrett's esophagus. Early stage tumors rarely cause any symptoms and are therefore difficult to diagnose. The most common symptom is progressively worsening difficulty in swallowing, starting with solid foods and ultimately a complete blockage if untreated. The first symptom may be when food, often a piece of meat, gets "stuck" when trying to swallow. Difficulty in swallowing may present as a sensation of fullness, pressure, or burning. These problems may be intermittent or they may get progressively worse over time. Initial difficulty may be seen when eating meats, bread, or dry foods. In some patients swallowing may also become painful. Loss of appetite due to the cancer itself or symptoms associated with diagnosis will often lead to weight loss. This weight loss is often a reason that someone will see their doctor prior to a diagnosis of esophageal cancer.

Early stage tumors rarely cause any symptoms and are therefore difficult to diagnose.

Patients may present with weakness, lack of energy, tiredness, or fatigue. Fatigue may be due to **anemia** caused by slow undetected bleeding from the tumor or to a compromised nutritional status.

As tumors block the esophagus, they may cause coughing due to **aspiration** of retained food and secretions in the esophagus. Aspiration also may occur due to paralysis of the vocal cords when the nerves to the vocal cords are involved by the tumor. In very advanced stages, tumors involving the upper esophagus may develop a communication or "fistula" (a tubular passageway) between the esophagus and the windpipe.

Cancer is just one potential cause of these symptoms. There can be a number of other, less serious medical conditions that may cause these symptoms. People with symptoms such as these should see their family doctor and a gastroenterologist. A **gastroenterologist** is a doctor who specializes in diseases of the digestive tract and is the appropriate medical professional to evaluate these symptoms.

Bart's comment:

The problem with this disease is that the early signs can be masked by other non-crucial types of problems. Heartburn, which is considered a common problem that occurs in millions of Americans, can be an early sign of esophageal cancer. Persistent heartburn (over a 6- to 12-month period) should be discussed with your doctor and a gastroenterologist to see if this has gone beyond the simple problem to a more serious problem. Having difficulty swallowing or food occasionally getting stuck in your esophagus could be considered a late sign of this disease and should be evaluated by a physician immediately.

Anemia
a condition where the number of blood cells, amount of hemoglobin, and/or the volume of packed red blood cells are less than normal. Symptoms include pallor of the skin, shortness of breath, palpitations of the heart, and fatigue.

Aspiration
the inspiratory sucking into the airways of fluid or any foreign material, especially gastric contents.

Gastroenterologist
a physician with special training in the function and disorders of the gastrointestinal system, including the stomach, intestines, and related organs of the gastrointestinal tract.

Risk and Prevention

15

11. Are there any screening recommendations for esophageal cancer?

Currently there are no screening guidelines for the early detection of esophageal cancer. The challenge for doctors and researchers is to identify individuals who may be at higher risk to develop esophageal cancer. Approximately 20% of adults in the United States have symptoms of GERD. Of these, roughly 10% will go on to develop Barrett's esophagus. The risk to that 10% of developing esophageal cancer is about 0.5% a year. Research is ongoing to help determine which patients will benefit most from medical surveillance of esophageal disorders and symptoms.

It is important that if you have any of the risk factors, such as chronic heartburn or reflux, you should see a physician or a gastroenterologist. These risk factors will probably not lead to esophageal cancer, but are uncomfortable to the individual experiencing them and may lead to other serious conditions. A gastroenterologist will be able to assess and manage your symptoms and can recommend the appropriate medical follow up.

12. I have GERD. Am I at risk of developing esophageal cancer? What should I do if the heartburn has lasted more than six months?

Occasional heartburn is usually nothing to worry about.

Heartburn is often described as a burning sensation behind the breastbone. It commonly occurs in the lower half of the esophagus but can occur all the way up to the throat. Many people will experience occasional heartburn or reflux, particularly after a spicy or high fat meal. Occasional heartburn is usually nothing to worry about, and there are many over-the-counter products to treat occasional heartburn. However, if symptoms persist for more than one month, you should see a doctor. Another common symptom is regurgitation, a backup of bitter-tasting fluid. These symptoms are usually worse after meals or when lying flat.

A diet high in fat or particular foods such as whole milk, citrus fruits, chocolate, mints, or tomatoes can lead to reflux. Eating large meals, smoking, alcohol consumption, or reclining after meals can also cause reflux. In addition, certain medical conditions such as a **hiatal hernia** (Figure 2), pregnancy, and obesity can increase an individual's risk of developing reflux.

Heartburn that is persistent and lasts at least two days a week for more than six months could be a sign of a

Hiatal hernia

a condition in which part of the stomach protrudes through the esophageal opening (esophageal hiatus) of the diaphragm.

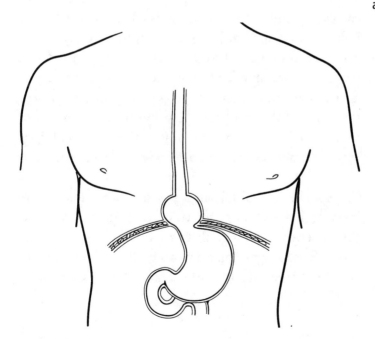

Figure 2. Hiatal hernia.

more serious condition known as gastroesophageal reflux disease or GERD, as discussed in Question 2. The esophagus is normally protected by a muscle located at the top of the stomach called the **lower esophageal sphincter (LES).** This muscle keeps stomach acid from backing up into the esophagus. If this muscle is weakened, stomach contents are allowed to enter the esophagus. One reason why it may be weakened is a hiatal hernia. A hiatal hernia occurs when a small section of the upper part of the stomach slides back and forth between the chest and the abdomen. The stomach lining has a special protective barrier against acid, but the lining of the esophagus does not. If the lower esophageal sphincter does not function properly and acid enters the esophagus, it can cause an uncomfortable burning sensation (heartburn), which over time can lead to irritation, inflammation, and damage to the wall of the esophagus. Left untreated, GERD can cause complications such as esophagitis, which is an inflammation and erosion of the esophagus caused from exposure to stomach acid. A stricture, or scar tissue, can develop as a result of acid exposure and cause the esophagus to narrow. Barrett's esophagus is a condition where the lining of the esophagus actually changes in response to repeated acid exposure. Each of these conditions requires evaluation and follow-up with a physician.

You should see a physician if you have persistent heartburn. It may be best to see your family doctor, who can then refer you to a specialist (gastroenterologist) if necessary. Several symptoms are more urgent, however, and you should see a doctor immediately if you experience:

- Difficulty swallowing or feeling as if food is stuck in your throat
- Unexplained weight loss

Lower esophageal sphincter (LES)

a muscle located at the top of the stomach that opens and closes to keep stomach acid and bile from backing up into the esophagus.

See a physician if you have persistent heartburn.

18

- Chest pain
- Hoarseness
- Dark stools or blood in stools

Each of these symptoms may be a sign of a more serious condition and should be evaluated by a physician.

Bart's comment:

You should see a doctor if you have persistent reflux. A drug may be recommended that you should take for a stipulated period of time. If the problem continues once you stop taking the medicine, then you should see a gastroenterologist and possibly have an endoscopy done.

13. Tell me more about "Barrett's esophagus." What is it? What causes it?

Barrett's esophagus is a condition that occurs as a complication of chronic GERD. Over time, chronic reflux of the acidic stomach contents or bile into the esophagus leads to changes in the cells that line the esophagus. The acid changes the squamous cells that normally line the esophagus so they are more like the lining of the stomach or the intestines. When viewed under a microscope, healthy tissue lining the esophagus is a whitish color. In an individual with Barrett's esophagus, the whitish lining has turned to an abnormal salmon pink color. This change is called **metaplasia** and is most often seen near the gastroesophageal junction, where the esophagus meets the stomach. Metaplasia is the process of the replacement of one tissue lining by another type of tissue. This cellular change in the tissue is thought to be a protective response because the lining in Barrett's esophagus is more resistant to injury from acid than the original lining of the esophagus.

Metaplasia

transformation of an adult, fully formed cell of one kind into an abnormal cell of another kind; an acquired condition (see Barrett's esophagus).

19

Barrett's esophagus does not have unique symptoms, and you will not even know you have it unless you have an endoscopy. The symptoms associated with GERD—heartburn and regurgitation—are often seen in an individual with Barrett's. However, not all individuals with Barrett's esophagus have symptoms of GERD.

Barrett's esophagus can only be diagnosed by an **endoscopy** and a **biopsy.** An endoscopy is a procedure performed by a gastroenterologist where a lighted scope is inserted through the mouth and the lining of the esophagus is visualized. This lining is viewed by the gastroenterologist, who can biopsy the tissue at the same time. When the biopsy is viewed by an experienced **pathologist,** the presence of intestinal type cells (called goblet cells because of their shape) confirms the diagnosis of Barrett's esophagus. Both the visual change and the biopsy result are required for a diagnosis of Barrett's esophagus.

An endoscopic biopsy may be misleading if there is inflammation in the esophagus, and the biopsy erroneously may be reported to show **dysplasia** (see Question 18). If there is inflammation, it is important to be treated for reflux with high doses of proton pump inhibitors (such as Prilosec®, Prevacid®, or Nexium®) and for the biopsy to be repeated. If there is no dysplasia in two consecutive biopsies, the American College of Gastroenterology's 1998 guidelines suggest an endoscopy and biopsy every two to three years.

The progression of Barrett's esophagus to cancer is a reasonably well-established phenomenon, with changes progressing from low-grade dysplasia to high-grade dysplasia and then to cancer. Reports indicate that of the patients with metaplasia who are on medication

Endoscopy

examination of the interior of a canal or hollow viscus by means of a special instrument, called an endoscope; the patient is sedated during the process.

Biopsy

a process of removing tissue from a patient for diagnostic examination.

Pathologist

a physician who practices, evaluates, and/or supervises diagnostic tests, using materials removed from living or dead patients, to determine the causes or nature of the disease change.

Dysplasia

abnormal development or growth of tissue, cells, or organs.

therapy, a proportion of them will be fine and the cells will not progress to cancer. This cell progression is not merely one way. In several studies, approximately 25% of patients who have low-grade dysplasia may have no dysplasia on subsequent exams. Similarly, some patients with high-grade dysplasia may regress into low-grade dysplasia or no dysplasia at all. Overall, in most cases there is progression towards cancer.

Pathologists can disagree about the definition of low-grade and high-grade dysplasia. It is important to have at least two pathologists review the slides and confirm the presence of a high-grade dysplasia before an invasive treatment is undertaken.

If a diagnosis of Barrett's esophagus is suspected but uncertain, it is best to obtain a second opinion at a center that has extensive experience with the disease. This can prevent you from worrying about your long-term risk of cancer or the need for additional medical tests if the diagnosis of Barrett's was incorrect. It can also allow you to start close surveillance for cancer if the diagnosis of Barrett's is confirmed. Barrett's esophagus is treated by treating the underlying cause: GERD.

14. Does having Barrett's esophagus or GERD increase my risk of developing cancer? What is H. pylori, and what part does it play in GI disorders?

Yes, Barrett's esophagus is associated with an increased risk of esophageal cancer. The type of cancer that occurs in individuals with Barrett's esophagus is called **adenocarcinoma,** which arises from the intestinal cells. **Squamous cell carcinoma** of the esophagus arises from

Adenocarcinoma

a malignant neoplasm of epithelial cells in a glandular or gland-like pattern.

Squamous cell carcinoma

a malignant neoplasm derived from stratified squamous epithelium cells, such as those that line the esophagus.

21

the squamous cells that line a normal esophagus and is not associated with Barrett's esophagus.

Esophageal adenocarcinoma has been increasing in frequency for the past 20 years, primarily in white males. It is not known why this is occurring. One possibility is that there is a decrease in **Helicobacter pylori** (*H. pylori*) infections in the stomach. *H. pylori* is a type of bacteria that is the major cause of ulcers. It is a very common infection and causes no symptoms in most of the individuals who are affected by it. If the infection goes untreated, it can lead to progressive inflammation of the stomach. This inflammation leads to a decrease in acid secretion. Due to better public health measures, this infection is diminishing worldwide. Some researchers speculate that the decreased acid production as a result of the *H. pylori* infection may actually have a protective effect to the esophagus—so the decline of *H. pylori* infections, while helpful in reducing the incidence of ulcers, actually contributes (in theory) to the increase in cancers. However, this link has not been proven and is still under investigation.

It is thought that approximately 10% to 15% of individuals with chronic GERD will develop Barrett's esophagus. It is unknown why some people with chronic GERD develop the condition and others do not. It is also unknown why Caucasian males seem to be more at risk to develop Barrett's esophagus than any other group. Relatively few patients with Barrett's esophagus will develop adenocarcinoma of the esophagus. However, Barrett's esophagus does put an individual at higher risk for cancer and routine surveillance is necessary. Periodic, routine endoscopy and biopsy are recommended procedures that can help to detect early cancers.

Helicobacter pylori

a specific type of microorganism that causes gastritis and peptic ulcer disease of the stomach. It may play a role in the development of dysplasia and metaplasia of gastric mucosa and distal gastric adenocarcinoma.

15. How are GERD and Barrett's esophagus treated?

The primary treatment for GERD and Barrett's is the suppression of acid reflux. Lifestyle changes may be able to relieve some of the symptoms of GERD. The following list contains some suggestions that may help:

- Do not eat large meals; rather, eat small, frequent meals.
- Do not lie down for about two hours after eating.
- Avoid late night snacks.
- Avoid highly seasoned foods, acidic juices, alcohol abuse, peppermint, products with caffeine, and fatty foods.
- Avoid tobacco products in any form.
- To reduce reflux, sleep with the head of your bed raised 45 degrees.
- If you are overweight, losing weight will reduce reflux.
- If your doctor has prescribed medication for you, take it as directed.

Mild symptoms can be treated with over-the-counter medications, such as antacids or low doses of medications called **H-2 blockers.** More persistent symptoms can be treated with higher doses of H-2 blockers. Examples of H-2 blockers are Tagamet®, Pepcid®, Zantac® and Axid®. **Proton pump inhibitors** are medications that are used for ongoing therapy or complicated GERD (associated with bleeding or strictures). Examples of proton pump inhibitors are Prilosec®, Prevacid®, Aciphex®, Protonix®, and Nexium®.

Proton pump inhibitors work by blocking the secretion of acid from the stomach. They can be effective in relieving heartburn and can allow the inflammation of

H-2 blockers

type of pharmaceutical drug used to treat GERD and Barrett's esophagus.

Proton pump inhibitors

type of pharmaceutical drug used to treat more complicated GERD (associated with bleeding or strictures).

Risk and Prevention

the esophagus (esophagitis) to heal. Proton pump inhibitors are usually well tolerated and have minimal side effects. If you are taking any of these medications, it is important that you do not stop them suddenly. This can lead to an increase in symptoms. It is best to discuss your medications with a gastroenterologist who can change them if needed or instruct you on how to taper your dose.

16. Will taking heartburn medications help prevent esophageal cancer?

It is not known if heartburn medications help to prevent esophageal cancer.

The long-term side effects of heartburn medications are still being investigated, and it is not known if they help to prevent esophageal cancer. Some laboratory studies have identified stomach tumors in rats after exposure to proton pump inhibitors; however, more than 15 years of experience with these medications has not identified a similar occurrence in humans. Some individuals on long-term medication therapy develop small benign **polyps** in the stomach. These polyps do not become cancerous and cause no problems.

Polyp

a general term used for any mass of tissue that bulges or projects outward or upward from the normal surface level; is visible as a roundish structure growing from a mound-like base or a slender stalk.

17. Is surgery used to treat GERD and Barrett's esophagus?

GERD, with or without Barrett's esophagus, is sometimes treated by surgery. This type of operation is called **fundoplication** or anti-reflux surgery, and is performed to stop the reflux of acid into the esophagus. The operation involves wrapping the stomach around the lower part of the esophagus, which tightens the lower esophageal sphincter and is intended to prevent reflux. These operations are typically performed by thoracic (chest) surgeons, gastric surgeons, or general surgeons. It is most often done laparoscopically,

Fundoplication

suture of the fundus of the stomach completely or partly around the gastro-esophageal junction to treat gastro-esophageal reflux disease.

without the need for a large incision. **Laparoscopy** is a type of surgery where the surgeon inserts several tiny telescopes thru the abdomen. The abdomen is then inflated with carbon dioxide to move the abdominal wall away from the internal organs. The surgeon can then work with instruments, visualizing the area through the telescopes to perform the surgery.

Your doctor will need to do several tests to determine if you are a candidate for this type of surgery. Most patients who have the surgery have serious complications from GERD and require high doses of medications. There is no evidence that this type of surgery reduces the risk of esophageal cancer.

18. I've been told that I have high-grade dysplasia. What does this mean?

Dysplasia is the development of changes within a cell that are not normally seen in cells in that part of the body. Cells that have these dysplastic changes appear malignant but do not invade other tissues like cancer cells. It is not yet known which patients with Barrett's esophagus will progress to dysplasia and which patients with dysplasia will progress to cancer.

Dysplasia is considered premalignant and is classified as either high-grade, low-grade, or indefinite. The indefinite classification means that the pathologist is unable to tell if low-grade dysplasia is present or not. For low-grade and indefinite dysplasias, routine endoscopic biopsy surveillance is recommended. On the follow-up endoscopy, some patients will be found not to have dysplasia or will be diagnosed as having lesser grades of dysplasia. This change may represent a sampling variation or actual biological reversal. The exact

Laparoscopy

a type of surgery using a laparoscope, comprised of fiber optics and low-heat halogen bulbs that aid the placement and use of other surgical tools. One or more tiny incisions enable precise incision, drainage, excision, cautery, ligation, suturing, and other surgical procedures.

Risk and Prevention

25

reasons why the dysplasia may regress are not currently known.

The presence of high-grade dysplasia indicates that cancer may already be present and surgery is the recommended treatment. Some patients with high-grade dysplasia may opt for follow-up biopsy surveillance. This is an important decision you should make only after a thorough discussion of the risks and benefits with a gastroenterologist and a thoracic surgeon. If you choose surveillance, it will be recommended that you have an endoscopy every three months for a year and then every four to six months afterwards. The reason surgery is recommended instead of close follow-up is because of the high likelihood that cancer may be missed by the biopsies.

If you are diagnosed with high-grade dysplasia, your gastroenterologist may repeat your endoscopy with more biopsies. If you are diagnosed with Barrett's esophagus with dysplasia, it is important that a pathologist experienced in this diagnosis review your pathology slides. It is a common practice to ask a second or a third pathologist to review the pathology slides. This is important to check for agreement among pathologists and to possibly get a more experienced opinion.

PART THREE

Diagnosis and Staging

How is esophageal cancer diagnosed?

What tests are preformed to aid in the diagnosis?

What does my doctor mean by "stage of disease," and why is staging important?

More . . .

19. How is esophageal cancer diagnosed?

Most patients with esophageal cancer are diagnosed after they experience symptoms and go to their doctor to be evaluated. They may go to their primary physician complaining that food is getting "stuck" during swallowing. Depending on the physician, she/he will either evaluate these symptoms themselves or refer the patient to a specialist such as a gastroenterologist for evaluation. Either way, if an abnormality is identified, an endoscopy and biopsy are performed.

It is not unusual for an early stage cancer to be discovered during a routine endoscopy. People who suffer from heartburn or GERD or have been diagnosed with Barrett's esophagus often have an endoscopy periodically to monitor potential damage to the esophagus.

Bart's comment:

When I complained to my doctor that a piece of meat had gotten stuck in my esophagus and there was significant pain, we did an endoscopy, and that determined that I had a tumor in my esophagus. We did a CAT scan and a PET scan to confirm the cancer and to see if there were any other cancer sites in my body. Once we determined that this was the only cancer site, we then began the plan on how we would attack this cancer. A discussion with the team of doctors produced a chemotherapy and radiation protocol, followed by surgery plan.

20. What tests are preformed to aid in the diagnosis?

There are a number of tests that are used to diagnose esophageal cancer. In most cases, multiple tests are required to fully evaluate the extent of the cancer. Each test will give the physicians different information.

- A **barium swallow** (also called an upper GI series or esophagram) is a type of radiology exam where you are asked to drink a barium solution before an x-ray is taken. This is often the first test done when a doctor is concerned about a problem in the esophagus. The barium coats the esophagus and stomach and shows up on an x-ray. The x-ray pictures will show the **radiologist** changes in the shape of the esophagus, stomach, and duodenum (the lower part of the stomach). It is often ordered to determine if and where in the esophagus an abnormality is located and if there is obstruction of the esophagus.
- A barium swallow is also used to identify such conditions as ulcers, hernias, blockages, and other abnormalities.
- In order to obtain a clear picture of your gastrointestinal system, you will be asked to not eat or drink anything for four to eight hours prior to the test. You will also be asked to remove any metallic objects, such as jewelry.

Barium can cause constipation as it moves through the digestive system. To help minimize this, drink extra fluids after the test and ask your doctor if you should take a laxative. Barium has a whitish color and may be noticeable in your stools for several days after the test.

- A **CAT (computed axial tomography)** scan of the chest and abdomen is often performed to assess for any anatomical abnormalities. A CAT scan is an x-ray procedure that uses a computer to generate cross-sectional views of the body. The pictures generated from a CAT scan show a 'slice' of the body.

Barium swallow
a type of radiology examination where a barium solution is drunk before the x-ray is taken to be able to visualize the esophagus, stomach, and duodenum.

Radiologist
a physician specially trained in the diagnostic and/or therapeutic use of x-rays and radionuclides, radiation physics and biology.

CAT scan
a type of x-ray procedure that is painless and provides multiple pictures of the body in specific sections for diagnostic purposes.

An example often used to illustrate the type of images of a CAT scan is that of a loaf of bread. Imagine the body as a loaf of bread and you are looking at one end of the loaf. As each slice of bread is removed, you can see the entire surface of the next slice. Similarly, CAT scan images give physicians multiple pictures of your body, which help to define normal and abnormal structures. CAT scans are painless and may be done with intravenous (IV) and/or oral contrast, which will help to enhance the pictures. Your physician will look for thickening of the wall of the esophagus or stomach; any enlarged lymph nodes, lung, or liver nodules; and fluid in the chest or abdomen. The CAT scan is usually done on both the chest and the abdomen.

- An endoscopy (also called esophagoscopy or EGD) is a test that is done under sedation. It is performed to visualize the esophagus and to obtain biopsies. The physician (usually a gastroenterologist) will take a small flexible, lighted tube and insert it through your mouth to your esophagus. The physican can then visualize the inside of the esophagus and take a biopsy of any suspicious area. An endoscopy is sometimes done with ultrasound or sound waves (**endoscopic ultrasound** or **EUS**) to see how far into the wall of the esophagus the tumor has grown and to determine if there are any lymph nodes involved.

- An endoscopy and endoscopic ultrasound are valuable procedures in the diagnosis and staging of esophageal cancer. The ultrasound is actually able to see through the wall of the esophagus with much more accuracy than a CAT scan. The depth of the tumor into the wall of the esophagus is an important factor in considering the appropriate treatment for

Endoscopic ultrasound (EUS)

a type of endoscopy that uses sound waves for diagnostic purposes.

you. An endoscopic ultrasound is the best method to determine this depth. An endoscopic ultrasound can also see any enlarged lymph nodes or suspicious lymph nodes present along the esophagus or the stomach. It is a relatively new technique, and not all gastroenterologists who perform endoscopy may perform endoscopic ultrasounds.

- The gastroenterologist will be able to discuss the visual findings from the exam that day. If any biopsies were taken, these may require several days to be read by a pathologist. Your doctor will let you know when to expect any biopsy results.

- A **Positron Emission Tomography** (**PET**) scan is used to determine the metabolic activity of different tissues in our body and whether an abnormality is likely to be a cancer or not. Cancer cells are usually more active than normal cells and are presumed to metabolize nutrients faster. This difference in metabolism can be identified by a PET scan. A PET scan assesses the entire body for evidence of cancer and utilizes an injection that works with the glucose in the body to identify areas that are likely to be a cancer. An abnormal focus of increased activity may suggest the possibility of cancer at that site. A PET scan is a relatively new test but has quickly become a valuable tool to help physicians identify areas that may be of concern.

- To prepare for this test, you will be asked to refrain from eating and drinking anything (except water) and to refrain from vigorous physical activity for several hours before the test. The reason for this is that the injection that is utilized for a PET scan works with the glucose in your body. Having sugar (even a piece of gum or candy) may interfere with the results of the test. After you receive the injec-

Positron emission tomography (PET) scan
a type of scan that measures positron-emitting isotopes with short half-lives that the patient has ingested to assess metabolic and physiologic function rather than anatomic structure.

31

tion, you will be asked to lie in a quiet room for about 45 minutes. After this time, you will be placed on a moveable table where the scan will take place. Your doctor should receive the results of the test in several days. PET scans complement the other staging tests you are having. In about 15–20% of patients a PET scan detects cancer that has spread beyond the esophagus. In addition, some recent research suggests that the level of activity measured by PET scan (often reported as Standard Uptake Value or SUV) is suggestive of prognosis.

Each of these tests will help your doctor to assess your condition. Each can identify an abnormality, but only with a biopsy can your physician say for sure whether it is a cancer or not. As your doctor orders tests, it is a good idea to check with your insurance company to determine whether you need pre-certification or authorization prior to having the test.

Bart's comment:

I was surprised at all of the tests they had available to further define this cancer and to see if there were any other tumors in my body. My suggestion would be that if you have had an initial diagnosis, you should go through a CAT scan, PET scan, and endoscopy before a plan is decided on by your medical team

21. What does my doctor mean by "stage of disease," and why is staging important?

Your doctor will determine the stage of your disease for several important reasons. By "stage," he or she is referring to the extent of the cancer in your body. This includes where it is located, how extensive it is, and whether it has spread to any lymph nodes, nearby organs, or elsewhere in your body. Treatment for esophageal cancer includes chemotherapy, radiation therapy, surgery, or a combination of any or all of these. The stage of the disease will determine what treatment option will be the most suitable for you. Staging also gives physicians a standard language to discuss your treatment with other medical professionals involved in your care.

Bart's comment:

When we had all of the tests done, the doctors told me that I had a stage 3 tumor with no lymph node involvement.

22. How is esophageal cancer staged?

All solid tumors use a classification called the TNM staging system. $\underline{T}$ relates to the primary tumor, $\underline{N}$ indicates whether the lymph nodes are involved, and $\underline{M}$ denotes the presence or absence of metastasis. Once each of these areas has been evaluated by tests such as a CAT scan, endoscopic ultrasound, or PET scan, an overall stage is assigned. The overall stages are listed below (see also Figure 3).

- Stage I—the tumor is localized to the top few layers of the esophageal wall.
- Stage II—the tumor has invaded deeper into the esophageal wall and may involve local lymph nodes.
- Stage III—the tumor has invaded the full thickness of the wall of the esophagus or involves local lymph nodes.

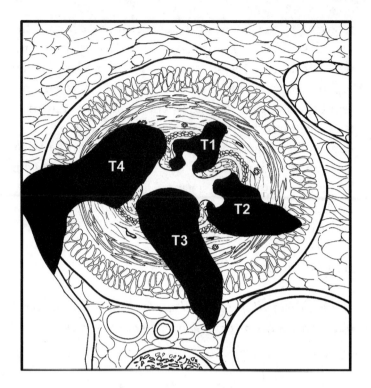

Figure 3. Esophageal cancer staging. Darkened areas demonstrate the level of invasion through the esophageal wall for each tumor stage.

- Stage IV—the tumor has spread beyond the esophagus to involve other parts of the body.

23. What are lymph nodes?

Lymph is an almost clear fluid that drains waste from cells. This fluid travels through vessels to our lymph nodes, which are small, bean-shaped structures located throughout our bodies that filter unwanted substances, such as cancer cells and bacteria, from the fluid. Since the job of the lymph nodes is to filter unwanted substances, like cancer cells, it is important to check them at diagnosis and during treatment (see Figure 4).

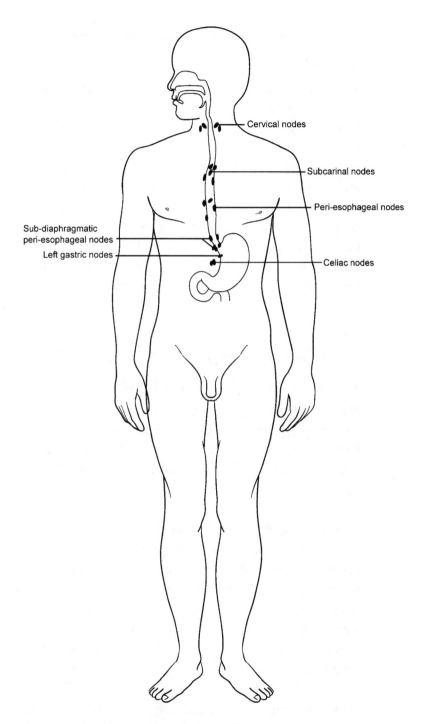

Figure 4. Regional lymph nodes near the esophagus.

24. Why are lymph nodes important in esophageal cancer?

Whether the cancer has spread to the lymph nodes is an important factor to consider when deciding the best treatment for you. Lymph nodes may appear enlarged on diagnostic tests such as a CAT scan or an endoscopic ultrasound. A biopsy is required to know if they are involved with cancer or if they are enlarged for another reason, such as an infection. At the time of surgery, your surgeon may remove your lymph nodes as part of the operation. This is done for surgical staging, and some surgeons believe that the removal of lymph nodes near the area of the tumor improves survival following surgery.

25. How important are survival statistics to an individual patient?

Survival statistics for esophageal cancer are not very encouraging and can be overwhelming when viewed from an individual perspective. It is therefore imperative that one understands how these statistics are compiled.

Survival statistics measure the five-year survival rate of all patients with a similar diagnosis, but they cannot predict prognosis in a single individual. Your survival depends on a number of factors, including the stage of your disease, how well you respond to treatment, and your overall medical health. You should also keep in mind that the statistics you are viewing were compiled on therapies and technology that are often outdated. Treatment for esophageal cancer has changed dramatically over the past decades, and published statistics may not reflect improved treatment advances.

Bart's comment:

When you are dealing with cancer statistics as to life expectancy given your respective cancer, there is always a concern, and the number is of interest to the patient. When the doctor tells you that statistics indicate that there is a 20% chance you will live 5 years or that 3 out of 4 people who contract this cancer die from it, these are shocking comments. But do they really apply to me as a patient hearing them?

One must look at the individuals who are part of the database that gave rise to these statistics. What are the ages of those in the statistical database? Are they all 61 like myself, or are some older and some younger? If a database states 'white males between 55 and 75,' then this immediately raises questions as to the validity of that database because I am 61, and how do people at other ages affect these statistics? Mine was a stage 3 cancer. What were the stages of the other patients in this statistical base and how do they fare? Do they add to the life expectancy or take from it? The comparisons can go on and on. Were the participants in this statistical base smokers or drinkers, or were they sickly all their lives, or did they have stressful jobs versus people who have no stress in their lives? What I am trying to say is that most statistical databases do not specifically apply exactly to you and therefore, as I like to say, "YOU ARE A STATISTIC OF ONE!"

All the statistics in the world do not compensate for the will of the individual to meet this challenge and actively fight this problem and beat the odds. "Problems are opportunities," a boss once told me, and having been told you have cancer is all you need to know to say, "I am going to meet this challenge and I will win. I will never give up."

Having a positive attitude goes a long way in fighting this disease. For you to stay in control, make sure you are a part of the decision process, and make sure you retain that positive attitude through all the treatments you have to endure. I am sure you will have positive outcome. God made each of us unique, and no two of us are exactly the same; it is this uniqueness that makes us special.

PART FOUR

Coping with the Diagnosis

I've been diagnosed with esophageal cancer.
What should I do now?

How do I select a surgeon or medical oncologist?

Should I get a second opinion?

What else can I do to strengthen
myself before treatment?

More . . .

26. I've been diagnosed with esophageal cancer. What should I do now?

If you've been diagnosed with cancer of the esophagus, you already may have been seeing your family doctor or a gastroenterologist. These physicians should explain to you what they think the next best step will be. An evaluation by a physician who specializes in esophageal cancer will be important in planning your care. Esophageal cancer is a rare type of cancer, and it may be necessary to go to a larger university hospital to see doctors that have experience treating esophageal cancer. It will be beneficial to see both a medical **oncologist** (a doctor who treats cancer with medications such as chemotherapy) and a surgical oncologist. Esophageal cancer is often treated in a **multimodality** fashion, and each of these specialists can offer their opinion as to the best treatment course for you. Radiation is often used to treat esophageal cancer, and a medical oncologist or surgical oncologist can refer you to a radiation oncologist for treatment if necessary.

When making plans to see a specialist, it is helpful to collect a copy of any physician's notes, test results, radiology reports and films, and any other medical information related to your diagnosis and past medical history. It is very important for the doctors to see the actual radiology films in addition to the paper report. The doctors you will be seeing will need a copy of your records, and it may save time and energy to ask for a copy of each report as you have each test rather than gathering all the information at a later date. If you have had a biopsy at a different hospital from which you will be treated, you will probably be required to bring in the glass slides made from your original biopsy. Most hospitals require review of previous biop-

Oncologist

a physician with specialized training in the science of the physical, chemical, and biological properties of cancer.

Multimodality

the use of specialists in two or more disciplines to treat a specific disease; may include diagnostic testing, radiation, pharmaceuticals, or surgery.

It may save time and energy to ask for a copy of each report as you have each test rather than gathering all the information at a later date.

sies by their pathologists prior to starting treatment or having surgery. The patient is responsible for obtaining the slides and pathology report from the hospital that performed the biopsy. If your primary care physician has been coordinating your care, his or her office may be able to help obtain some of this information.

Bart's comment:

The first step in the process is to determine the institution that has experience treating this kind of cancer. Visiting web sites of the different cancer centers will give you insight into the facility the particular center has, the attention they pay to thoracic cancers, and the team they have assembled to handle this kind of cancer.

27. How do I select a surgeon or medical oncologist?

It is important to be sure that you are getting the best care possible, and this starts with your choice of doctors. A recommendation from a reliable source, such as your primary care physician or gastroenterologist, is a good place to start. You can also call the nearest cancer center or university hospital to find a specialist. The National Cancer Institute (NCI) has a toll free phone number (1 800 4-CANCER) where you can call to find a specialist near you. The leading cancer centers are identified by the National Cancer Institute as NCI-designated comprehensive cancer centers. The American College of Surgeons' web site (*http://www.facs.org*) lists its members by specialty. At the main page of their web site, you can go to the "public information" tab, and from there you can search for members with a specialty in thoracic surgery or general surgery, or for a surgeon located near you. The American Society of Clinical Oncology also has a web site, People Living with Cancer (*http://www.plwc.org*). From the main page you can go to "Find an oncologist" and then search for a medical oncologist, radiation oncologist, or surgeon near you.

After you have identified a specific doctor, it is important to evaluate whether this person is a qualified physician and whether you are comfortable with him or her. Some things to consider include:

- Clinical experience—It will be critical to determine whether a physician has experience with the treatment of esophageal cancer. Oncologists treat patients with all types of cancer, but ideally you want to find one who specializes in esophageal cancer. Surgical oncologists also may treat many types of cancer, so it is helpful to look for one who has experience with esophageal cancer. You should also ask the physicians what percentage of their practice is esophageal cancer and how many esophageal surgeries they perform over a given amount of time (i.e., within a year).
- Hospital affiliation—Cancer centers and university hospitals conduct research and provide access to the newest treatments and clinical trials. They also have experience with less common types of cancer such as esophageal cancer. When choosing a physician, keep in mind that you are not only choosing the physician, but also the nursing and ancillary staff. You should feel comfortable and confident with the entire team who will be helping to take care of you.
- Credentials—Basic professional information for licensed U.S. physicians is available through the American Medical Association's Physician Select web site (*http://www.ama-assn.org/aps/amahg.htm*). At the

web site you can search by physician's name or specialty. To find a surgeon, click on the "search from an expanded list of medical practice specialties." Each listing offers information on the physician's medical school, residency and fellowship training, board certification, and office location. Board certification ensures proficiency in a specified area, such as medical oncology, radiation oncology, general surgery, or thoracic surgery. Residency or fellowship training at a major cancer center can be a plus, as that involves rigorous post-graduate education with experts in the field of oncology.

Other factors that you should also consider:

- *Is the doctor covered by your insurance plan?* Financial constraints are a reality, and insurance coverage should be considered when selecting a doctor. Your doctors should be covered under your policy unless cost is not an issue for you. However, there may be reasons you need to see a specialist outside your insurance plan. Esophageal cancer is a relatively rare form of cancer and not every doctor or surgeon has experience treating it. In some cases, insurance companies may make exceptions for coverage to a specialist not participating in your policy. It may be helpful to speak with a **social worker** at the hospital where you are being treated or the benefits representative at your place of employment if you cannot find a specialist in your plan who treats esophageal cancer or if you have questions regarding insurance issues. You may also want to call your insurance company to see about out–of–network coverage.
- *Distance.* Treatment for esophageal cancer, such as chemotherapy or radiation therapy, may require mul-

Social worker
a degreed mental health professional who can provide counseling services to individuals and groups as well as help the patient network with community services and resources.

tiple, or even daily, trips to the doctor or hospital. Surgery usually requires an extended hospital stay. If you feel this may become a significant issue for you and your family, it may be helpful to speak with the hospital's social worker about transportation alternatives or possibilities for inexpensive lodging.

Bart's comment:

Once you have selected the cancer center, you need to evaluate the surgeons and medical oncologists associated with that cancer center. Reputation and years of service play a role in your selection. Also, frequency at which the surgery is performed at this center is important to know and, more specifically, how many surgeries of this nature the surgeon you are thinking about has performed.

28. Who are the other members of the medical team? What is multidisciplinary care?

You likely will see more than one specialist for your esophageal cancer care.

Dietitian

a degreed professional who can develop a nutritious eating plan for an individual.

Esophageal cancer is a complex disease, and its treatment frequently involves some combination of surgery, chemotherapy, and radiation. You likely will see more than one specialist for your esophageal cancer care, including medical oncologists, thoracic surgeons, radiation oncologists, and **dietitians.** Ideally, these specialists work together in a multidisciplinary setting where they can easily consult with each other and reach a consensus about your treatment options. This multidisciplinary approach not only offers you high-quality care, but also has practical advantages that may include fewer trips to the doctor, less time from diagnosis to start of treatment, and more efficient coordination of treatment logistics. Multidisciplinary care is commonly offered in cancer centers and in larger treatment centers such as university hospitals, but it is beginning to be implemented in some community hospitals as well.

Each specialist you see is a member of your treatment team, but one doctor will have primary responsibility for managing and directing your care. There are also a number of other doctors, along with support staff, who will be involved in your care. It is helpful to understand what each of these health care professionals does, and what role he or she plays in your care. The following list contains a brief description of health care professionals who may be involved in your care.

- Medical oncologist: a physician who performs comprehensive management of cancer patients throughout all phases of care. Medical oncologists specialize in treating cancer with medicine, using systemic treatments such as chemotherapy.
- Surgical oncologist: a physician who specializes in performing cancer surgery. Some surgeons have received additional training in chest surgery and are considered thoracic surgeons.
- Radiation oncologist: a physician who specializes in treating cancer with radiation.
- Gastroenterologist: a physician who specializes in diagnosis and treatment of gastrointestional diseases.
- Pathologist: a physician trained to examine and evaluate cells and tissue. The pathologist evaluates your biopsy tissue and furnishes a biopsy report to your oncologist or surgeon.

- Oncology nurse: a specialized nurse trained to provide care to cancer patients, including administering chemotherapy and monitoring side effects.
- Psychiatrist: a physician who specializes in treating people for depression, anxiety, and other psychological illness. Psychiatrists provide psychotherapy and can also prescribe medication.
- Psychologist: a person trained in psychology who can provide psychotherapy.
- Oncology social worker: a social worker trained to provide counseling and practical assistance to cancer patients. Social workers can help you locate services such as transportation, support groups, and home care. They can also provide assistance with insurance and financial issues.
- Rehabilitation specialist: a person trained to help patients recover from physical changes brought about by cancer or cancer treatment. Physical therapists can help patients recover range of motion and strength following esophageal surgery.
- Nutritionist or dietitian: a person trained to provide nutritional or dietary counseling. Patients with esophageal cancer may experience weight loss as a result of their cancer or its treatment. Treatment side effects, such as nausea from chemotherapy or heartburn from radiation, can negatively affect appetite. Nutritional or dietary counseling services can help patients to increase appetite and gain weight.

29. Should I get a second opinion?

The quality of the care you will receive is very important. A second opinion is a good way to be sure you are receiving the best possible care while having peace of mind that you have explored all of your options. A second opinion can offer new options, confirm recommendations, or bring to light substandard care. It is a good idea to check with your insurance company prior to getting a second opinion. They may be able to help you find a specialist that is covered by your plan.

A second opinion requires some logistics—everything you gathered for your first appointment will also be needed for a second opinion.

There are certain instances when a second opinion is particularly important:

- If you have been told you are not a candidate for surgery but you have reason to think you may be. Surgery offers the best chance for a cure, and decisions regarding who is an appropriate surgical candidate are changing and may differ from surgeon to surgeon.
- If a doctor tells you there are no treatment options. This is rarely the case, and a second opinion may bring additional choices for treatment. Larger hospitals or cancer centers may have access to new treatments through clinical trials that may benefit you.
- You should have a second opinion if you are uncomfortable with your doctor or have doubts about his/her recommendations for your care. It's vital to have a good doctor/patient relationship, and you should look for a doctor you have confidence in and are comfortable with.

If you do get a second opinion and receive conflicting advice, seeking a third opinion or the advice of another doctor (such as your primary care doctor) can help to resolve any outstanding issues.

It is important to keep in mind that getting a second opinion can be emotionally draining and may consume time and energy you do not have. It may even create confusion and delay treatment. It is important to consider this prior to getting another opinion. A second opinion may or may not be covered by your insurance company and you may incur additional costs.

Some patients worry that they will offend a doctor by getting a second opinion. It is your right to seek a second opinion. If you sense that your doctor is threatened by your intention to get a second opinion, you might consider that to be reason enough to pursue another perspective.

Bart's comment:

Any major procedure or life-changing illness should be verified with a second opinion. However, time is of the essence, and it may take an unreasonable time to get a valid second opinion. At this point you need to determine how confident you are in the first opinion, if you feel comfortable with the hospital's experience and the surgeon's credentials, and how your meeting with the surgeon left you. If there is uncertainty, then wait for a second opinion. If you are comfortable with what you have heard and found out, then it would be prudent to proceed.

30. What questions should I ask my doctor?

Write down any questions you think of before you see the doctor.

This book will provide you with information that may prompt questions you would like to ask your doctor. It is always helpful to write down any questions you think of before you see the doctor to ensure that all of your questions are addressed. Listen to what the doctor has to say, since he or she may answer many of your questions when talking, and then ask any additional questions that were not covered. Having a close friend or family member with you during the visit is also very helpful. The more minds that are listening and asking questions, the better the chance your concerns will be addressed. It may also help to take notes during the conversation. Be sure you understand what the extent of your disease is (stage) and what treatment your doctor is recommending and why.

Bart's comment:

You should ask him how many of these operations he has done in the last six months and, perhaps more importantly, how many the hospital has done in that same period. After surgery, the hospital staff will be taking care of you, and knowing you are in the hands of a capable staff can rest your mind and speed your recovery.

31. How can I relate best to my doctor? What can I do to make my medical visits as productive as possible?

The doctor/patient relationship lies at the heart of patient care. This relationship will guide and support you throughout the course of your esophageal cancer. It is your job, and your doctor's, to nurture this relationship and to work toward a partnership based on mutual trust and respect. Although difficulties between doctor and patient may occur at times, just as they do in any relationship, these problems will be minimized if good communication is maintained. Remember that your doctor is not a mind reader. It is your responsibility to be open and honest in your communications and to bring up any concerns, needs, or preferences you may have. It is especially important that you feel comfortable discussing sensitive issues such as your use of alternative medicine treatments, your lifestyle (smoking, drinking, drugs), end-of-life issues, and sexual concerns. Keep in mind that conversations between doctor and patient are confidential and that the more your doctor knows about issues that may impact your health, the better care you will receive.

At your first visit, you should address the issues of how much information you want from your doctor and how involved you would like to be in the decisions that are made about your care. Some patients want to know everything about their condition, and they want to make all of the decisions themselves. Some patients find too much information anxiety-provoking. These patients would prefer to hear less information (often only the good news) and are more comfortable allowing their doctor to make all the decisions. Many patients fall somewhere in between. Whatever your preferences may be, and they may change over time, it is your responsibility to communicate them to your doctor. If you feel that your doctor is not responsive to your needs, or if you have other concerns regarding your relationship, you should bring them up before they reach a crisis stage. If you and your doctor cannot resolve disagreements in a productive and satisfactory manner, you should look for another doctor.

Think about what you are going to say to your doctor ahead of time. Remember, he or she has a finite amount of time to spend with you, so before your appointment consider which concerns are most pressing and write them down in order of importance. This tactic will help you focus and make the most effective use of the limited time you have with your doctor. If you choose to review events in great detail, you risk running out of the time that your doctor has for addressing your critical questions.

If you have symptoms to report, describe them clearly and concisely. Be prepared to answer your doctor's questions, such as when the symptoms started, how often they occur, and how long they last. Don't be afraid to mention the emotional and social issues that are affecting you, in addition to any physical problems you have.

Always bring someone with you to your appointment. It is impossible to remember all that is said during an office visit, and emotions can cloud what a patient hears. It helps to have someone else along who can write down what the doctor says. It is important to understand everything your doctor tells you. If something is unclear, say so, and ask questions until you are satisfied that you understand completely.

Be sure that all necessary tests are completed prior to your visit and that you have all the information you need. This includes having the required referrals, if any, and a current list of the prescriptions and nonprescription drugs you are taking. Bring a notebook or binder that contains your medical information and paperwork to each appointment. If you can present your doctor with the information needed to care for you in an efficient and clear manner, you will go a long way toward increasing the quality of your relationship with your doctor and, ultimately, the quality of your care.

32. Can exercise help me cope with diagnosis and treatment?

Studies have shown that engaging in some form of moderate exercise helps one both physically and mentally. Simply walking for twenty to thirty minutes daily can increase appetite, lift your spirits, and increase energy. Exercise becomes even more important when undergoing cancer therapy. All forms of treatment are a drain on energy stores both physically and emotionally, and it is important to stay as fit as possible. Fatigue is a common symptom during and after cancer treatment, and physical activity can help to reduce this fatigue. Starting with a slow exercise program, such as walking, can help to restore energy. There will be days, however, when you will be just too fatigued for any form of exercise. Do not push your body further than it can go, but remember to resume your exercise routine when you are able. If your fatigue persists, see your doctor. Sometimes fatigue is a result of a medical problem such as anemia, which can be corrected with medication.

Little is known about the impact of exercise after diagnosis of esophageal cancer. In the absence of more definitive information, the American Cancer Society recommends that survivors of gastrointestional cancers follow the ACS guidelines for the prevention of cancer. The ACS guidelines on physical activity for cancer prevention follow (Brown et al, 2003).

Adopt a Physically Active Lifestyle
- Adults: Engage in at least moderate activity for 30 minutes or more on five or more days of the week; 45 minutes or more of moderate to vigorous activity

on five or more days per week may further enhance reductions in the risk for breast and colon cancer.

• Children and adolescents: Engage in at least 60 minutes per day of moderate to vigorous physical activity at least five days per week.

Maintain a Healthy Weight Throughout Life
• Balance caloric intake with physical activity.
• Lose weight if currently overweight.

Bart's comment:

Exercise is always good and important for you whether you do it before treatment or during the chemotherapy and radiation protocol, and it is even advisable to continue an exercise regimen during the entire recovery process. After completing the surgical procedure, the nurses will have you up and walking within minutes of having arrived from the recovery room. Exercise plays an important part in helping you stay clear of complications, especially pneumonia. An exercise regimen should be continued through the home recovery process as well. The more exercising you do, the faster you will heal, your appetite will come back sooner, and your overall condition will vastly improve.

33. What else can I do to strengthen myself before treatment?

It is important to take care of yourself before, during, and after treatment for cancer of the esophagus. Maintaining a healthy diet, getting enough rest, and using support services, if needed, can help.

Eating healthy is important whether you have a diagnosis of cancer or not. However, cancer of the esophagus may lead to problems with swallowing and a loss of appetite that make maintaining a healthy diet difficult. In fact, weight loss is one of the more common symptoms that initially bring someone to the doctor's office prior to a diagnosis of esophageal cancer. After diagnosis, it is important to maintain your weight and prevent additional weight loss. If you are having difficulty swallowing, discuss exactly what you are able to eat and what you are not able to eat with your doctor. A discussion with a dietitian may be helpful to talk about ways to increase your calories with softer or easier-to-swallow foods. In some cases, if weight loss is severe or if swallowing more than liquids is difficult, your doctor may recommend placing a feeding tube to help maintain your nutritional status. A **feeding tube** can be inserted through the nose into the stomach, but most often is surgically placed directly from the abdomen to the stomach. This type of tube is called a **gastrostomy tube** (or **G-tube**), **a percutaneous endoscopic gastrostomy** (**PEG-tube**), or **jejunostomy tube** (**J-tube**). This type of tube is inserted thru a small incision in the abdomen during an outpatient surgical procedure. The different names indicate different placement locations within the stomach or small intestine. After placement of a feeding tube you will be able to take meal supplements thru the tube. You should also take food by mouth, if you are able.

In addition to nutrition and exercise, it is important to get adequate rest before, during, and after treatment. In you are having difficulty sleeping, exercise may help you sleep better. A diagnosis of cancer is a very stressful situation and maintaining a healthy lifestyle, including getting adequate rest, can help you to manage the stress of diagnosis and treatment.

Each person and their family will cope in different ways with a diagnosis of cancer. It is important to find

Feeding tube

a flexible tube passed through the nose and into the alimentary tract, through which liquid food is passed.

Gastrostomy tube (G-tube)

a type of feeding tube that is inserted directly into the stomach; procedure is done surgically and requires sedation.

Percutaneous endoscopic gastrostomy (PEG-tube)

a type of feeding tube for those who have an intact gastrointestinal tract but are unable to consume sufficient calories to meet metabolic needs.

Jejunostomy tube (J-tube)

a type of feeding tube that is placed through the skin directly into the small bowel; this is a surgical procedure that will require a hospital stay.

a strategy that works for you and helps you to cope during this difficult time. Individuals often find that psychological support is helpful. Check with your doctor or hospital about counseling services. Psychiatrists, psychologists, and social workers can help you to develop coping strategies and gain perspectives on your situation. Social workers can also assist with more practical matters such as transportation, financial concerns, and the effects of cancer treatment on employment. Religious or spiritual counseling may also be of benefit.

During this time it is important to take care of yourself and your loved ones and not to let cancer control everything you do. This is easier said than done, but if you are having difficulty coping with your diagnosis, talk about it with your family, a dear friend, or your medical team.

Bart's comment:

Continue to eat balanced meals, exercise, and get enough rest. In effect, make yourself as strong as you can be—physically, mentally, and spiritually.

34. What are advance directives? Are a power of attorney and a living will the same thing?

Advanced directives is a general term that refers to the oral and written instructions of your wishes for medical care if you are unable to speak for yourself. A medical power of attorney and a living will are both forms of advance directives. Each state regulates the use of advance directives differently. We will provide you with some general information about each of these, but

Coping with the Diagnosis

Take care of yourself and your loved ones; do not let cancer control everything you do.

Advanced directives

oral and written instructions containing your wishes for medical care if you are unable to speak for yourself; includes medical power of attorney and living will.

you should check with your local hospital or state government (usually the Department of Health) for specifics regarding your state regulations.

A *living will* is a document where you can put your wishes in writing about the medical care you would like to receive in case you are unable to communicate for yourself at the end of life. State laws may limit when the living will can go into effect and may limit the treatments that apply. A living will is also called a directive to physician, declaration, or medical directive.

A *medical power of attorney* (also called a *health care proxy, appointment of health care agent,* or *durable power of attorney for health care*) is a document that allows you to appoint someone to make decisions about your medical care. This is different from a power of attorney, which is a document that authorizes a person to make financial decisions for you and cannot be used to make health care decisions. You must complete a medical power of attorney in order to have someone make medical decisions for you. The person you appoint through a medical power of attorney is usually authorized to speak for you any time you are unable to make your own medical decisions, not only at the end of life.

Each document offers something the other does not, and both are important. The primary difference between a medical power of attorney and living will is that a living will does not authorize you to appoint someone to make medical decisions for you. Having both documents will help to protect your treatment decisions.

If you have questions about these documents or the specific regulations in your state it may be helpful to talk with a social worker at the office or hospital where you are being treated.

35. So much information is available on the Internet. How do I evaluate this information to be sure that it is accurate, complete, and up-to-date?

There are more Internet sites offering health-related information every day, and it is an excellent resource for valuable health information about esophageal cancer and its treatment. However, it is important to know that there is no regulation or control of the information that is posted on the internet. Many Web sites may have misleading or incorrect information. It is necessary that you distinguish good medical information from misleading or incorrect information as you look online. To do this, here are some helpful tips adapted from a National Cancer Institute fact sheet:

- Who runs the web site?

  You must consider where the information is coming from before you consider the content. The site should clearly state who is responsible for the information. For example, a web address ending in '.gov' denotes a federal government-sponsored site, '.org' is from a nonprofit group, and '.edu' sites are from an educational institution. Many university hospitals and comprehensive cancer centers have web sites with searchable online patient education information. The purpose and owner of the web site can influence what content is presented, how the content is presented, and what the site owners want to accomplish on the site. You should be wary of sites run solely by insurance or drug companies, which may be promoting their own products or services.

The purpose of the site can usually be found by clicking "About This Site" on the web page.

- Where did the information come from?
  Many web sites post information collected from other web sites or sources. The source of the information should be clearly stated. Ideally, medical facts and figures will have a reference to a medical journal.

- How current is the information?
  Web sites should be reviewed and updated on a regular basis—the best sites are updated every six months. Medical information can change frequently, so it is important to look for a site that has been updated recently. The most recent update or review date should be clearly noted and usually can be found at the bottom of the web page.

- What personal information does the site collect, and why?
  Web sites routinely trace the paths visitors take through their sites to determine what pages are being used. Some sites may ask for you to subscribe or become a member. Others may charge a fee or want your personal information in order to personalize health information for you. A credible site asking for personal information should tell you exactly what they will and will not do with this information. Many commercial sites sell collected data about their users to other companies—information such as what percentage of their users has cancer, for example. In some cases they may collect and reuse information that is personally identifiable, such as your postal zip code, gender, and birth date. Be certain that you read and understand any privacy

policy or similar language on the site prior to submitting any personal information. If you can't easily find one, then do not submit any information. It is never a good idea to sign up for something you do not fully understand.

Always remember that the Internet can't replace time with your doctor, but it can help to make you a better informed patient. Knowing what questions to ask when you see the doctor will be beneficial to getting the best health care.

CAREGIVER CONCERNS

36. Is depression a possibility?

Most people who face a diagnosis of cancer will experience a wide range of emotions from denial to despair. Your state of mind can influence all aspects of your treatment, and upon receiving a diagnosis of cancer there will need to be a period of time for adjustment and incorporation of diagnosis and treatment plans into one's life. Most people are able to make this adjustment. Feelings of sadness, helplessness, and hopelessness are normal during this time. However, it is important to distinguish normal feelings of sadness and grief with a clinical depression. Clinical depression occurs when the depression is of such a magnitude that the person is unable to enjoy any of the activities that normally give them pleasure. Even though it is normal and natural to feel sad and down about a diagnosis of cancer, sometimes these feelings of sadness become so overwhelming that they take on a life of their own and become a problem in and of themselves. Patients can become so discouraged, hopeless, or full of despair that they are unable to enjoy their family or the little things in life.

If you find yourself sitting at home, no longer interested in your usual activities, or withdrawing from family and friends, you may be depressed.

Most depression is treatable.

The good news is that most depression is treatable, and the medications are usually well tolerated with minimal side effects. The bad news is that it frequently goes undiagnosed. Several factors complicate the process of diagnosing depression in patients with cancer. The first is that many of the symptoms of depression (such as changes in eating or sleeping habits) are also symptoms associated with cancer and its treatment. Second, medical factors and some cancer treatments can cause depression. Third, patients often do not openly share emotional symptoms— a major component of the depression diagnosis—with their doctors. If you think you might be depressed, it is very important that you discuss this possibility with your doctor, who can then refer you to a psychiatrist for further evaluation and treatment.

Most frequently, patients with cancer have a type of depression called reactive depression. This is of limited duration and can be helped with counseling. Major depression is more severe and long lasting, and treatment most often includes medications such as antidepressants. When depression is treated effectively, patients experience relief of distressing symptoms and are better able to cope with their cancer and the demands of cancer treatment. Early recognition of the signs of depression will facilitate prompt diagnosis and successful treatment.

Sometimes patients are unwilling to undergo treatment for depression, thinking that it represents a sign of weakness and that they should be able to control their feelings. Nothing could be further from the truth. When you are hungry, you cannot trick your mind into thinking you are not. If you are depressed, why would you be able to trick your mind into thinking that you are not?

37. What is the right thing to say to my loved one?

It is natural to feel unsure of the right things to say when someone you care about has been diagnosed with cancer, is undergoing difficult treatment, or is perhaps facing the end of his or her life. You may feel uncomfortable asking the person how he or she is doing because you are unsure of the response. You may worry that if you say the wrong thing, you will hurt him or her, or that if you talk about your own sadness, or even cry, the person will be upset. Because of your own discomfort, you may try to withdraw from the situation, distancing yourself from the person, calling less often, and putting off visits. This can result in leaving the person feeling alone at a time when he or she needs your presence more than ever before.

There is no script you can follow as a guide in knowing what to say. In fact, if you make assumptions about what the person is thinking or feeling, you may unintentionally say things that will be upsetting. The best way to start is by listening. Let the person know that if he or she would like to talk about their illness you would like to listen. At the same time, remember that not everyone communicates in the same way. Some people are very open and want to share all their thoughts and feelings. Others are more private and prefer not to talk about these things. Even for those who are generally more communicative, there may be times that he or she may feel like talking and other

The best way to start is by listening.

times when he or she doesn't. You should let the person know that you are available to listen, and should let them control when and how much they choose to share. This is a great gift that you can give.

However, listening to things that are painful or being with someone who is emotionally upset or crying may be uncomfortable. You may want to change the subject or even offer reassurances that everything will be okay, even if that may not necessarily be true. Although this may help in dealing with your own discomfort as the listener, it does not help the person speaking. In addition, it may give the message that you do not really want to hear what he or she has to say. Try to overcome your own discomfort and remain to hear what he or she is saying. It is okay to tell the person that this is difficult for you and that you are not sure how to respond to what is being said.

You may want to speak to the person who is ill about thoughts or feeling that you are having. You may want to tell him or her about your love and concern, or of your own sadness or feelings of helplessness. You may want to try to resolve previous conflicts. You may want to talk with him or her about your own worries and concerns related to the illness. We often leave a great deal unsaid in an attempt to protect those we love. Yet in fact, it is the unsaid things that are often the most important to say.

38. As a caregiver, how do I take care of myself during this difficult time?

Communication is very important during this time. Including your loved one in decisions will help you both cope during this difficult time. If you feel you need help, ask for it. Often family and friends want to help but may not know how or what you need. While some may not help as you would like, others will provide significant support. Here are some tips when asking for help from family and friends:

- Identify areas where you need help, and make a list or note them on a calendar.
- Ask family and friends about when they are available and what jobs they feel most comfortable doing. You may also contact a person with a specific request, being as clear as possible about what you need.
- As you hear back from each person, note it on your list to ensure everything is taken care of.

There are many resources available to caregivers. Many hospitals and community agencies now have support groups or services specifically for caregivers. Talk with a nurse or social worker, or contact your local American Cancer Society for services that are available in your area.

It is important at this time that you take care of yourself in addition to taking care of your loved one. Balancing your normal day-to-day tasks, such as cleaning, work, and caring for children or grandchildren, with the stress of a loved one diagnosed with cancer can be challenging at best. It is important not to feel guilty or selfish if you take time for yourself. By taking time for yourself, you will be better able to take care of your loved one.

Here are some tips to help you take care of yourself during this difficult time:

- Make your own health a priority. Keep doctor appointments, get enough rest, eat properly, and exercise regularly.

- Take time for leisure activities that you enjoy.
- Organize a schedule with family and friends who are willing to help.
- If you need some time from work, speak with your supervisor or benefits department. If your company has an Employee Assistance Program, look into the services it offers. Some offer counseling services for financial issues, stress, and depression.
- Consider joining a support group for caregivers or using counseling services.
- Respect your spiritual and religious needs, and continue them as much as possible.

Despite the demands and challenges of caring for someone who has cancer, the role of a caregiver can be fulfilling and satisfying. Communication can help to work through difficult times. Asking for help can also take some of the pressure off and allow you time to take care of yourself.

39. As a caregiver, how do I know what is normal and what is urgent, and when I should call the doctor for help?

It is important to designate one person to be a key contact for communicating medical information about your loved one to family and friends, and to contact the doctor, if necessary, to ask questions. As your loved one goes through treatment, the doctor, nurse, and other members of the medical team should alert you to expected symptoms or problems and to potentially serious problems. Before each visit with the doctor, write down your key concerns and a list of questions. You may want to ask other family members or friends if they have any questions as well. Be sure to ask your most important questions first. As you are talking with the doctor, take notes. If you don't understand something, ask for it to be explained again.

Keep important phone numbers in an easy-to-locate place, and ask your doctor for a number to call in an emergency, at night, or over the weekend. If you have questions after you leave the doctors office, call and ask to speak with someone. They may be able to answer the question or will refer you to the doctor if necessary.

Any acute or sudden symptoms such as difficulty breathing or chest pain are an emergency and warrant a call to 911 or a visit to your local emergency room.

PART FIVE

Treatment Options

What things should I consider
when making treatment choices?

Will I have pain? What are my
options to treat it if I do?

What are the latest developments
in esophageal cancer treatment?
How do I find out about them?

More . . .

40. What do I need to know about this disease that will help me care for my loved one while he or she is undergoing treatment?

Your love and support are tremendously valuable at this critical time. Just knowing that there is someone with whom they can share their fears and concerns is the best gift you can give. It is very important that you also keep in mind that you, as the caregiver, will have many demands made on your time and resources. Not only will you be expected to perform your usual chores, you will often be asked to assume the tasks routinely done by the patient. It will also fall on you to schedule and coordinate appointments, provide transportation, run errands, obtain medications, and so forth.

There will be times that you will feel overwhelmed. Do not hesitate to ask for and accept help from other family members and friends. Find out what resources are available in your community and whether you qualify for these services. Remember that treatment is going to take months and be a major disruption of your lives. Take advantage of whatever is available to you to make the process as smooth as possible. Every family is different, and each member of the family may react to this health crisis of a loved one in different ways. Being honest about what is happening with the loved one and talking about the treatment plan are important (keeping in mind age-appropriate communication styles with young children and adolescents.) But this is only one side of the picture. For many families, this is an important opportunity to create one-on-one time and family experiences outside of the boundaries of the cancer. Such things as visiting a museum, flying kites, doing community projects, simply walking together, or continuing regular enjoyable family activities as much as possible can help the family as well as you, the care-giver. Your social worker can provide individual and family counseling services, as well as group counseling and suggestions for community resources and activities.

41. What things should I consider when making treatment choices?

Before deciding on a treatment, be sure you are well informed as to your options. It is important to under-stand the treatment as well as why your doctor thinks it is the best option for you. You should consider other factors such as the location of the treatment center and insurance coverage for the treatment. You should also feel comfortable with the doctor and the medical team who will be treating you. This includes the nurses, spe-cialists, and support staff at the facility you choose.

42. Will I have pain? What are my options to treat it if I do?

Pain is uncommon in patients with early or locally advanced esophageal cancer. If you have surgery, your pain will be managed both in the hospital and at home until it resolves. It is important to remember that after surgery you will need to be out of bed as much as possi-ble to prevent complications that can occur following surgery. In this case, your doctor will work closely with you to monitor your pain so that you are comfortable enough to walk, take deep breaths, and cough, but are not too drowsy from the medication. You will also need to help your doctors and let them know how you are feel-ing. In most cases you will be given a **patient-controlled analgesia (PCA)** following your surgery. This is a

Patient-controlled analgesia (PCA)
medication for pain that the patient can self-administer by pressing a button; after surgery while in the hospital, a small tube is inserted so the medication can be pumped into a vein.

Treatment Options

method to deliver better pain control to patients in the hospital. With a PCA, pain medicine is administered by a computerized pump either through a vein or through an **epidural catheter.** Pain medicine is programmed by the pump to be administered at a low dose continuously or when the patient presses a button. The pump is controlled so that the patient cannot receive more medication than is prescribed by the physician.

If you have pain during or after treatment, discuss it with your doctor. Medications are available to help relieve the pain and make you more comfortable.

43. What are the latest developments in esophageal cancer treatment? How do I find out about them?

There are many treatment studies being researched in order to find more effective treatments for cancer of the esophagus. Researchers are constantly looking at methods to minimize side effects and improve symptoms of the disease. New medications are also being tested for their effectiveness in treating esophageal cancer. Talk with your doctor to find out about the latest research and treatments, or call the National Cancer Institute (1-800-4-CANCER) and ask for a PDQ® clinical trials search. A cancer information specialist will assist you in finding clinical trials. You can also search for clinical trials on the NCI's web site (www.cancer.gov/search/clinicaltrials). In order to search, you will need to know the type (esophageal) and stage of cancer. It is helpful to know the types of trials that are relevant to you (for instance, treatment, diagnostic, prevention, etc.). You will also be able to search for a specific drug, or a particular clinical trial by zip code or city that is convenient for you. PDQ® is the most comprehensive resource available to find can-

Epidural catheter

a small tube placed in the spinal fluid through which medication can be administered to a patient, via a pump mechanism either at a low constant dose or when the patient presses a button, according to the physician's prescription.

cer clinical trials. If you do search for clinical trials for esophageal cancer, bring your results with you to your physician to discuss what treatment is right for you.

44. What is a clinical trial?

Currently, there are over 2,000 clinical trials for cancer in the United States and abroad. Clinical trials, or research studies, test new treatments for all kinds of diseases, including cancer. The overall goal of oncology clinical trials is to find better, more effective ways to treat cancer and help patients with cancer. Most often, we think of testing new drugs when we think of clinical trials, but research is also conducted on new approaches to surgery, diagnosis, radiation, or entirely new treatment methods such as gene therapy or biologic therapy.

Clinical trials are important for several reasons. First, the patients who participate in clinical trials may be helped personally by the treatment they receive as part of the trial. There is no guarantee, however, that the treatments will help individual patients. New treatments may also have unknown side effects or risks. Clinical trials used to be thought of as a last resort and only used after standard treatment had failed. Today, for some types of cancer, the first treatment recommended may be in a clinical trial. Another important reason for clinical trials is that they contribute to our knowledge and treatment for cancer. If a new treatment is effective in a trial, it often becomes the new standard of care and can help many patients.

45. What are the different types of clinical trials?

There are several types of clinical trials, and it is important to understand the differences among them. Trials are classified into three phases, based on the type of question the trial is attempting to answer.

- Phase I: these trials are the first step in testing a new treatment. The goal of a Phase I trial is to determine the best method (intravenous, by mouth, or by injection) and the best dose of a medication. In addition, Phase I trials watch for side effects of new drugs or new doses of existing drugs. Because of their preliminary nature, these studies usually include only a limited number of patients who would not be helped by other, more known, treatments.
- Phase II: in these studies the goal is to determine whether the new treatment has an anticancer effect. For instance, does it shrink the tumor? These trials also test new treatments for specific cancers. Phase II trials also have risks and unknowns associated with them and involve small numbers of patients.
- Phase III: these studies compare the results of a new treatment with the results of people taking the standard treatment. These trials attempt to answer questions such as which group has better survival rates or which treatment has fewer side effects. Phase III trials often include large numbers of patients and are conducted nationwide.

When deciding to take part in a clinical trial, consider the decision with your family and close friends as well as the medical professionals caring for you. Clinical trials have potential benefits as well as potential drawbacks. Remember that taking part in a clinical trial is always voluntary and may be only one of your treatment options. Ask questions about the purpose of the study, possible risks and benefits, the schedule of care involved in the study, and insurance coverage for treatments, tests, or other procedures. Talking with your doctor and clearly understanding your options will enable you to make the best decision.

46. What follow-up will I need after treatment?

Your follow-up will depend on the treatment you received and how you responded to that treatment. Your doctor will discuss how often you need to be seen and what is involved in the follow-up visit or treatment. In most cases, your doctor will see you in the office and you will have a CT scan every few months (see Question 20). He or she may also add a PET scan or an endoscopy periodically to check that your cancer has not recurred. If you notice any change in how you are feeling, let your doctor know so that your follow-up schedule can be adjusted.

47. How do I find out about complementary and alternative therapies?

Complementary medicine and alternative medicine are broad terms that describe a wide variety of therapeutic approaches that are outside the realm of conventional Western medicine. These health care practices are not intended to replace the current treatment prescribed by your physician and other medical professionals, but may be used in tandem. There is a growing body of scientific evidence about the effectiveness of these treatments, and physicians are frequently integrating once non-conventional approaches into their treatment plans. However, because some can interfere with your individual healing process, it is important to discuss these options with your primary physician.

Several reliable sources provide information about complementary and alternative therapies. Because of the rapidly changing state of knowledge about this area of medicine, the Internet provides the most up-to-date information. Resources with general information on complementary and alternative therapies include:

- Cancer Information Service of the National Cancer Institute
- National Center for Complementary and Alternative Medicine of the National Institutes of Health
- The Richard and Hinda Rosenthal Center for Complementary and Alternative Medicine at Columbia University
- MD Anderson Complementary/Integrative Medicine Education Resources
- Oncolink, from the University of Pennsylvania

Resources with information specifically about dietary supplements, including vitamins, minerals, and botanicals, include:

- Office of Dietary Supplements of the National Institutes of Health
- Center for Food Safety and Applied Nutrition of the U.S. Food and Drug Administration
- American Botanical Council (*www.herbalgram.org*)
- Supplement Watch (*www.supplementwatch.com*)
- Quackwatch (*www.quackwatch.com*)
- Memorial Sloan-Kettering Cancer Center (*http:// www.mskcc.org/mskcc/html/11570.cfm*)

For scientific bibliographic citations related to particular therapies, see the following:

- National Library of Medicine (*www.nlm.nih.gov/ nccam/camonpubmed.html*)

TREATMENT OPTIONS

48. How is cancer of the esophagus treated?

There are treatment options for all patients with esophageal cancer. Three kinds of treatment are used: surgery, **chemotherapy,** and radiation therapy. We will discuss each of these in more detail in this section of questions. Briefly, surgery is the removal of the cancer during an operation, chemotherapy is the use of drugs to kill cancer cells in the body, and radiation therapy is the use of high-dose x-rays to kill cancer cells.

Chemotherapy
the use of drugs to kill cancer cells.

Treatment recommendations are based primarily on two factors: the extent of the disease (or stage) and the general health of the patient. The extent of disease is determined by staging tests such as CT scans, endoscopy, and PET scans (see Questions 21 and 22 for more information on these tests and staging). The general health of the patient is determined by the doctor based on previous health conditions and tests such as heart and lung function studies.

49. What is the current standard of care for esophageal cancer?

The recommended treatment of early esophageal cancer is surgery as a single treatment. Historically, the treatment of locally advanced esophageal cancer (cancer that was not diagnosed very early but had not yet spread to other organs) was either surgery alone or radiation therapy alone. Unfortunately, neither of these treatments had good long-term results. In order to improve these results, physicians decided to try a combination of radiation and surgery. The results were better, but more work needed to be done. Chemotherapy,

Palliation

treatment to reduce the severity or relieve the symptoms of a disease, but is not a cure of the underlying condition.

when used as a single treatment, has very good results for **palliation** of symptoms in a high percentage of patients. Therefore, researchers have devised strategies to combine all three modalities, and the standard of treatment continues to evolve. A number of clinical trials have been conducted to determine the effectiveness of using chemotherapy and radiation prior to surgery. More research is ongoing to improve these results, but it is generally accepted, especially in North America, that pre-operative chemotherapy and radiation therapy followed by surgery is the accepted treatment choice for locally advanced esophageal cancer.

50. How do I decide which treatment is best for me?

There is a lot for you to consider when choosing the best way to treat your cancer.

At this point, your test results have been reviewed by a diagnostic team of specialists, and you know the diagnosis and stage of the esophageal cancer. You may have also obtained a second opinion about the diagnosis. Based upon the expertise and recommendations by the diagnostic team of health care professionals, your doctor has suggested a few treatment options and developed a proposed treatment plan for what he or she believes will be the best individual treatment for you. It is important to talk with your doctor about the recommended treatment as well as any anticipated side effects of this treatment.

You have read the literature provided by your physician as well as the recommended web sites on the Internet. You have also discussed these options with your family and/or primary caregiver. Those who are spiritual have prayed for help and health, and perhaps asked others to pray for you.

For most patients, the best treatment plan will be obvious. Expert opinion from the treatment team will align with your primary physician's recommendation, a review of the literature, and your personal wishes. Some patients, however, need a bit more time to continue their research, or to be still and think about his or her options before coming to a decision. Ultimately, whatever the treatment plan is decided upon, be confident that it will be the right one for you.

51. What is the difference between local and systemic treatment?

There are two different approaches to the treatment of cancer: local treatment and systemic treatment. Local treatment refers to the treatment of the original tumor. Systemic treatment refers to treatment that is directed at the entire body to treat any cells that may have left the original tumor site.

In most cases, surgery is considered a local treatment because it is aimed at treating the original site of the tumor. Radiation therapy is often used as a local treatment as well. Chemotherapy is considered a systemic treatment because it is given through your blood system and goes to your entire body.

SYSTEMIC TREATMENT: MEDICAL TREATMENT (DRUG THERAPY)

52. What are the current medical treatments for esophageal cancer?

The standard medical treatments for esophageal cancer are chemotherapy and radiation alone, or a combination of chemotherapy and radiation followed by surgery. The combination of chemotherapy and radiation may reduce the risk of distant recurrence of disease. The most aggressive approach to treatment combines chemotherapy and radiation followed by surgery. In about 60% to 70% of patients treated with chemotherapy and radiation, their tumor shrinks or is down-staged. This means their disease is at a lower stage than prior to when they received treatment. About 80% to 90% of these patients are then able to have surgery following chemotherapy and radiation. This still means that 10% to 20% of patients are not able to have their cancer removed following this treatment, either due to local extent of the cancer or that it has spread to other parts of the body. More research is being conducted to identify combinations of treatment regimens that will provide better results.

53. What is chemotherapy?

Chemotherapy is the use of drugs to kill cancer cells. Most often the drugs are given into a vein (**intravenously**) or by mouth. Chemotherapy drugs are also called **cytotoxic drugs,** that is, they are cell-destroying medications.

Intravenously

injection or infusion of liquid, usually medication, directly through the skin into a vein.

Cytotoxic drugs

a type of pharmaceutical substance that is detrimental or destructive to cells.

Many different types of chemotherapeutic drugs exist that affect cancer cells in different ways by altering or interfering with different parts of the cell cycle. Drugs are often given in combination to try and achieve better control of the cancer.

Chemotherapy works by stopping cancer cells from growing and dividing, and chemotherapy drugs affect rapidly dividing cells in the body, including cancer cells. The reason that side effects occur from chemotherapy is partly because healthy cells can also be harmed by chemotherapy. In addition, some chemotherapy agents have other side effects that are specific to that drug or class of drugs. Side effects of chemotherapy are related to the dose and frequency of administration of the drugs as well as to characteristics of the patient. Medication is sometimes required to minimize or counteract the side effects of chemotherapy. Question 54 discusses the most common chemotherapy drugs and their side effects.

54. What are the most common drugs given?

Different drugs are given, and the choice depends on the kind of cancer you have, the stage of the disease, and your general overall health. Some of the more common agents used to treat esophageal cancer are listed below. Ask your nurse about more specific information for the medications used for your treatment.

Cisplatin (Platinol®)—prevents cancer cells from growing by interfering with DNA, the genetic material in cells. It is given intravenously (by vein).

Immediate Side Effects (beginning within 24 hours):
- Nausea or vomiting can begin within two hours after you have received cisplatin and last about 24 hours. Nausea may continue or recur for several days.
- Loss of appetite may occur 24 to 48 hours after treatment.
- Allergic reactions can occur, but are rare.

Early Side Effects (beginning within one week):
- Diarrhea may occur, but usually subsides within a day.
- Kidney damage may occur unless cisplatin is given with large amounts of intravenous and oral fluids.

- A ringing or "stuffy" sensation in the ears or difficulty hearing may occur within one week after treatment and may persist. The "stuffy" sensation usually subsides in two to three weeks.

Late Side Effects (beginning after one week):
- A temporary decrease in blood cell counts—red blood cells, white blood cells, and platelets—may occur 7 to 14 days after treatment. This is usually mild.
- Temporary thinning or loss of hair may occur several weeks after treatment.
- Numbness, tingling, or burning in the hands or feet may occur after several treatments, but is uncommon.
- This medication may have temporary or permanent effects on your hearing, such as ringing or a stuffy sensation in the ears, hearing loss of high frequency sounds, and difficulty hearing when there is background noise. Discuss any change in your hearing with your doctor.

Special Points:
- Drink fluids as instructed by your doctor.
- Take your anti-nausea medication as instructed.
- Do not take aspirin, ibuprofen (e.g., Motrin®, Advil®), products containing them, or similar products unless your doctor prescribes them. [Ask your doctor or nurse for a complete list of NSAIDs (non-steroidal anti-inflammatory drugs) and products containing aspirin, or ask your pharmacist for a list.]
- Tell your doctor or nurse if you are taking any other medications, including over-the-counter preparations that do not require a prescription, herbal remedies, vitamins, or dietary supplements. Some of these may interfere with your chemotherapy.

Call Your Doctor or Nurse If You:
- Are urinating less frequently than usual or in small amounts.
- Have excessive nausea, vomiting, or diarrhea and are unable to eat or drink for more than 24 hours after receiving the drug.
- Have a fever of 100.5°F (38°C) or higher.
- Have black bowel movements, bruising, a faint red rash, or any other signs of bleeding.
- Have any unexpected, unexplained problems.
- Have any questions or concerns.

5-FU (Fluorouracil, Adrucil®)—interferes with an enzyme that cancer cells need to live and grow. It is given intravenously (by vein).

Early Side Effects (beginning within one week):
- Mild nausea and vomiting may occur while you take this drug.
- You may experience diarrhea with this medication.
- You may develop soreness in the mouth.

Late Side Effects (beginning after one week):
- A temporary decrease in blood cell counts—white blood cells and platelets—may occur one to two weeks after treatment.
- Dryness and scaling of the nails, cuticles, and skin of the hands may occur four to six weeks after treatment.
- Darkening of the nail beds, the skin, and the veins in which the drug was given may begin four to six weeks after receiving the drug and may persist.
- Temporary thinning of the hair may occur three to four weeks after each treatment.
- Nasal stuffiness and watering of the eyes may occur three to four weeks after treatment.

Special Points:
- Do not take aspirin, ibuprofen (e.g., Motrin®, Advil®), products containing them, or similar products unless your doctor prescribes them. (Ask your doctor or nurse for a complete list of NSAIDs and products containing aspirin, or ask your pharmacist for a list.)
- Protect your skin from overexposure to the sun. Wear protective clothing and use a sunscreen with a sun protection factor (SPF) of 15 or greater when in the sun.
- Tell your doctor or nurse if you are taking any other medications, including over-the-counter preparations that do not require a prescription, herbal remedies, vitamins, or dietary supplements. Some of these may interfere with your chemotherapy.

Call Your Doctor or Nurse If You:
- Have a fever of 100.5° F (38° C) or higher.
- Have more than three loose bowel movements a day over your normal bowel routine.
- Have black bowel movements, bruising, faint red rash, or any other signs of bleeding.
- Develop mouth sores.
- Have any unexpected or unexplained problems.
- Have any question or concerns.

Irinotecan (Camptosar®, CPT-11)—is a partly man-made drug derived from an extract of a plant that grows in Asia. It kills cancer cells by interfering with an enzyme that helps DNA unwind so that cells can reproduce. It is given intravenously (by vein).

Immediate Side Effects (beginning within 24 hours):
- Abdominal cramping can occur while the drug is being given.

- Mild sweating, with or without feeling warm, can occur while the drug is given.
- You may experience nausea and vomiting.
- Diarrhea may occur with this medication.

Early Side Effect (beginning within one week):
- You may experience a runny nose.

Late Side Effects (beginning after one week):
- A temporary decrease in white blood cell count (cells that help fight infection) can develop.
- Possible temporary thinning or loss of hair can occur.
- Diarrhea can occur after the second or third cycle of treatment.
- You may experience fatigue.

Special Points:
- Diarrhea that occurs during or within a few hours of treatment usually goes away by itself. Do not take Imodium® (loperamide) under these circumstances, as it can lead to constipation.
- If diarrhea occurs other than on the day of treatment, begin taking Imodium® when diarrhea starts. Although the package cautions not to take this amount, take two Imodium® tablets at the first sign of diarrhea. Then take one tablet every two hours (or 2 tablets every 4 hours at night) until you have gone 12 hours without diarrhea. If Imodium® is not effective after 36 hours, call your physician.
- Do not take aspirin, ibuprofen (e.g., Motrin®, Advil®), products containing them, or similar products unless your doctor prescribes them. (Ask your doctor or nurse for a complete list of NSAIDs and products containing aspirin, or ask your pharmacist for a list.)

- Tell your doctor or nurse if you are taking any other medications, including over-the-counter preparations that do not require a prescription, herbal remedies, vitamins, or dietary supplements. Some of these may interfere with your chemotherapy.

Call Your Doctor or Nurse If You Have:
- A fever of 100.5° F (38° C) or higher.
- Black bowel movements, bruising, faint red rash, or other signs of bleeding.
- Diarrhea of any sort, including an increase in frequency of bowel movements.
- Any unexpected, unexplained problems.
- Any questions or concerns.

Paclitaxel (Taxol®)—works by interfering with the cancer cell's ability to grow. It is given intravenously (by vein).

Early Side Effects:
- In rare circumstances, patients may develop an allergic reaction with a rash, facial flushing, or have trouble breathing. Benadryl® (diphenhydramine), Decadron® (dexamethasone), and Zantac® (ranitidine) are given before paclitaxel to help prevent this reaction.
- Mild nausea and vomiting, though uncommon, may occur while you are taking paclitaxel.
- Fatigue can occur during treatment.
- Joint pain and body aches may occur and can usually be relieved by acetaminophen (e.g., Tylenol®).

Late Side Effects:
- Mouth sores may develop within four to seven days.
- Hair thinning or loss may occur, depending on your treatment schedule.

- Numbness and tingling in the hands and feet may occur.
- A temporary decrease in blood cell counts—especially white blood cell counts—may occur about one week after treatment.

Special Points
- Tell your doctor if you are also taking ketoconazole (Nizoral®).
- You or your partner should not get pregnant while you are taking paclitaxel. You must use an effective contraceptive during treatment.
- Speak with your doctor before you get any vaccine (e.g., a flu shot).
- Check with your doctor or pharmacist before you take any prescribed or over-the-counter medicine, herbal remedy, or vitamin supplement, as some can interfere with your chemotherapy treatment.
- Do not take aspirin, ibuprofen (e.g., Motrin®, Advil®), products containing them, or similar products unless your doctor prescribes them. (Ask your doctor or nurse for a complete list of NSAIDs and products containing aspirin, or ask your pharmacist for a list.)
- You must not breastfeed during your treatment.

Call Your Doctor or Nurse If You:
- Develop a fever higher than 100.5°F (38.0°C).
- Develop mouth sores that prevent you from eating or drinking.
- Have joint aches or pain not controlled by Tylenol® (acetaminophen).
- Have uncontrolled nausea or diarrhea.
- Have pain in your back.
- Have any unexpected or unexplained problems.
- Have any questions or concerns.

Docetaxel (Taxotere®)—works by interfering with the cancer cell's ability to multiply and grow. It is given intravenously (by vein).

Immediate Side Effects (beginning within 24 hours):
- Flushing of the skin, chest tightness, shortness of breath, and back discomfort may occur occasionally during the infusion. These symptoms disappear when the infusion is stopped. A medication will be prescribed to prevent these symptoms before you receive docetaxel.

Early Side Effects (beginning within one week):
- A temporary decrease in blood cell counts, particularly white blood cell counts, may occur within one week of treatment.
- A red, raised, itchy rash; peeling of the skin on hands and feet; and ridging and splitting of fingernails and toenails may occur after any dose.
- Redness or swelling may occur at the injection site.

Late Side Effects (beginning after one week):
- Temporary thinning or loss of hair may begin two to three weeks after treatment.
- Swelling of arms and legs, bloating, and weight gain may occur after receiving docetaxel for several months. Fluid can also accumulate around the lungs or in the abdominal cavity.
- Numbness, tingling of fingers and/or toes, or both may also occur after receiving docetaxel many times.

Special Points:
- Before receiving docetaxel, you will be given a prescription for a medication to prevent side effects. The nurse will review with you the schedule for taking this medication. Please inform the nurse if you are unable to take the medication as ordered.

- Do not take aspirin, ibuprofen (e.g., Motrin®, Advil®), products containing them, or similar products unless your doctor prescribes them. (Ask your doctor or nurse for a complete list of NSAIDs and products containing aspirin, or ask your pharmacist for a list.)
- Tell your doctor or nurse if you are taking any other medications, including over-the-counter preparations that do not require a prescription, herbal remedies, vitamins, or dietary supplements. Some of these may interfere with your chemotherapy.

Call Your Doctor or Nurse If You Have:
- Shortness of breath.
- Difficulty swallowing.
- Pain, redness, swelling, or blistering near the injection site.
- Nausea or vomiting and are unable to eat or drink.
- A fever of 100.5° F (38° C) or higher.
- Swelling of the arms or legs.
- Any unexpected, unexplained problems.
- Any questions or concerns.

Mitomycin (Mutamycin®)—stops cancer cells from growing by interfering with DNA, the genetic material in cells.

Immediate Side Effect (beginning within 24 hours):
- Nausea and vomiting are unusual, but may begin several hours after treatment and last for several hours.

Early Side Effect (beginning within one week):
- Mouth sores can begin five to seven days after treatment.

Late Side Effects (beginning after one week):
- A temporary decrease in blood cell counts—red blood cells, white blood cells, and platelets—can occur two to three weeks after treatment. The platelet count can remain low for several weeks.
- A temporary thinning or loss of hair can begin two to three weeks after each treatment.
- Damage to lung tissue resulting in shortness of breath can occur after several doses.

Special Points:
- Do not take aspirin, ibuprofen (e.g., Motrin®, Advil®), products containing them, or similar products unless your doctor prescribes them. (Ask your doctor or nurse for a complete list of NSAIDs and products containing aspirin, or ask your pharmacist for a list.)
- Tell your doctor or nurse if you are taking any other medications, including over-the-counter preparations that do not require a prescription, herbal remedies, vitamins, or dietary supplements. Some of these may interfere with your chemotherapy.

Call Your Doctor or Nurse If You:
- Experience shortness of breath.
- Experience pain, redness, swelling, or blistering at or near the injection site.
- Have excessive vomiting and are unable to eat or drink for more than 24 hours after treatment.
- Have a fever of 100.5° F (38° C) or higher.
- Have black bowel movements, bruising, faint red rash, or any other signs of bleeding.
- Develop mouth sores or a sore throat.
- Have any unexpected, unexplained problems.
- Have any questions or concerns.

Vinorelbine (Navelbine®)—works by interfering with cancer cells' ability to multiply and grow.

Immediate Side Effects (beginning within 24 hours):
- Discomfort in the veins may occur during administration of the drug.
- Pain at the site of the tumor during administration of the drug.
- Mild nausea and vomiting may occur within 24 hours of treatment.

Early Side Effect (beginning within the first seven days):
- Constipation may occur one to three days after treatment.

Late Side Effects (beginning after seven days):
- A temporary decrease in blood cell counts—white blood cells, red blood cells, and platelets—can occur within the first two to three weeks of treatment.
- Temporary thinning or loss of hair may begin two to three weeks after each treatment.
- Tingling or numbness or both in your fingers and toes as well as muscle weakness may occur after several treatments.
- Discoloration of the veins into which the drug was infused.

Special Points:
- Do not take aspirin, ibuprofen (e.g., Motrin®, Advil®), products containing them, or similar products unless your doctor prescribes them. (Ask your doctor or nurse for a complete list of NSAIDs and products containing aspirin, or ask your pharmacist for a list.)
- Tell your doctor or nurse if you are taking any other medications, including over-the-counter prepara-

tions that do not require a prescription, herbal remedies, vitamins, or dietary supplements. Some of these may interfere with your chemotherapy.

Call Your Doctor or Nurse If You:
- Have a fever of 100.5° F (38° C) or higher.
- Experience pain, redness, swelling, or blistering near the injection site.
- Have severe constipation that is not helped by laxatives.
- Are unable to eat or drink for more than 24 hours after treatment.
- Have any unexpected, unexplained problems.
- Have any questions or concerns.

55. Are chemotherapy and radiation given before or after surgery?

Adjuvant therapy

chemotherapy given after surgery to lessen the chances that cancer will recur.

Neoadjuvant therapy

chemotherapy given before surgery to shrink or isolate the tumor.

Chemotherapy and radiation can be given either before or after surgery. **Adjuvant therapy** is treatment given after surgery to lessen your chances that the cancer will return. **Neoadjuvant therapy** is the same type of treatment, except that it is given before surgery.

Physicians differ on their preference for treatment, and past research has not found a clear benefit for one treatment over another. A slight survival advantage has been reported when chemotherapy and radiation are given following surgery. However, it may take some time to recover from surgery, and some patients may not be able to tolerate the complete treatment. Some physicians, therefore, recommend giving chemotherapy and radiation prior to surgery. It is thought this may relieve symptoms such as dysphagia and increase the chances of complete removal of the tumor at the time of surgery. Neither option has proven to be clearly superior. Research is ongoing to identify the best schedule of treatment.

Discuss each of these options with your physician to better understand the benefits and drawbacks of each approach.

56. When would someone need chemotherapy?

Surgery is recommended as a single treatment for patients with Stage I or early Stage II esophageal cancer. Chemotherapy is recommended for patients with Stage II disease or higher. The advantage of chemotherapy is that it travels throughout the entire body and, potentially, may kill cancer cells that have spread beyond the original tumor site. Additionally, when chemotherapy is combined with radiation, more cancer cells are killed. Chemotherapy should be included in the treatment plan for all patients with esophageal cancer that was not found at a very early stage.

57. What is radiation therapy?

Radiation therapy uses x-rays to kill cancer cells and shrink tumors. Radiation is like surgery in that it is a localized type of treatment that affects defined areas in the body, and it is different from chemotherapy, which circulates throughout the body. Radiation can come from a machine outside the body, which is called **external beam radiation therapy.** It also can be delivered directly to the tumor in a treatment called **brachytherapy.** External beam radiation is the most common type of radiation used to treat cancer of the esophagus. External beam radiation is usually delivered daily, Monday to Friday. A treatment course, depending on the area being treated and on the size of the cancer, can be anywhere from 5–10 treatments to 28–35 treatments. Very specific targets are marked on

External beam radiation therapy
a type of x-ray therapy that comes from a machine outside of the body, usually delivered daily in a specific series of treatments.

Brachytherapy
a type of radiation therapy where a source of irradiation (such as radioactive seeds) is implanted directly into or near the tumor permanently or for a specified time.

Simulation

a process where the medical professional marks specific areas on the patient's body, sometimes using computed tomography, in preparation for targeting the tumor(s) with radiation therapy.

your body, using complicated CT scanning to determine the exact area to be treated. This process (called **simulation**) can take several hours. From there, medical physicists and the radiation oncologist plan the total dose of the radiation, the number of treatments, and the field size. Usually, a couple of days before beginning radiation you will undergo a "beam check" to ensure that the radiation prescription is exact and appropriate. Each daily radiation treatment takes approximately 10 minutes.

58. Is radiation a recommended treatment for esophageal cancer?

Radiation as a single treatment for esophageal cancer is not effective for a curative approach. Instead, it is combined with chemotherapy so that the radiation provides local control (to the area of the primary tumor) and the chemotherapy provides systemic control (from spread of the cancer through the blood or lymph systems).

Radiation is also used as a palliative treatment to relieve symptoms such as difficulty swallowing, pain, or other symptoms.

MEDICAL TREATMENT: SIDE EFFECTS

59. What are the common side effects of chemotherapy and radiation? Are these side effects temporary or permanent?

Chemotherapy works by targeting the rapidly dividing cells in the body. Cancer cells divide rapidly, but many beneficial cells in the body also divide rapidly and are negatively affected by chemotherapy. The lining of the digestive tract is affected, which can lead to nausea, vomiting, diarrhea, poor appetite, and sores in the mouth. Hair cells divide rapidly, so chemotherapy can lead to loss of hair. Our body's blood cells divide rapidly, so chemotherapy can lead to anemia, reduced blood clotting ability, and decreased ability to fight an infection. Medications and treatments can lessen the intensity of these side effects, and the occurrence of the side effects varies based on the general health of the patient and dose of the drug given. These side effects usually go away gradually after treatment stops. Some drugs may have longer-term side effects. An example of one is Cisplatin, which can have temporary or permanent effects on hearing. If you have hearing loss prior to treatment, you doctor may recommend a different drug or may monitor you closely for hearing changes during treatment.

Radiation works by using x-rays to kill cancer cells. The x-rays are aimed at the part of the body with the tumor to kill cancer cells while minimizing damage to surrounding healthy tissue. When being treated with external radiation therapy, the patient is not radioactive, so no special precautions are necessary. Radiation therapy can lead to fatigue or feelings of tiredness as treatment progresses. It can also cause skin problems to the area being treated, an upset stomach, diarrhea, difficulty swallowing, and a cough. These side effects may worsen as the treatment progresses. Radiation continues to work even after the treatment has finished. Side effects, therefore, may take some time to resolve, but do gradually improve following treatment.

60. How can side effects be treated?

Some general side effects of both radiation and chemotherapy are listed next with suggestions to help manage them. As always, discuss any side effects you may be having with your doctor or nurse who can help you manage them.

- Fatigue: a feeling of tiredness or lack of energy that is a common side effect of chemotherapy and radiation. The exact cause is not known and may be related to a variety of factors. Rest does not always relieve this type of fatigue. Some suggestions to help manage fatigue include planning rest periods during the day and taking short breaks or naps instead of one long rest. Continue to do the activities you enjoy but at easier levels or for shorter periods of time. Short walks or light exercise have been found to help with fatigue. Eating well and drinking plenty of fluids may help with fatigue.
- Nausea and vomiting: frequent side effects of chemotherapy that are seen less frequently with radiation therapy. New drugs are available to help prevent nausea and vomiting and help to make them less severe when they do occur. If you do experience nausea or vomiting, discuss it with your doctor or nurse, especially if you are unable to keep liquids or medications down. Some suggestions to help manage nausea and vomiting include eating small meals instead of larger ones and chewing food well for easier digestion. Drink liquids at least an hour before or after meals, instead of with meals, and drink frequently in small amounts. Eating foods cold or at room temperature can help if strong smells bother you. Drinking decaffeinated sodas that have lost their fizz may also help.
- Hair loss: a common side effect of chemotherapy but does not occur with all drugs. Discuss this with your doctor if you are at risk for this side effect. When hair loss does occur, it can become thinner or may fall out completely and occurs on all body parts. The

hair usually grows back once the treatment is over and may grow back a different color or texture.

- Anemia: caused by a decrease in red blood cells' ability to carry enough oxygen. Anemia may lead to feelings of shortness of breath, tiredness, and weakness. Your doctor will check your blood counts frequently during treatment. Medications are available to help boost the growth of red blood cells in your body. If your blood count falls too low, you may need a blood transfusion to help raise the number of red blood cells in your body.

- Low white blood cell count: can lead to being at higher risk for an infection. White blood cells help our body fight off infections. These cells divide rapidly and may be destroyed by chemotherapy. Your doctor will check your blood counts regularly during treatment and will be able to tell you if you are at risk for an infection. Medications are available to help speed the recovery of white blood cells and can greatly lower the risk of serious infection. Several simple steps can help to prevent an infection: Washing your hands before you eat and after using the bathroom will help. Avoid standing water, for example, from flower pots, or vases of cut flowers, or humidifiers. Wear gloves when gardening or cleaning up. Do not eat any raw fish, seafood, meat, or eggs. Stay away from anyone you know who is actively sick or has the flu, chicken pox, or a fever. Call your doctor immediately if you experience a temperature over 100°F, chills, sore throat, cough, or burning on urination.

- Low platelet counts: Platelets are a type of blood cell that help your blood to clot. If your platelets are low, you will be at risk to bleed and will bruise more easily. Your doctor will check your platelet count frequently during treatment and will alert you if you are at risk for bleeding. If your platelet count gets too low, you can receive a platelet transfusion to replace some of your platelets. There are also medications that can help increase your platelets. If you do have a low platelet count, you will need to avoid behaviors or activities that may cause bleeding or bruising. Some of these include using a soft toothbrush, blowing your nose gently, avoiding activities that may result in injury, and using an electric shaver instead of a razor.

- Mouth sores: sores in the mouth or throat are called stomatitis or mucositis. Mouth sores can be painful and may become infected. Some steps to help prevent or minimize mouth sores involve practicing good oral hygiene. Brush your teeth after every meal and before going to bed. Avoid mouthwashes with alcohol as they may be irritating to the oral mucosa. Your doctor or nurse can recommend a non-irritating, gentle mouthwash that will help. If you do develop mouth sores, avoid irritating or acidic foods such as orange juice or tomatoes, spicy foods, or dry, coarse foods such as crackers, popcorn, and raw vegetables. Foods that are cold or room temperature are usually more soothing than hot foods.

- Skin irritation: radiation can often cause irritation of the skin that is being treated. This area can often become red or dry. Do not expose this area to the sun, and avoid wearing clothes that rub the area. Your radiation oncologist or nurse will recommend a soap or lotion that you should use. Do not use any lotions or soap without checking first.

61. What happens if I don't have side effects? Is the treatment working?

Medications have been developed to help manage the side effects of chemotherapy. Today we have medications to help with nausea and vomiting, decreased blood counts, and other side effects of chemotherapy. In addition, side effects of both chemotherapy and radiation tend to be cumulative and may get worse as someone has had more treatment.

If you do not have side effects, don't worry. Continue to take care of yourself by eating well and getting some exercise. Your doctor is managing your treatment well and is preventing any side effects. The only way to tell if the treatment is working is to repeat CT scans or other staging procedures after several cycles of chemotherapy and radiation to assess how your cancer has changed.

MEDICAL TREATMENT: SURGERY
62. What is an esophagectomy?

An **esophagectomy** is the surgical removal of part of or most of the esophagus and proximal part of the stomach. It is often the only treatment for cancer of the esophagus, especially when the cancer is in an early stage. In most cases, however, surgery is combined with chemotherapy and radiation to treat esophageal cancer.

During an esophagectomy, the surgeon removes the part of the esophagus that contains the tumor with additional length of normal esophagus and possibly part of the stomach to ensure complete removal of the cancer. The next part of the operation is to make a new esophagus either with the stomach or part of the small or large intestine. Most surgeons prefer to use the stomach because of certain advantages: it has the most dependable blood supply, and it takes only one connection **(anastomosis)** to attach the stomach to the remaining

Esophagectomy

the surgical removal of part or most of the diseased esophagus and part of the stomach, and then rebuilding a new esophagus using tissue from stomach or the small or large intestine.

Anastomosis

a natural communication or connection, direct or indirect, between two blood vessels or other tubular structures; the surgical connection of severed organs to form a continuous channel.

esophagus. When the colon is used, three connection sites are necessary: one connecting to the esophagus, one to the remaining stomach, and another attaching back to the colon itself. The anastomosis is the name for the site where the remaining esophagus is connected to the "new" esophagus (see Figure 5).

In addition to removing the tumor in the esophagus, the surgeon may remove or sample adjacent lymph

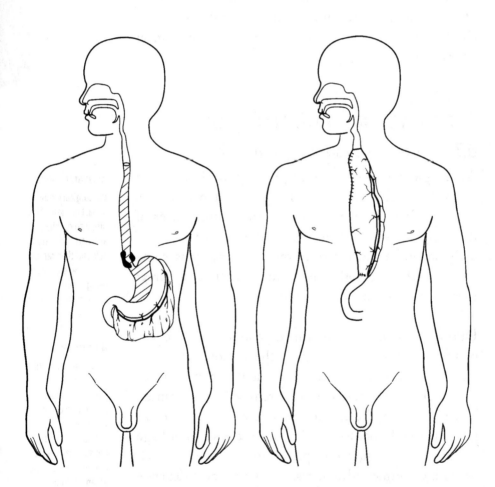

Figure 5. (Left) Normal anatomy (striped area is removed at the time of resection). (Right) Reconstruction of the esophagus and repositioning of the stomach.

nodes and tissue near the tumor. All of the tissue that is removed will be checked by a pathologist for the presence of cancer cells.

An esophagectomy is a major surgical procedure that carries potential risks, complications, and mortality. Surgeons with training in thoracic or gastrointestinal surgery have experience performing this operation, and in some hospitals the two will work together, with the thoracic surgeon doing the chest part of the operation while a gastric surgeon will do the abdominal part of the operation. Recently, some studies have found that patients undergoing major or complicated procedures such as esophageal resection at hospitals that performed a low volume of esophagectomies were at increased risk of postoperative complications and death. Therefore, it is vital to seek care at a hospital with high volume of such procedures being performed so that you are being treated by an experienced surgeon and his or her team.

63. What are the different types of esophagectomy?

There are several techniques that can be used to remove the tumor and any adjacent lymph nodes that might be involved, and to reconstruct the esophagus using either the stomach or the colon or, less frequently, the small bowel (see Figure 6 for diagrams of the surgical incisions for transhiatal and transthoracic esophagectomy).

Transhiatal esophagectomy is performed through an incision in the neck and another incision in the abdomen, extending from the lower part of the breast bone to almost the umbilicus. After the stomach is isolated, the esophagus is dissected through an open-

Transhiatal esophagectomy
surgical type of resection of the esophagus where the incision is made from the cervical section of the neck from above and up from the abdomen from below.

99

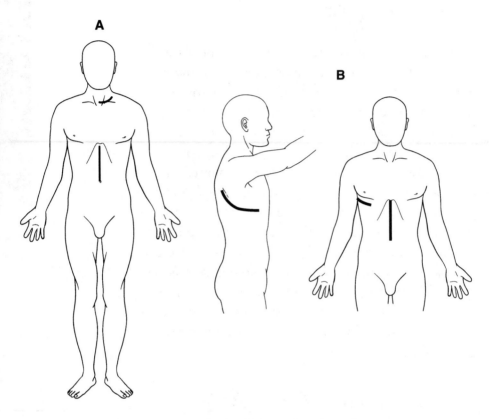

Figure 6. Surgical incisions for (A) transhiatal and (B) transthoracic esophagectomy.

ing in the diaphragm and through the incision in the neck. Most of this can be done under direct vision but, in the mid-chest, it is usually done by the surgeon using feel rather than direct vision. Surgeons call this a "blind dissection." The stomach is brought up into the neck and the esophagus, from the neck down to the stomach, including a small rim of the stomach, is removed. The stomach is attached to the esophagus in the neck either by a stapling device or by manually suturing the two together. The advantage of this particular surgical technique is that it avoids a more painful incision in the chest where the ribs need to be spread. However, because of the "blind dissection," some of the tissues (including the lymph nodes around the esophagus) may not be widely excised. It is possible that remaining lymph nodes have cancer that later could spread to other organs in the body.

Transthoracic esophagogastrectomy. A surgical procedure started in the mid-1930s by two British surgeons that remains the gold standard of surgery for esophageal cancer. It requires an incision in the abdomen from the breast bone to the umbilicus, plus an incision on the right side of the chest. Working through the chest incision, the esophagus can be dissected with the surrounding lymph nodes and wide margins. The stomach may be attached to the esophagus in the chest if there are adequate margins next to the tumor or, for better margins, the surgeon may elect to go into the neck. The advantage of this surgical procedure is that the tumor is removed with the surrounding tissues and lymph nodes adequately. The pain associated with spreading the ribs can be effectively controlled by placing an epidural catheter, allowing the patient to control the amount of pain medication needed for satisfactory relief.

Minimally invasive surgery. A relatively recent advance in surgical techniques that has also been applied to removal of the esophagus. A number of variations on this procedure using a number of small incisions over the abdomen and chest have been described. These techniques are new and have to prove themselves as far as adequacy, completeness of removal of a tumor, and cure rates are concerned.

Transthoracic esophago-gastrectomy
surgical type of resection of the esophagus through a thoracotomy incision (breast bone to the umbilicus, plus another incision on the right side of the chest).

Minimally invasive surgery
an operative procedure that results in the smallest possible incision or no incision at all; includes laparoscopic, laparoscopically assisted, thoracoscopic, and endoscopic procedures.

64. What are the risks and complications of surgery?

An esophagectomy is a major surgical procedure and carries a number of risks associated with it. Some of the complications are the same as what may occur after any type of surgery and others are specific to esophageal surgery. Your medical history and general overall health will impact your recovery from the operation and chances to develop a complication after surgery. We'll review some of the more common risks and complications here. Your surgeon will review the risks and potential complications of your surgery with you.

Two of the most common complications after surgery are pneumonia and infection. An infection can occur after any surgical procedure but is minimized with good surgical procedures. The hospital staff will monitor you closely after surgery for any signs or symptoms of an infection.

Postoperative pain and limited or no activity leads to an individual taking shallow breaths. This results in parts of the lung being not fully expanded. Incompletely expanded lungs collect secretions. Just as a stagnant pool of water can grow all kinds of organisms, secretions that are settled in the lung start growing bacteria and cause pneumonia. Pneumonia is the most common complication of surgery and the most common cause of the patient not surviving the operation. It can be prevented by preparing oneself prior to surgery. Aerobic exercises, such as walking for about an hour a day, will get the patient in better physical condition (see Question 33). Stopping smoking is also very important to preparing yourself for surgery (see Question 8).

After the surgery, it is important to be taking deep breaths and coughing even though you may not bring up any sputum. Coughing is the best way to re-expand your lungs and keep them expanded. Expanded lungs will not collect any secretions and hence you will reduce the chances of getting pneumonia.

During the preoperative teaching, nurse will give you an **incentive spirometer** (Figure 7) and explain to you how it is used. An incentive spirometer is a small plastic device that you will use to inhale and expand your lungs. Just as the name implies, it induces you to take deep breaths, and you should use it frequently before and after surgery. You will also be asked to cough after walking or using the incentive spirometer in order to move any secretions that may be in your lungs.

Incentive spirometer

a device used to help the patient inhale and expand the lungs.

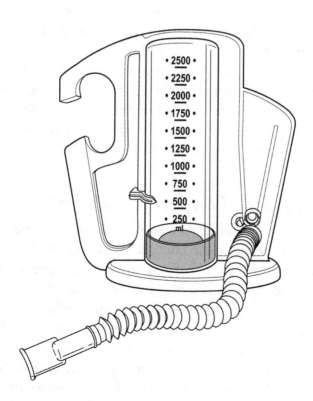

Figure 7. Incentive spirometer.

Cardiac complications are also common after surgery. Irregular heart rhythms or other heart problems can occur after a major surgery such as an esophagectomy. Depending on your age and your previous medical history, assessment of your heart is usually done before surgery. A cardiologist may examine and perform certain tests to ensure that you are able to tolerate the surgery. In some cases, medications or special monitoring may be necessary following surgery. If you have pre-existing cardiac problems, such an assessment becomes important, and a cardiologist may get involved in your care prior to and after the surgery.

Anastomotic leak

leakage of liquids or saliva into the chest cavity when the tissues have not healed completely from an esophagectomy.

There are some complications that are specific to the surgical procedure of an esophagectomy. One of these is an **anastomotic leak.** At the time of the operation, the stomach or the colon is attached to the remaining esophagus with sutures or staples. Tissues have to heal to permanently seal it off. If there was a problem with healing, liquids or saliva can leak into the chest cavity. This is a rare but potentially serious complication. Your surgeon will probably not allow you to eat or drink until it heals. Treatment for an anastomotic leak includes allowing more time for the site to heal or more surgery.

65. How do I prepare for surgery?

Anyone who undergoes a surgical procedure needs to be in the best possible physical shape they can be, and this is especially true of those undergoing an esophagectomy. It is a major undertaking and a drain on one's physical reserves. Getting into the best physical condition has to be the primary goal in the patient's mind. This is no less a task than an athlete getting into shape for his event at the competition. For those patients who are receiving preoperative treatment, it is very important that they develop and maintain a program of physical activity throughout the course of treatment. There will be times when feelings of fatigue will interrupt the routine, but even walking 15 to 20 minutes a day will help. There is a hiatus of four to six weeks from the end of preoperative chemotherapy and radiation to surgery. This is a good time to recuperate from the effects of treatment and restart or intensify your exercise routine.

Good mental health is as important as good physical health, and if at all possible this would be a good time to get away for a week or two. You may also find it helpful to speak with someone who has undergone the surgery and is now fully recovered. Some institutions have a patient-to-patient volunteer program, but if yours doesn't, your doctor or nurse may be able to arrange for you to speak with someone.

66. What is the hospital stay like?

Unless there is a specific reason for early admission, patients are admitted on the same day as the surgery. The average hospital stay is 10 to 14 days. During the surgery, some tubes and drains may be placed to drain fluid from the stomach and/or the chest. The different types of tubes and drains you will need depend on the type of surgery your physician performs. Your doctor and nurse will have spoken to you about the tubes you should expect beforehand. Most surgeons will obtain a barium swallow after about a week to check on the healing of the anastomosis. The barium swallow will tell your surgeon if the anastomosis is healed. If the barium swallow looks normal, you will be started on sips of clear liquids, and your diet is slowly advanced until you are able to eat regular food. It is also at this time that your tubes and drains are removed. It is rare that someone will be discharged with any drainage tubes.

67. What is the success rate for surgery?

Nationally, about a third of the patients having an esophagectomy will develop some minor complications. However, in about 5% of the patients undergoing an esophagectomy, the complications are fatal. In a center with expertise in this disease and the procedure, the mortality rate for surgery may be half of that percentage. The addition of chemotherapy and radiation as a multi-modality treatment has also allowed more patients to be able to undergo surgery and has not increased the complications of surgery.

68. How long will it take to recover?

Everyone will recover from surgery at their own pace, and recovery depends on a number of factors. Your overall medical condition prior to surgery will impact the time it takes to recover. Complications are a risk of any surgery, and if you experience any complications it may take you slightly longer to recover.

Exercising for about an hour a day is usually recommended. You may not be able to do that much at one time and may want to break it up into shorter segments with an aggregate of an hour a day. You may have to start for shorter time and progressively increase to the recommended duration. Exercise is very important after surgery to prevent complications such as pneumonia and blood clots. Your doctor will advise you about walking in the hospital after surgery and continuing this at home after discharge. Moderate exercise can also help improve your appetite and fatigue following surgery.

If you are working and have taken time off from work for surgery you may require 8 to 12 weeks prior to returning to your job. This will depend on the type of work you do on a day-to-day basis. Keep in mind, however, that it can be difficult to go back for "just a few hours" or a few days a week. Once there, you may be asked to do more than you are ready to do. Therefore, it is often better to take the maximum amount of time your doctor advises.

69. What is laparoscopic surgery?

Laparoscopy is a type of surgery where small incisions are made into the abdominal wall and specially designed ports are placed through the incisions. A gas is then used to inflate the abdomen so that the organs and structures can be visualized with a telescope, and a camera introduced into the abdominal cavity through a "port." Instruments are then placed thru additional ports and, with the help of a camera, the abdominal cavity is visualized. Surgical procedures or biopsies are then able to be performed. The advantage of laparoscopic surgery is that healing of the incisions is quicker and the pain is less when compared to larger incisions. In most cases, laparoscopy for diagnosis or small procedures is an outpatient procedure and patients go home the same day. They may experience some abdominal discomfort or shoulder pain, but these are minimal and usually subside after a day or two.

For patients with esophageal cancer, laparoscopy is most often performed as a diagnostic test to determine the extent of disease. In some patients, esophageal cancer can spread to the lymph nodes, abdominal wall, or liver, and for these patients an esophagectomy would not be the recommended treatment. A laparoscopy can determine if this spread has occurred and prevent unnecessary surgery. Research has found diagnostic laparoscopy to be a useful tool to detect if cancer has spread to the lymph nodes or other parts of the abdomen. Discuss with your surgeon if any of your staging tests (CT, endoscopy, or PET scan) indicate that a diagnostic laparoscopy would be recommended.

Some surgeons are investigating utilizing a laparoscopic approach to perform an esophagectomy. This is a new procedure that requires specific skills from the surgeon, and the long-term results of these procedures are not known. Research is ongoing to determine if this approach is adequate for a cancer operation.

70. What is laser surgery or ablative therapy?

Laser surgery

a surgical procedure using a device that concentrates high energies into an intense narrow beam of nondivergent monochromatic electromagnetic radiation.

During **laser surgery** or ablative therapy cancer is treated by procedures that destroy the cancerous tissue. Lasers or electrocoagulation are utilized to destroy the tissue. One instance where these procedures are used is for patients with Barrett's esophagus with dysplasia. This treatment has had mixed results. Ablation is successful in about half of the patients treated, but rates of recurrence differ widely at different centers. The difficulties in this type of treatment are related to the fact that this is a relatively new treatment and differences exist in ablation techniques. In addition, after treatment with ablation, the patient requires acid suppression therapy, either with surgery or with medications, to prevent the return of the Barrett's.

The benefits of this type of treatment are still being investigated, and until more is known, the treatment must still be considered experimental. If you have Barrett's esophagus with dysplasia, discuss with your gastroenterologist the benefits and risks of this type of treatment. As this is a new procedure and not all gastroenterologists or surgeons may be familiar with it, you may also want to find a center that has experience in this type of treatment for Barrett's esophagus.

71. Someone mentioned photodynamic therapy as a treatment for esophageal cancer. What is this?

Photodynamic therapy has been used as treatment for Barrett's esophagus with high-grade dysplasia or for palliation in advanced obstructing esophageal cancer. For this treatment, a type of laser light destroys cancer cells after the patient has been administered certain drugs that are **photosensitizing.** Treatment with photodynamic therapy is a two-step process. The first step involves the intravenous injection of a photosensitizing agent. Photofrin (porfimer sodium) is a photosensitizing agent that is FDA approved in the United States for the palliative treatment of advanced esophageal cancer. The agent remains in cancer cells for a longer period of time than it does in normal cells. The second step is to treat the area with cancer with a laser light. The laser light is directed to the area through an endoscope in a procedure similar to a regular endoscopy. When the cancer cells are exposed to laser light, the photosensitizing agent absorbs the light and the cancer cells are destroyed. Sometimes, a second endoscopy may be necessary to mechanically remove the dead cells or the debris. Timing of the light exposure is critical—it must be timed to occur when most of the photosensitizing agent has left the healthy cells but is still present in the cancer cells.

Photodynamic therapy (PDT)

a type of surgery that uses an injection of photosensitizing drugs to highlight the cancerous cells and laser light through an endoscope to kill them.

Photosensitizing

a type of treatment where target cancer cells are illuminated by bioluminescent drugs.

A side effect of the photosensitizing agent Photofrin is photosensitivity. The skin and eyes are sensitive to light for six weeks or more following the injection of the drug. During this time, patients are at risk to develop damage to the skin or the eyes and must remain out of the sunlight and avoid bright indoor light. Patients are advised to wear dark sunglasses when outdoors or in bright light. Other temporary side effects can include coughing, difficulty swallowing, and abdominal pain.

The advantage of photodynamic therapy is that it causes minimal damage to normal tissue that is near the dysplasia or cancer. However, the laser light cannot penetrate deep into the tissues, and therefore this treatment is used to treat early superficial tumors or dysplasia, or to remove cancer cells that may be causing an obstruction in the esophagus.

72. How is photodynamic therapy used to treat high-grade dysplasia?

Photodynamic therapy (PDT) is the most common experimental treatment for patients with Barrett's esophagus and high-grade dysplasia. Dysplasia can be eliminated in more than 75% of patients treated with PDT. After treatment, patients need ongoing surveillance for persistent or recurrent Barrett's.

For patients with high-grade dysplasia, the risk of developing an invasive cancer is not inevitable but is high. Historically, patients with this condition faced two options: close endoscopic surveillance or surgical resection of the esophagus. Surgery is highly curative for high-grade dysplasia and early cancer, and for patients who can tolerate an esophagectomy, this is the preferred method of treatment. For patients who are not able to tolerate surgery, ablation therapy is an option. Recent research has found that this treatment holds promise for select patients with high-grade dysplasia who cannot tolerate surgery for medical reasons. As this is still considered an experimental treatment, long-term studies are needed to demonstrate whether this treatment will prevent esophageal cancer in these patients.

73. How is photodynamic therapy used to treat advanced esophageal cancer?

Cancer that has advanced within the esophagus can cause a blockage or obstruction that can lead to difficulty or inability to swallow, decreased oral intake, and aspiration of food or saliva in the lungs that can lead to pneumonia. In some cases, palliative treatment can improve these symptoms and the patient's overall quality of life. Palliative treatment is meant to relieve symptoms and make the patient more comfortable, but is not meant as a cure for the disease.

One method of palliation that has been used for esophageal cancer is photodynamic therapy (PDT). When the tumor is within the esophagus and is causing obstruction or bleeding, PDT can be used to treat the tumor and remove some of the tissue, thus opening the obstruction or stopping the bleeding. The advantage of PDT over other treatments is that it can improve symptoms within days of treatment, there is minimal pain with the treatment, and PDT is administered in most cases on an outpatient basis. Disadvantages such as photosensitivity, risk of perforation of the esophagus, and the need for possible repeat treatments must be considered.

Other treatments for palliation of obstructing esophageal cancer include external beam radiation, laser therapy, or stents. Each has advantages and disadvantages, and a thorough discussion with your physician will help you decided which treatment is best for you (see Question 89 for more information on palliative treatment).

SIDE EFFECTS OF SURGICAL TREATMENT

74. I have trouble swallowing after surgery. What can I do?

After surgery, as the anastomosis (area where the esophagus was reconnected) heals, a stricture can form. A **stricture** is a narrowing or tightening of the esophagus. This can also occur after other treatments, including laser therapy or photodynamic therapy. After surgery, the anastomosis forms a scar. If you think about having a scar on your hand or your knee, the skin around the scar pulls up or puckers. A similar process can occur in your esophagus, and as this area heals the tissue pulls and tightens. This can lead to difficulty swallowing.

One way to help prevent this from occurring is to eat solid foods. As you are swallowing solids, they will naturally help to stretch the esophagus and keep it open. A stricture can still develop even if you have been trying to eat solids. If you do start to experience difficulty swallowing, alert your surgeon or your nurse. They will assess what you are able to eat and when your difficulty occurs.

Treatment for a stricture can be done in your surgeon's office or as an outpatient procedure in the hospital. In some cases, your surgeon can see you in the office and,

Stricture

a narrowing or tightening of the esophagus.

while you swallow, inserts a weighted tube, called a **bougie,** which will open the stricture. Sometimes several treatments are required to keep the esophagus open. For some patients who require repeated treatments, the surgeon will instruct them to do this procedure at home. In other cases, your surgeon may wish to stretch the esophagus during an endoscopy at the hospital. This is similar to a regular endoscopy and a balloon is used to open the esophagus. Your surgeon will discuss which procedure is best for your situation.

Bougie

a cylindrical instrument used for dilating constricted areas in a tubular organ (such as the esophagus).

Treatment Options

Bart's comment:

If you are experiencing problems with swallowing, where food seems to be taking a long time to clear your esophagus, it could be that scar tissue that formed where your surgery took place could be tightening, so you will need a dilation to stretch your opening. This is a procedure that can be done either in your surgeon's office or in the hospital.

75. What are some other side effects of surgery?

Esophageal surgery has other potential side effects. Some are temporary and some will require permanent lifestyle changes. Your surgeon will discuss possible side effects with you and the risks of each of them, given your situation and planned treatment.

Some patients experience a change in their voice following surgery. Some changes in your voice may be temporary; however, some may be lasting. The location of your tumor will determine whether your voice is affected by surgery. If your tumor is located at the top of your esophagus, your surgeon will discuss the implications of surgery on your voice.

It is not unusual for someone who has received anesthesia to experience a decrease or loss of appetite. For those who have had an esophagectomy it may take longer for their appetite to return. Also, because the gastrointestinal tract has been reconfigured and the stomach is smaller, patients often complain of feelings of fullness and discomfort when ingesting much smaller portions. These symptoms do resolve with time. It is recommended that people who have an esophagectomy eat six small meals a day (see Question 81 for more specifics on diet changes after an esophagectomy).

Patients who have had their esophagus removed will need to adjust their sleep position. In most cases, when the esophagus is removed as part of an esophagectomy, the sphincter, or valve, at the lower end of the esophagus is removed as well. Normally this valve prevents acid and stomach contents from coming back up into the esophagus and lungs. Without this valve there is a possibility that if you sleep flat, some stomach acid or contents could travel up the esophagus and leak into the lungs. This leaking can lead to serious complications such as pneumonia. In order to prevent this, it is recommended that you sleep with the head of your bed elevated about 10 to 12 inches. This change is permanent and will need to be maintained for the rest of your life.

Raising your bed to this height requires more than just extra pillows. There are several methods to raise the head of your bed. One is to place blocks or risers under the two posts at the head of the bed. An advantage of this is that the entire bed is then on an incline and you won't be able to 'wiggle down' to a flat position. You can also purchase a wedge that will raise the top part of your body. It is important to consider a wedge that raises your entire torso, from your hips to your head. Wedges are available that only raise the head and shoulders, but this would not be adequate for people who have had their esophagus removed. Some wedges are even inflatable and can be packed in your suitcase for travel. A good company to check for a wedge is Back Be Nimble (*www.backbenimble.com* or 800-639-3746). You can also check your local medical supply pharmacy for wedges.

Bart's comment:

My experience after my adenocarcinoma surgery has been that the only time I find my voice changing is after I eat, especially when I have eaten too much. Your stomach, which now starts in the middle of your chest, fights for space with your lungs and not getting enough air into your lungs can impact your projection of words.

After my surgery, which took a portion of my stomach as well as the cancer in my esophagus, I found that I had to eat smaller meals and eat more often to get the nourishment my body needed while still paying attention to the new size of my stomach. A well-balanced meal is always important, and more so with a limited amount of food you can take in at a given point of time. Drinking, which also is important, should be kept to a minimum during your eating, only sipping a drink during this time. The major part of your fluid intake should occur two hours before and two hours after your meals.

Also, you should finish your food intake for the day at least two hours before you go to bed. In this way you give your system time to digest the food, so it does not sit in your stomach overnight that could cause acid or bile reflux to occur.

If your surgery involved taking a portion of your stomach, then the valve that holds your food down undoubtedly had to be removed. Since there is no replacement for that valve, you need to sleep at a 30° incline so the food in your stomach stays there. This position can be accomplished in several ways. You can buy and sleep on a wedge. You can put wood blocks under the head portion of the bed that will in effect raise the head portion of the bed so that the entire bed is at a 30° angle. The other option would be to purchase adjustable beds so you can set your bed at one level and your partner can set their section of the bed at the level they desire.

76. What is "dumping"?

Dumping syndrome

postsurgical rapid gastric emptying; early dumping symptoms includes nausea, vomiting, bloating and diarrhea and late dumping symptoms include weakness, sweating, and dizziness.

Dumping syndrome is a common occurrence following surgery and is also called rapid gastric emptying. This occurs when the lower end of the small intestine fills too quickly with undigested food. Dumping can occur either 'early' or 'late.' Early dumping occurs soon after a meal and symptoms include nausea, vomiting, bloating, and diarrhea. Late dumping occurs one to three hours after eating and symptoms include weakness, sweating, and dizziness. Although both types are possible after surgery, late dumping is more common.

77. What should the postoperative patient do to minimize the discomfort associated with dumping syndrome?

If you do experience dumping, changing your eating habits may help. Try eating more slowly or eating smaller meals more frequently. Also, avoiding high fat or high sugar foods can help. In some cases your doctor can prescribe medications to slow your digestion. It is a good idea to keep some juice and a snack, such as nuts, available with you at all times in case you start to feel symptoms of weakness or dizziness. If you do experience these symptoms, discuss them with your doctor.

Bart's comment:

Dumping is a product of your eating habits. If you eat too much sugar or carbohydrates and you eat too fast, you do not give your system proper time to digest what you have eaten. As a result, your stomach just releases what you have eaten into your lower intestines and a dumping syndrome ensues.

You know that you are experiencing a dumping syndrome when you feel weak, have shortness of breath, are sweating profusely, and need to rest from the overall weak feeling. Usually some orange juice or a small candy or anything sweet will get you out of this feeling within 20 or 30 minutes.

78. What is palliative treatment?

Palliative treatment is given not with the intent to cure, but with the intent to prolong survival, shrink the tumor, and improve symptoms. Generally, chemotherapy for advanced esophageal cancer is palliative treatment. It is administered with the intent to shrink the tumor or at least keep it stable. In doing so, one hopes to prolong life and decrease symptoms, thereby improving quality of life.

79. What palliative treatments are used to treat cancer of the esophagus?

Unfortunately, many people with cancer of the esophagus are diagnosed when the cancer has spread from the esophagus and are not candidates for curative treatment. For these individuals, the goal of treatment is relief of symptoms to improve quality of life. Chemotherapy, surgery, and radiation can all be used as palliative treatments. The choice of treatment is based on each technique's advantages and disadvantages, the area to be treated, as well as the patient's overall condition. Your doctor will individualize treatment to your specific case. Discuss with him/her the plan for treatment as well as the advantages and disadvantages.

Surgery

Surgery is a difficult decision when cancer is at an advanced stage. Occasionally, a palliative esophagectomy or surgery to bypass the esophagus may be considered. The goal of surgery in this situation is the relief of dysphagia. Some studies have found that over 80% of patients had complete and lasting relief of dysphagia following palliative esophagectomy. Despite these benefits, surgery in these patients carries a high risk of morbidity and mortality and requires careful consideration.

Radiation Therapy

Radiation therapy is an important method of palliation for patients with esophageal cancer. In 50% to 70% of patients radiation can lead to relief of dysphagia. An important factor to consider is that it takes about four to six weeks for the effects of radiation therapy to be seen. Thus, this would not be an appropriate treatment for someone with a complete obstruction who requires immediate relief. Complications of radiation therapy are esophagitis, narrowing of the esophagus, and **fistula.** Radiation therapy is noninvasive. This is advantageous to patients; however, it does require time and travel to the hospital every day for several weeks.

Fistula

an abnormal passage from a hollow organ to the body surface or from one organ to another.

Brachytherapy

Brachytherapy is a type of radiation therapy where radiation is delivered directly to the tumor by radioactive seeds that are placed directly in or near the tumor. Brachytherapy can directly treat an esophageal tumor and shortens treatment time. The radioactive seeds can be permanent when they are implanted directly into the tumor or they can be placed in a hollow tube and passed near the tumor for a set number of minutes. A complication of brachytherapy is esophagitis. The majority of patients treated with brachytherapy will have relief of their dysphagia.

Brachytherapy may be combined with external beam radiation therapy. The goal of this treatment is to improve the local control of the tumor. This combination can restore normal swallowing in the majority of patients.

Chemoradiation

Chemotherapy has been utilized alone or in combination with radiation therapy in the palliative treatment of esophageal cancer. Research has found that this approach provides good, long-lasting relief of dysphagia. Toxicity from **chemoradiation** is a concern and is higher when the treatments are combined than when they are given as single treatments.

Chemoradiation
where chemotherapy is used in combination with radiation therapy.

Dilatation

Dilatation, or stretching of the esophagus, is an important first step in the palliative treatment of patients with obstructing esophageal tumors. This treatment can offer relief of dysphagia with a low risk of complications. The duration of relief is short so dilatation is rarely used alone as a palliative treatment. The advantage to this treatment is its simplicity, avail-

Dilatation
(also dilation) An outpatient treatment used to stretch the esophagus.

ability, low cost, ability to be performed in the outpatient setting, and applicability to many types of tumors.

Stents

Stent

a thread, rod or catheter that is inserted into the cell wall of the esophagus to keep it open.

Plastic or metal **stents** are often utilized for palliative treatment. They can be a thread, rod or catheter that is inserted into the wall of the esophagus to keep it open when it becomes constricted (see Figure 8). Advantages of this treatment are its simplicity, short hospitalization, and immediate improvement in swallowing. Complications occur rarely but include perforation, hemorrhage, pneumonia, and tube dislocation. A disadvantage of this treatment is that the tumor can overgrow the stent and that food may become impacted. Recently, metal stents have been introduced that reduce some of the complications seen with plastic prosthesis.

Laser Therapy

Lasers are used to destroy the tumor and open the esophagus to allow for better swallowing. Tradition-

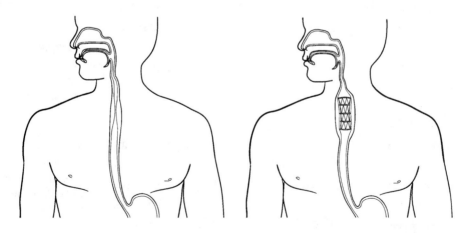

Figure 8. (Left) Narrowing of the esophagus caused by tumor. (Right) Esophageal stent placement.

ally, a type of laser called the Nd:YAG laser was utilized. This laser is placed at or near the tumor to destroy the cancer cells. The advantage of laser therapy is its high success rate with low complications. Almost immediate relief is seen and the treatment can be repeated indefinitely. Laser therapy is performed as an outpatient with local anesthesia. Complications are rare but include perforation, bleeding, and fistula formation.

Photodynamic Therapy

Photodynamic therapy is also used in palliative treatment of esophageal cancer (see Question 85).

Each palliative treatment has advantages and disadvantages and may be indicated for specific symptoms. Your physician will discuss with you the techniques he or she is recommending and why.

80. Am I at risk for a blood clot? What is a pulmonary embolism?

A blood clot that occurs in a deep-lying vein in the leg or pelvis is known as a **deep vein thrombosis** (DVT). If the blood clot breaks off and travels up through the heart and into the lungs, it is called a **pulmonary embolism** (PE). A pulmonary embolism is a potentially serious condition, because if it is a large blood clot, it can block off a blood vessel going to the lung and cause significant problems with breathing, or even death.

Lots of things can cause a DVT, particularly in the elderly, including poor circulation, sitting for long periods of time, or being bedridden following surgery. For unclear reasons, patients with cancer have a higher tendency to get blood clots.

Deep vein thrombosis

a blood clot that occurs in a deep-lying vein in the leg or pelvis.

Pulmonary embolism (PE)

a blood clot that has broken away from the blood vessel wall and travels into the lung; a large clot can cause breathing problems and even death.

Treatment Options

To prevent a DVT from happening, your doctor may put you on an anticoagulant (anti-clotting drug), such as coumadin (Warfarin) or heparin. These drugs do not cause the blood clot to dissolve. Instead, they prevent the blood clot from becoming even bigger, allowing it to shrivel up and become "glued" to the wall of the vessel. Although coumadin can work well in some cancer patients, in others it does not. Those patients often need to be treated with heparin. Heparin can be administered in several ways. Until recently, patients were often admitted for intravenous heparin, but now low-molecular-weight heparin has become available, which can be administered once or twice per day subcutaneously. Note that the commonly used phrase "thinning the blood" is not quite accurate. These medications make the blood less likely to clot, allowing the body to take care of the clot as described above.

PART SIX

Living with Esophageal Cancer

I don't seem to have much of an appetite after treatment. How can I improve my appetite and nutrition during and after treatment?

Will I be able to work during and after treatment?

How do I get my life back to normal?

More . . .

81. I don't seem to have much of an appetite after treatment. How can I improve my appetite and nutrition during and after treatment?

Treatment for esophageal cancer can affect your appetite in different ways. Chemotherapy can cause nausea or may alter your taste for food. Radiation can cause irritation to your esophagus and make swallowing painful. An esophagectomy reduces the size of your stomach and may change the rate at which food leaves your stomach and is absorbed by the body. In addition, each of these treatments can lead to a decrease in your general appetite, and you may not feel you have a taste for food. In fact, some patients have even said they developed an aversion to food following treatment.

Maintaining your nutritional level and weight during and after treatment is a challenge, and is vitally important to recovery and healing. We will provide some general tips to increase your appetite and maintain your nutrition, and then give some specific advice of each type of treatment.

If you have difficulty swallowing or pain when swallowing, discuss these symptoms with your doctor. Some of the following tips may be difficult to try if you are having trouble swallowing. In that case, it may be helpful to meet with a dietitian or nutritionist who works with your medical team. He or she can be a valuable resource as you navigate treatment and recovery.

Maintaining Calories and Stimulating Appetite

- Large meals can seem overwhelming, so try frequent, small meals instead of three large meals.

- Drink beverages high in calories such as milkshakes, fruit juices, and nectars instead of diet drinks, coffee, or tea.
- Keep snack foods that you like readily available at home and work.
- Eat your favorite foods any time of the day—if you feel like an omelet for dinner, have one.
- Pleasant aromas such as bread baking or bacon frying can help to stimulate your appetite.
- Avoid foods that are labeled "low fat," "nonfat," or "diet."
- Snack on dried fruits and nuts or add them to hot cereals, ice cream, or salads.
- Add sour cream, half-and-half, or heavy cream to mashed potatoes, cake and cookie recipes, pancake batter, sauces, gravies, soups, and casseroles.

Increasing Protein in Your Diet

Protein can help your body to heal from surgery or wounds and helps your body to function efficiently.

- Eat foods high in protein such as chicken, fish, pork, beef, eggs, milk, cheese, beans, and tofu.
- Drink 'Double Milk' by adding 1 envelope of non-fat dry milk powder to 1 quart of milk and blending. Refrigerate after blending.
- Add powdered milk to cream soups, mashed potatoes, milkshakes, and casseroles.
- Snack on cheese or nut butters (such as peanut butter, cashew butter, etc.) with crackers, apples, bananas, raisins, or celery.
- Add chickpeas, kidney beans, tofu, hard-cooked eggs, nuts, cooked meats, or fish to your salads.
- Add grated cheese to sauces, vegetables, soups, baked or mashed potatoes, casseroles, and salads.
- Add wheat germ to cereals, casseroles, and yogurt.

82. How will chemotherapy and radiation affect my nutrition and digestive system? Can these side effects be managed?

Chemotherapy

Many chemotherapy agents can affect the digestive system and cause nausea and vomiting, diarrhea, sore mouth, dry mouth, weight loss, and changes in the taste of food. These side effects depend on the drugs you receive and doses used and vary from person to person. New medications are available to manage some of these symptoms. Some patients may experience very mild symptoms or no symptoms at all. The tips that follow can help to manage some of these side effects, but if you do experience any of these, discuss them with your nurse and your doctor (see Question 54 for more side effects of chemotherapy).

Bart's comment:

The chemotherapy protocol is what I like to call "patient friendly." They usually are given once a week so people can continue to work during their treatments. Patients can work the remaining part of the week, and my experience in talking to some patients has been that they can work even on the day they take their treatment. This is a good area to measure the progress that has been made over the last few years.

My chemotherapy protocol was 24 hours a day for 5 days a week, for 6 straight weeks. While I was going through this protocol I was also taking radiation therapy each day (28 treatments) as well.

Radiation Therapy

Radiation to the esophagus can cause a sore mouth, sore throat, difficulty swallowing, and taste changes. Follow the tips below to help manage these side effects. In addition to the tips listed, it would be helpful to avoid acidic foods such as orange juice and tomatoes, which may irritate the esophagus (see Question 58 for more side effects of radiation).

Bart's comment:

I did not have any bad side effects from my radiation therapy. It was painless for me. I did not have any radiation burns and, along with the chemotherapy I took, overall reduced the size of my tumor from 5 cm to 1 cm.

Nutrition Tips to Manage Side Effects During Chemotherapy and Radiation

- Diarrhea: if you experience diarrhea check with your doctor before treating it yourself. Drink at least 8 cups (8 oz.) of liquid to replace water and electrolytes you may be losing. Try well-cooked, pureed and peeled, canned vegetables and fruits such as bananas, peeled apples, and diluted juices. Try white breads, cereals, rice, pasta, and farina. Avoid whole grain breads, breads with nuts or seeds, and fatty breads or pastries. Avoid large amounts of sugar, spices, rich gravies, and caffeine.
- Sore or dry mouth: mouth dryness or sores can make eating difficult or painful. For a dry mouth, try soft and pureed foods and cold foods. Sugar-free mints or gum can help to stimulate saliva production for a dry mouth. For mouth sores, try bland, soft, pureed foods such as creamed soups, casseroles, macaroni and cheese, and scrambled eggs. For both a dry mouth and mouth sores, avoid rough or dry foods

such as meat without sauce, crackers, pretzels, and raw fruits and vegetables.

• Taste changes: changes in taste vary from person to person, but the most common changes are bitter and metallic tastes in the mouth. Occasionally, food may seem to have no taste at all. When food seems tasteless, use spices and flavoring, as tolerated. For example, add sauces and condiments, such as soy sauce and Creole spice. Marinate meats in salad dressing or another favorite sauce. Try herbs such as rosemary, basil and oregano, mint and different types of mustard. Try sour and tart foods as these may help to stimulate taste. Look for recipes from different regional American and international cuisines in the grocery store and on the Internet. If you have a bitter or metallic taste in the mouth, rinse with water before meals. If meats taste bitter, try marinating them in fruit-based sauces or fruit juices. Use plastic utensils to reduce a metallic taste and try sugar-free mints or gum.

• Nausea: nausea is a common side effect of treatment and medications are available to help control nausea. Talk with your doctor or nurse if you have nausea before trying the following suggestions. Try high-carbohydrate, low-fat, bland foods such as gelatin, dry toast, skinless chicken, light pasta salads, and popsicles. Avoid high-fat, spicy or overly sweet foods, fatty meats, and fried foods.

83. How will surgery affect my digestive system? How can I manage these side effects?

Surgery results in two physical changes that impact the way you eat and digest food. Your stomach will be smaller, which will lead to feeling full more quickly after eating than you did before surgery. The valve that controls the rate at which food leaves your stomach and enters your intestines may be altered, which means nutrients may not be absorbed as well as before. Before or after your surgery you should meet with a dietitian to discuss your particular needs. Some general tips are listed below.

- Eat six or seven small meals daily instead of three main meals. This will help you to eat the proper amount of food even though your stomach is smaller. The amount of food you are able to eat at each meal will increase over time but may not reach your pre-surgery capacity.
- Eat slowly and chew your food thoroughly. This helps digestion and lets you know when you are full, so you can stop eating before you feel uncomfortable.
- Drink no more than 4 ounces of liquid at meal times. This allows you to eat more solid foods and slows the passage of food to the small intestine.
- Drink liquids before and after meals to prevent dehydration. You should drink about 8 to 10 cups of fluid a day.
- Eat sweets in moderation. Sugar in drinks and foods such as sodas, fruit juices, candy, and cake can cause food to flow more quickly into the small intestine, which can lead to cramping, stomach pain, or diarrhea (see Question 60 for more information on this side effect).
- Test your tolerance for fats. Try a small amount first and increase slowly. You may have trouble digesting large amounts of fat.
- Sometimes people become lactose-intolerant after surgery. This usually goes away after a few months. After surgery, gradually introduce dairy products into your diet. If you think you may be lactose intolerant, contact a dietitian for guidance.

After surgery and when you are able to tolerate liquids, you may want to start with soft, tender foods. As the esophagus heals, the area that was reconnected (anastomosis) will form a scar and may shrink or tighten. Eating solid foods will help to keep this open. However, if you experience coughing or the sensation of food getting stuck when you swallow, inform your doctor.

During an esophagectomy, the valve between your stomach and esophagus (the gastroesophageal sphincter) is removed. This can cause contents of your stomach to move upwards and enter the esophagus. It is important to prevent this. Sit upright during and for at least 30 minutes after meals. Wear loose fitting clothing and allow at least two hours between your last meal and bedtime. Keep the head of your bed elevated to a 30° angle.

Bart's comment:

This is major surgery and I was in the hospital for 10 days. The key element to being in the hospital is you need to work while you are there. Walking, coughing, and using the breathing machine are all things I had to do to avoid complications in the recovery process.

When you first go home after surgery, you will find that you will need to eat by the clock. If the clock says 12 noon it is time to eat lunch, and at 6 pm it is time for dinner. As your time from surgery lengthens, you will begin to get your appetite back. I have found for myself that exercising during the recovery process will bring your appetite back sooner than what other people were telling me.

84. When can I consider myself cured of esophageal cancer?

Surviving cancer is a process and it is difficult to pinpoint a time when you can consider yourself "cured." As you transition from treatment to life after treatment, you may face many challenges. More and more hospitals and community agencies are focusing support services and educational programs to individuals who have completed their treatment for cancer. Contact your hospital or local American Cancer Society for local resources. Two good Web sites for survivorship information are the National Coalition for Cancer Survivorship (www.canceradvocacy.org) and the National Cancer Institute's Office of Cancer Survivorship (http://dccps.nci.nih.gov/ocs/).

Bart's comment:

I do not consider myself as being cured of esophageal cancer, but rather, I consider myself as having successfully gone through chemotherapy, radiation, and surgery. All tests taken from surgery to date (CAT scans and endoscopies) have indicated that no further cancer has been identified in my body.

In the first year I took a CAT scan every six months with an alternating endoscope every six months as well, in effect visiting my surgeon four times that first year. I am repeating these tests on a six-month basis. This is to say, I have visited my surgeon twice the second and third years. We will continue this through my fourth year of recovery and then we will go to annual visits.

85. Will I be able to work during and after treatment?

How someone responds to treatment varies greatly. Chemotherapy may be given from one to several days a week. Most often it is given on an outpatient basis, but occasionally patients are required to stay overnight in the hospital. Some patients are able to work throughout chemotherapy and only take a few days off, while others need more time. Radiation therapy is given Monday through Friday, and even though the treatment may only take a few minutes, the distance to the facility must be considered. Surgery usually requires a 10- to 14-day hospital stay and a 6- to 8-week recovery before going back to work. Your doctor will outline your treatment schedule, which will allow you to estimate if you'll need time away from work.

If you believe that you may need some time away from work during your treatment and recovery, you may need to talk with your supervisor about taking sick leave or perhaps changing your responsibilities during this time. If you are unable to work full-time and must switch to part-time hours, speak to your company's human resources or benefits department staff. Be aware that the Family and Medical Leave Act allows eligible employees up to a total of 12 weeks of unpaid leave during any 12-month period. For information about this legislation, contact the human resources department where you work or the United States Department of Labor (*http:// www.dol.gov/dol/esa/fmla/htm*).

You may be concerned about discussing your diagnosis with your supervisor or co-workers. The Americans with Disabilities Act protects you from discrimination at work and requires that employers make reasonable adjustments as long as you can perform the essential functions of the job. Unfortunately, some employers do not always respond in the way we hope they will or in the way the law requires. If you do need to talk with a supervisor or co-worker, prepare ahead for the conversation. First, determine how you can get the most important parts of your job done. Then, determine how you need to alter the hours you work to balance getting the job done with taking care of your medical needs. Being open at the beginning can be helpful in obtaining information about your rights and benefits. If you are not comfortable talking about this with your supervisor, talk with someone in the human resources department. If conflicts arise, you may need to contact an attorney for assistance. For more information about the Americans with Disabilities Act and how it applies to you, contact the United States Department of Justice (*http://www.usdoj.gov/crt/ada/ada-him1.htm* or 1-800-514-0301) or the United States Equal Employment Opportunity Commission (*http://www.eeoc.gov* or 1-202-663-4900).

Bart's comment:

Most people can work during the chemotherapy and radiation treatments they encounter. After surgery, you may need 2 to 3 months to get back into a working mode. Some patients have done this sooner and to a great extent it is up to how the patient feels and what he thinks he can handle.

86. How do I get my life back to normal?

The transition from treatment to normal life can include many conflicting emotions. If your treatment has been successful, you probably will be relieved and happy. At the same time, you may feel distressed and this emotional conflict is not unusual. You probably have made friendships with those involved in your care as well as other patients and their families. Now that you are not going to your health care facility regularly, you may not see them as often or perhaps never see them again. What had become a routine focus of your life is changing. This is a time of transition. It is normal to find it difficult to finish treatment and carry on with your life.

A support group may be helpful to you at this time. Here, you may find other cancer survivors who are facing similar circumstances. You will also be able to reach out to newly diagnosed patients. This effort to help others can make you feel good about yourself and remind you about how far you have come. If your anxiety causes you to feel depressed or interferes with your functioning, you should talk to your doctor and ask whether counseling or medication might help to alleviate your distress. You should also let your family and friends know that you still need their support even though you are no longer in treatment. They may assume everything is okay unless you take the time to explain your ongoing needs.

An important part of getting your life back to normal is to be vigilant about your follow-up care and "wellness care." Although follow-up care for cancer of the esophagus varies among doctors, you should be aware of your doctor's recommendations for office visits, scans, and follow-up tests. In addition to your cancer concerns, you should discuss "wellness care" with your doctor. It is important that you take good care of your general health so that you can be strong in your survival.

What will be most effective for getting back to normal and resolving your emotional distress is the passage of time. As each day passes, you will feel more comfortable with your status as a cancer survivor. You will adjust to the emotional, physical, and social changes brought about by your cancer experience and find a new equilibrium—a new normal—that will carry you through your life.

Bart's comment:

I like to say that my life has a slightly different definition of normal. I can now eat the same foods I ate before, and I can play golf as I did before, although I am probably three strokes worse. So why do I say a 'slightly different' definition of normal? Simply put, I now eat more than the three meals a day because my stomach is smaller then it was before surgery. Immediately after surgery I was eating 6 meals a day, which now after 4 years post-surgery has been reduced to three meals a day with a snack or two in between because my stomach has stretched since surgery.

Another slightly different routine than what I had before is with sleeping. I now sleep on an angle of approximately 30 degrees.

When you think about these two changes, eating smaller meals and sleeping on an angle, they are changes for the better that people who have not gone through this treatment should also follow. Eating smaller meals is good for everyone, and sleeping with a small elevation is also good for everyone.

87. Will I be able to do the things I used to do, such as travel, going out to eat, and playing sports?

You will be able to do as much of any activity you would like after being diagnosed with cancer of the esophagus. You may need to modify your activities during treatment, depending on how you feel.

Immediately after treatment it is best to check with your doctor before traveling long distances. After being cleared, you're free to travel where you would like! As always, it is best to verify with your insurance company the policy for health-related emergencies while away from home and to know the location of the closest medical facility. If you've had an esophagectomy you will need to keep the head of your bed elevated. Extra pillows may not be enough; some medical supply companies sell inflatable wedges that pack easily for travel. Check with your local medical supply retailer or try Back Be Nimble (see the Appendix) for an inflatable wedge that is convenient for traveling.

Eating out is a good way to relax and see friends and family. If you have difficulty swallowing, order softer foods or ask for sauces or gravies on your entrée. If you are only able to eat small meals, order an appetizer and salad or share a dinner with a family member or friend. Leftovers are a great snack for later!

As we've talked about in other questions, exercise is a great way to build and maintain your strength during and after treatment. Certainly pace yourself, and start slow if you haven't exercised in awhile or if you are just starting to exercise after not feeling well. It is always a good idea to have a companion with you in case you need anything. If you have any questions about when to start exercising following treatment, discuss them with your doctor.

Bart's comment:

The answer to all these questions is yes. You can travel, but keep in mind that you need to sleep on an angle, so you need to tell the hotel that you need additional pillows.

Going out to eat is also doable. Here you need to remember that a full course meal of appetizer, soup or salad, main entrée, and dessert is something you more than likely cannot do, but if you pace yourself and do not eat everything at each course, you could certainly enjoy all the courses.

I play golf at least once a week, and I attribute my poor play to this cancer, but that is not really the case!

88. Will I continue to have acid reflux following treatment?

You may continue to have reflux, but this depends on the type of treatment you received and your general medical condition. If you've had surgery, the reflux is not usually caused by stomach acid but by bile. Your surgeon can prescribe medications to help prevent this and alleviate any symptoms you may have. If you do experience reflux during or after treatment, discuss it with your doctor.

Bart's comment:

Because the surgery removes several acid-producing glands, the likelihood of getting acid reflux is remote. However, bile reflux is a possibility and if that persists, you need to see your doctor as there are medications that can be taken to protect your esophagus from the effects of bile reflux.

89. How can I cope psychologically with cancer? I feel depressed. Is this common?

Just as each individual is different, each person's response to the diagnosis of cancer is different. It's normal to feel scared, depressed, angry, or any number of other emotions after being diagnosed with cancer. Developing a coping strategy can help you to get through difficult times during treatment and recovery. Relaxation techniques, such as meditation, can be useful while waiting for treatments to begin or to see your doctor in the office. Communicating openly and honestly with your friends and family can help you to gain strength from each other. Some people may prefer to discuss emotions and feelings with someone other than a close friend or family member. Professionals, such as social workers or psychologists, are good resources to discuss your feelings and can help you to develop effective coping strategies that work for you. A source of spiritual support can also be a valuable resource for difficult times. In addition, set aside some time to be alone as well as time to do activities you enjoy. Don't let cancer control your life—try to live as normally as possible and appreciate the good things in your life. If you do find you are having difficulty coping or are feeling depressed, discuss it with your doctor so that you can be referred to the appropriate person for assistance.

Bart's comment:

Depression has a way of finding its way into a cancer patient's thought process. No matter how much control you think you have, when cancer strikes it renders you helpless, and as such you can become depressed because you seemingly lose control. I have found an aggressive regimen of exercise can fight off the depression feelings you can develop. Being around a supportive group of family and friends also helps in handling the depression that may occur. There are social workers attached to your local cancer centers who are trained to recognize depression and plan an appropriate course of action, and if depression persists you should avail yourself of these services.

90. Are support groups available?

Support groups are a good way for patients and families to face the challenges and uncertainties that are common following a cancer diagnosis. Support groups can help you feel less alone and can help you cope with diagnosis, treatment, and recovery. There are many support services offered by hospitals, cancer centers, community agencies, and private groups. Some groups are general cancer support groups while others are more specialized, such as a group for men with cancer, or may be specific to a certain type of cancer. Because cancer of the esophagus is a more rare type of cancer, it may be difficult to find a group specific to the patient with esophageal cancer. Contact the closest cancer center to you or your local American Cancer Society for a list of local support groups.

Support groups are often led by a professional, such as a social worker, nurse, or psychologist, but can also be led by patients and survivors. Some groups are strictly supportive, where participants discuss their feelings, reactions, and how they are coping. Other groups have an educational component and may address symptom management or educational needs of the participants. Groups vary in size, approach, and how often they meet. Many of these support groups are free but some do require a fee. Check with your insurance company to find out if your plan will cover the cost. It's important for you to find a group that is comfortable and convenient for you and that meets your needs. More support groups are being offered online and over the telephone to accommodate all patients. CancerCare is an organization that offers professional counseling individually or through professionally facilitated support groups. Both of these services are available online, through the telephone, and on-site in New York, Long Island, New Jersey, and Connecticut. All CancerCare services are free of charge. You can find more information at www.cancercare.org or 800-813-HOPE.

91. What support is available for my significant other and family?

Family and friends are also affected when someone they care about is diagnosed with cancer. Just as their loved one may benefit from support, they may also benefit from talking with a professional or other families who are having similar experiences. Some support groups are designed specifically for family and friends of people diagnosed with cancer. Others may encourage family members and patients to participate in the same group. In addition to your local hospital or American Cancer Society, the National Cancer Institute has a fact sheet about services for people with cancer that lists organizations that provide different support groups. The NCI fact sheet entitled: *National Organizations That Offer Services to People with Cancer and Their Families* is available on the Internet (*http://cis.nci.nih.gov/fact/8_1.htm*) or by calling the Cancer Information Service (1-800-4-CANCER).

Bart's comment:

There are several support groups that cater to patients and their families when it comes to esophageal cancer. Memorial Sloan-Kettering has a post-treatment support group available every couple of months. In addition, there are patient-oriented support groups where patients can become part of an e-mail network and share their experiences and questions with fellow patients. You can check their web sites at www.eccafe.com and www.fightec.org.

92. What medical insurance issues am I likely to face?

Medical insurance can be complicated, and navigating your insurance coverage and policies can be overwhelming at times. With any serious illness, it is important to review your coverage because there may be restrictions as to which doctors and facilities are covered by your plan. If you have insurance through your employer, it may be helpful to contact your benefits department and ask a representative to help you understand your coverage. They may be able to advocate for you directly with the insurance company and could help with any difficulties you experience. Some questions you may want to ask your insurance company are:

- Can I see any doctor or go to any hospital, or only those in your plan?
- How much more will I have to pay if I would like to use a doctor outside your plan ("out of network")?
- Do I have coverage for a second opinion?
- Do I need authorization before having diagnostic tests or treatments? If so, what is the process for doing this?
- What coverage do I have for prescription medications?

Your hospital may have a financial counselor who can help to determine the estimated costs of your care. You may be able to work with them to calculate what you will have to pay out-of-pocket based on your insurance coverage. If you are not able to pay this fee, discuss how you can work out a realistic payment plan. If you have difficulty paying for care, meet with a social worker to find out what financial assistance is available. You may be entitled to government or charitable assistance, and the American Cancer Society or Cancer Care may also be able to provide assistance.

The cost of prescription medications can be significant, and many pharmaceutical companies have assistance programs to provide medication at a reduced cost. To find out about financial assistance available for particular medication, ask your nurse or social worker for information. CancerCare has a web site (*www.cancercare.org/*

hhrd/drug_assistance.asp) that lists pharmaceutical companies with assistance programs.

Throughout your treatment, track all of the financial costs that you have incurred as a result of this illness. Generally, it is a good idea to keep receipts of all medical expenses for you, your spouse, and your children as certain medical expenses may be tax deductible. The IRS allows itemized medical deductions only to the extent they: (1) exceed 7.5% of the taxpayer's adjusted gross income and (2) are not compensated for by insurance or otherwise. Typically, expenses not covered by insurance are your annual deductible costs, co-pays (the fees you pay up front for specific services), and coinsurance (the part of the bill your insurance company doesn't cover). Other typical out-of-pocket expenses (e.g., prescription medications or the mileage for trips to appointments) may also be tax deductible. Unfortunately, the list of deductible medical expenses is too lengthy to discuss here, so please speak with your accountant or tax service when you are first diagnosed for information on what is tax deductible and what records you will have to keep.

Cancer of the esophagus is a rare type of cancer and not all facilities have experience taking care of patients with this diagnosis. If you have an HMO and do not have out-of-network coverage to see a specialist, work with your primary care doctor and the patient financial services department at the hospital where you want to be treated. They will be able to advocate on your behalf and write a letter of medical necessity as to why you need to see a specialist. Even with these efforts, your insurance company may still reject your claim. You may also call your insurance company directly and ask about out-of-network coverage to see a specialist. Keep track of who you speak with, the date of your conversation, and what the result was so that you will have documented records if needed.

93. What problems may I face in getting life insurance after a cancer diagnosis?

Life insurance companies evaluate new policies based on personal information such as age, occupation, and health to measure your risk as a new policyholder. Unfortunately, having a pre-existing medical condition like cancer makes it unlikely that companies will cover you for life or extended care insurance. The longer you are away from diagnosis and treatment, the easier it will be to obtain coverage. Most companies will sell insurance to cancer survivors at normal rates if they're healthy for at least five years after diagnosis.

If you are employed or retired, check with your company to see if they have provided coverage as part of your current or retirement benefits. Some insurance companies specialize in providing insurance to people with medical conditions and some even provide coverage specifically for individuals who have had cancer. The insurance company will want to know the specific type of cancer, dates of treatment, treatment methods, and if the cancer has spread to other sites. They may also require copies of your medical records and pathology reports. Look for a company that is rated A or better by A.M. Best (*http://www.ambest.com*) or Standard and Poor's (*http://www.standardandpoors.com*). Even with these specialized insurance companies, you may not be able to get coverage until you've been cancer free for at least two years, but they may be able to evaluate your case on an individual basis.

94. Should I take vitamin or herbal supplements? Are there alternative therapies recommended during treatment and recovery?

If you are eating a balanced diet you should not need to take a vitamin supplement. However, during treatment for cancer of the esophagus, it may be difficult to eat a balanced diet. In this case, a multivitamin may be beneficial. Check with your doctor before starting a new vitamin or taking high doses of vitamins, because some may have adverse side effects with treatment. For instance, high doses of vitamin E may thin the blood and are not recommended prior to surgery or biopsies.

Herbs or botanicals are a type of dietary supplement that have a long history of use and of claimed health benefit. However, some herbs may cause health problems or may react with medications. Since herbs are not classified as drugs by the Food and Drug Administration, no federal standards exist and their actual content cannot be identified. In addition, many herbs and supplements claim to have benefits that have not been proven. A more scientific approach to the benefits of herbs is underway and many clinical trials exist to test specific herbs and botanicals for benefits in the treatment of cancer. Check with your doctor or the Cancer Information Service (1-800-4-CANCER) for a list of clinical trials involving herbs or botanicals for cancer of the esophagus.

It is important to know that just because an herbal supplement is labeled "natural," this does not mean that it is safe and without any harmful side effects. Herbs are not benign and can act in a similar fashion to drugs, causing side effects and medical problems if taken incorrectly or at the wrong dose. For these reasons, it is important to consult your health care provider before using any supplements, especially if you are currently undergoing treatment. They can discuss the known benefits and possible side effects of the supplement, or refer you to someone who can. Many hospitals and cancer centers now have staff who are knowledgeable about the use of herbs and supplements for cancer. These staff may be in the "Integrative Medicine" or "Complementary Medicine" department.

For more information, contact the National Center for Complementary and Alternative Medicine (1-888-644-6226 or *http://www.nccam.hih.gov*). Memorial Sloan-Kettering Cancer Center has a web site that lists herbs and botanicals, and provides objective information for health professionals and the public including a clinical summary for each agent, adverse effects, and potential benefits or problems. You can access this site at *http://www.mskcc.org/aboutherbs*.

95. How do I cope with the fear of recurrence?

Cancer recurrence is the return of cancer after treatment and a period of time when no cancer was detectable. Having a fear of cancer recurrence is normal. If you feel afraid or anxious about your cancer recurring, it is important to realize that these feelings are normal and you should not criticize yourself for feeling this way. Try not to feel guilty and accept how you feel, and realize there are strategies that can help manage these feelings. One method is to express your feelings and talk about them with someone you trust. Joining a support group for survivors is a good way to discuss your feelings with others who are experiencing the same fears and anxieties. Keeping a journal is also a good way to explore your thoughts and feelings. It may also be helpful to discuss your fears with your physician. He or she may be able to discuss the normal recovery from cancer of the esophagus as well as symptoms to look out for. Being knowledgeable about what to expect can help to relieve unnecessary fears and worries. A good web site to check is People Living with Cancer (*www.plwc.org*). This is the patient information web site for the American Society of Clinical Oncology (ASCO) and provides oncologist-approved information on specific cancers and their treatment, clinical trials, coping, and side effects. The site includes information on cancer of the esophagus and is designed to help people with cancer make informed health care decisions.

As we've talked about in earlier questions, maintaining a healthy lifestyle by eating a well-balanced diet (Question 33), exercising regularly (Question 32), and getting enough sleep (Question 75) can help you cope with life after treatment for cancer. You'll feel better physically and emotionally, and will lower your chances of developing other health problems.

Coping strategies that helped as you went through treatment can also help after treatment with the fear of recurrence. If you've tried meditation, or joined a support group and found that to be beneficial, continue to do so after treatment has finished. If you've tried some strategies and are having difficulty coping with the fear of cancer recurrence, talk with your doctor about a referral to a social worker, psychologist, or other mental health professional. They will be able to help you focus on your feelings and work on ways to reduce anxiety and stress. It's important to remember that while you can't control whether your cancer is going to recur, you can control how much you let the fear of cancer recurrence impact your life.

Bart's comment:

Recurrence is always a concern, especially as my routine CAT scans and endoscopy check-ups come up throughout the year.

When cancer occurs, it quickly affects your control of what you plan to do in the future. There is always the stigma about planning for tomorrow when the uncertainty of being here weighs so heavily at times.

What has helped me is my ability to be able to live each day to the fullest. I appreciate seeing a sunrise and stopping to smell the roses and I thank God for that awareness. I appreciate the smaller things in life and this has enabled me to handle the recurrence issue. A positive self image adds to the equation.

Someone 30 years ago gave me a banner that says, "Make where you are better because you are there." It is a great motto to live by and it has given me a positive outlook on life without losing the realism that we all have to die someday. Whether cancer takes my life or another reason, taking the time now to live out this motto will serve me well when that time comes. At least I now think that way.

PART SEVEN

If Treatment Fails: Advocacy and Support

Where does esophageal cancer usually spread? What are the symptoms that indicate my cancer has spread?

What happens if the cancer comes back?

My treatment doesn't seem to be working. What should I do to prepare myself and my family for the future?

More . . .

96. Where does esophageal cancer usually spread? What are the symptoms that indicate my cancer has spread?

Esophageal cancer can spread at or near the primary site (local recurrence), to the lymph nodes or tissues near the esophagus (regional recurrence), or to other organs or tissue far away from the original site (distance recurrence). Some common sites are the liver, abdominal cavity, and lymph nodes in the chest. You may have new symptoms such as difficulty swallowing or pain, but often the recurrence is found at a follow-up visit with your doctor prior to developing symptoms. It is important to follow up with your surgeon or oncologist after your treatment is completed. Follow-up tests such as CT scans, endoscopy, and PET scans may be able to identify recurrence early, and your physician can then determine the best treatment options.

Treatment for recurrent esophageal cancer depends on the site and extent of recurrence. Most often this treatment is considered palliative, and the goal is to relieve symptoms and improve quality of life. Surgery, chemotherapy, and radiation each may be used for treatment of recurrent esophageal cancer. Your surgeon and medical oncologist will discuss treatment options with you, including clinical trials.

97. What happens if the cancer comes back?

Recurrence
when a particular type of cancer has been treated, but later returns either in the same type of tissues or in other areas of the body.

When cancer that has been thought to be cured or inactive returns, it is called a **recurrence.** This can occur weeks, months, or years after the initial diagnosis and treatment. When you were first diagnosed, treatment was aimed at destroying all the cancer cells in your body. Sometimes, even with the best treatment, a small number of cancer cells are able to survive and may not be able to be detected until much later.

Depending on the site and extent of the recurrence, surgery, chemotherapy, radiation, or a combination of these may be the best treatment. Discuss with your doctor the treatment he or she recommends as well as the side effects and goals of that treatment.

This may be a difficult time that can lead to fear and anxiety as you begin treatment again. One way that may help to alleviate some of this fear is to learn as much as you can about what's happening and find support to help cope with your feelings and emotions. Discuss questions and fears you may have with your doctor, nurse, or other members of your treatment team. Write down your questions so that when you see your doctor, you will have a list of concerns in hand and won't forget to ask about something. It is also helpful to have a friend or relative go with you who can help you remember what was discussed.

It is also important at this time to take care of yourself mentally, physically, spiritually, and emotionally. As we've talked about in other questions, maintaining a healthy diet and getting moderate exercise can help you to feel better. Support groups are a good venue to discuss your feelings and emotions with others who may be experiencing the same things. Take time to do things that you enjoy, and spend time with people you enjoy.

When cancer returns it may often lead to a sense of loss of control over your illness. It is important to know that this loss of control is not a loss of control over your future. You are able to control the way you approach each day.

Bart's comment:

From a patient's perspective, you are always in fear of hearing that the recent test you have taken has indicated a tumor and the signs are you have a recurrence. I experienced that in December 2003 when the doctors indicated a suspicious area on my CAT scan and indicated I should have a PET scan. When that came back positive, my surgeon ordered an endoscope with ultrasound with the idea of getting a tumor sample to see first-hand if I had a recurrence. When the gastroenterologist indicated he could not find a tumor to biopsy, you can imagine how I felt.

There was a period of time, though, between tests when I thought I had a recurrence, and my mind immediately went to how long do I have to live? and will I see certain milestones in my life? I thought back on my life and recalled a banner that someone had given me many years ago—"Make where you are better because you are there"—and thought about those words and how important they were to me.

If I get a recurrence it does not mean a death sentence. With the drugs they have today and are developing for next year and the year after, I still can live a fruitful life and maintain good quality of life even with a recurrence. Sometimes we need to "stop and smell the roses" and think not of ourselves, but of our families and friends and the journey that we share.

I often think of the soldiers in their late teens or early twenties who have given their lives for us and how they were not given the opportunities that I have enjoyed, and how thankful I should be for having that special length of time.

There is another saying that I heard many years ago, and it stated "for all that is happening we thank you God and for all that there is to come." YES! I truly believe that there is nothing that God and I together can't handle, and it is that mainstay that has caused me to do the things I do, to help the people I help and feel great about each day of my life.

We never give-up, we never yield to the cancer, we simply fight with all our strength.

98. My treatment doesn't seem to be working. What should I do to prepare myself and my family for the future?

When treatment doesn't appear to be working, you may be faced with conflicting and difficult emotions. You may be concerned about loss of control over your illness, the impact of this on your family and friends, and the choices you must make regarding your care and treatment. It is important to live your life as well as you can. We've included some information in this question that we hope will help to ease your concerns.

At this time, you may think about death and dying. We all know that death is inevitable but we do not usually spend time thinking about it. When faced with thinking about death, a person often changes how they look at life, and this change in perspective can lead to a change in what we value and hold dear. Some patients describe this as a time when they realized the importance of living one day at a time. You may have considered these feelings when you were first diagnosed and your perspective may already have changed. It is important to keep in mind that there is no right or wrong way to feel. Consider your emotions and beliefs about life and death, and find meaning for yourself in these thoughts and beliefs.

Your family and friends can be important sources of emotional support to you throughout your illness. They need to understand as much as you do and will need time to consider your illness and their own feelings of anger, helplessness, fear, and concern. Let them know their support and love will help you cope during this difficult time. Honest and open communication at all times during your illness has tremendous benefits for you as well as your loved ones. Discussing concerns or feelings helps your loved ones understand what is important to you and it may also help to alleviate some of the fears or anxieties you each are feeling. Keep in mind, however, that everyone handles difficult situations in their own way and may need time to cope with their feelings. Talking with a professional, either in a group or individual setting, is a good option for you and your family. Members of the clergy are also a good resource to discuss concerns.

Treatment options at the end of life are varied. As part of your treatment decisions, discuss your wishes with your doctor and medical team. Home care is a comfortable and realistic option for many patients. Home care can provide medications, nutritional supplements, physical therapy, and other complex nursing and medical procedures. Treatment in the home can ease the emotional and logistic burden of traveling to the hospital for care. A home health aide can assist with personal tasks such as bathing, dressing, and other personal care. The home health care team will work closely with you, your family, and your medical team to plan your care.

Hospice is another option for care at the end of life. The goal of hospice care is to maximize quality of life and minimize pain and is based on a team approach to care. Hospice can be provided at home, in the hospital, or at a separate facility. Hospice care not only focuses on the medical aspects of care, but also the emotional, spiritual, and social aspects. Your doctor, nurse, or social worker can discuss hospice care with you and provide information on services in your community.

In addition to your medical care, you may also want to plan for financial, legal, and emotional difficulties your family may face after your death. This is often very difficult, but planning for matters such as wills and debts now can eliminate problems your family may face later. You may want to consult with a social worker, lawyer, or your insurance company about questions related to financial or legal issues. Organizing documents and records can also help your family cope with the practical aspects of life. You may also consider planning a funeral or memorial service that conveys how you would like to be remembered. Discuss this with your family and clergy so that the service has a personal and special touch.

This is a difficult time for your and your family. Keeping lines of communication open and living each day to its fullest will allow you to cherish the good things all around you.

ADVOCACY

99. Where can I get more information?

It is always helpful to learn as much as you can about esophageal cancer and its treatment. Discuss questions or concerns with your doctor or nurse and take notes during your doctor visits. Information is available on the Internet and also at your public library or hospital library. We hope that this book provided you with some helpful and meaningful information as you navigate the complex and often distressing course that a diagnosis of esophageal cancer can lead you on. We've also included some information on organizations that may be able to provide additional assistance.

Bart's comment:

Two web sites that focus on patient experiences and are linked to individual patients who work through e-mail networks to develop questions and respond to those questions are http://www.eccafe.com and http://www.fightec.org

100. What are some helpful web sites and telephone numbers?

The Appendix that follows provides a list of many helpful web sites, organizations, and other resources for patients and caregivers.

American Cancer Society (ACS)
1599 Clifton Rd., NE
Atlanta, GA 30329
Voice: 800-ACS-2345
Fax: 404-325-2217
http://www.cancer.org

Cancer Care, Inc.
275 Seventh Avenue
New York, NY 10001
Voice: 800-813-HOPE
Fax: 212-719-0263
http://www.cancercare.org

Cancer Fund of America

Eastern Region	Western Region
2901 Breezewood Lane	2223 N. 56th Street
Knoxville, TN 37921-1099	Knoxville, NY 37921
Voice: 865-938-5284	Voice: 408-654-4715
Fax: 865-938-2968	
http://www.cfoa.org	

National Cancer Institute
http://www.cancer.gov
http://www.cancer.gov/cancerinfo/types/esophageal/ (esophageal specific)
1-800-4-CANCER (Cancer Information Service)

National Coalition for Cancer Survivorship
http://www.canceradvocacy.org/
1-877-NCCS-YES

OncoLink
http://www.oncolink.com/
http://www.oncolink.com/types/article.cfm?c=5&s=12&ss=769&id=9465
(esophageal specific)

Cancer Treatment Centers of America
http://www.cancercenter.com/
http://www.cancercenter.com/esophageal-cancer.cfm
(esophageal specific)
1-800-615-3055

American College of Gastroenterology
http://www.acg.gi.org/patientinfo/index.html
(patient information)
Web site includes a physician locator for gastroenterologists

People Living With Cancer
http://www.plwc.org

GENERAL HEALTH

WebMD
http://www.webmd.com
good general health web site

Mayo Clinic
http://www.mayoclinic.com
good general health web site for illnesses and medications

PRODUCTS

Back Be Nimble
http://www.backbenimble.com
1-800-639-3746
Inflatable wedge for sleeping at 30°

GOVERNMENT AGENCIES THAT PROVIDE FINANCIAL ASSISTANCE

Hill-Burton Funds

Federal assistance is available to those who are unable to pay, and is provided by the Hill-Burton Act of Congress. Public and non-profit hospitals, nursing homes and other medical facilities may provide subsidized low-cost or no cost medical care to fulfill their community service obligation.

Voice: 800-638-0742

TDD: 800-537-7697

http://www.hhs.gov/ocr

Social Security Administration (SSA)

Office of Public Inquiries

Windsor Park Building

6401 Security Blvd.

Baltimore, MD 21235

Voice: 800-772-1213

http://www.ssa.gov

Appendix

Glossary

Adenocarcinoma: A malignant neoplasm of epithelial cells in a glandular or gland-like pattern.

Adjuvant therapy: Chemotherapy given after surgery to lessen the chances that cancer will recur.

Advanced directives: Oral and written instructions containing your wishes for medical care if you are unable to speak for yourself; includes medical power of attorney and living will.

Anastomosis: A natural communication or connection, direct or indirect, between two blood vessels or other tubular structures; the surgical connection of severed organs to form a continuous channel.

Anastomotic leak: When the tissues have not healed completely from an esophagectomy and liquids or saliva leak into the chest cavity. To treat this condition, more time must be allowed for the tissues to heal completely or the patient undergoes further surgery.

Anemia: A condition where the number of blood cells, amount of hemoglobin, and/or the volume of packed red blood cells are less than normal. Symptoms include pallor of the skin, shortness of breath, palpitations of the heart, and fatigue.

Aspiration: The inspiratory sucking into the airways of fluid or any foreign material, especially gastric contents.

Barium swallow: (also called upper GI series or esophagram) A type of radiology examination where a barium solution is drunk before the x-ray is taken to be able to visualize the esophagus, stomach, and duodenum.

Barrett's esophagus: A chronic ulceration of the lower esophagus from esophagitis or esophageal cancer, causes the normal lining to be replaced by cells similar to the stomach or intestine, which can tolerate the acid or bile without damage.

Benign tumor: A growth or mass of abnormal cells that do not invade or destroy adjacent normal tissue.

Biopsy: A process of removing tissue from a patient for diagnostic examination.

Brachytherapy: A type of radiation therapy where a source of irradiation (such as radioactive seeds) is implanted directly into or near the tumor permanently or for a specified time.

Bougie: A cylindrical instrument used for dilating constricted areas in tubular organ (such as the esophagus).

Cardia: Junction between the stomach and esophagus, also called the gastroesophageal junction.

CAT scan: (computed axial tomography) A type of x-ray procedure that is painless, and provides multiple pictures of the body in specific sections for diagnostic purposes.

Cell: The smallest unit of living structure capable of independent existence. Cells are highly specialized in structure and function.

Chemoradiation: Where chemotherapy is used in combination with radiation therapy.

Chemotherapy: The use of drugs to kill cancer cells.

Computerized axial tomography (CAT) scan: Diagnostic studies of internal bodily structures in which computer analysis is used to construct a three dimensional image.

Cytotoxic drugs: A type of pharmaceutical substance that is detrimental or destructive to cells.

Deep vein thrombosis: A blood clot that occurs in a deep-lying vein in the leg or pelvis.

Dietitian: A degreed professional who can develop a nutritious eating plan for an individual.

Dilatation: (also dilation) An outpatient treatment used to stretch the esophagus.

DNA (Deoxyribonucleic acid): A type of nucleic acid found principally in the nuclei of animal and plant cells; considered to be the autoreproducing component of chromosomes and many viruses as well as the repository for hereditary characteristics.

Dumping syndrome: Post-surgical rapid gastric emptying; early dumping symptoms includes nausea, vomiting, bloating and diarrhea and late dumping symptoms include weakness, sweating, and dizziness.

Dysplasia: Abnormal development or growth of tissue, cells or organs.

Endoscopic ultrasound or EUS: A type of endoscopy that uses sound waves for diagnostic purposes.

Endoscopy: (also called esophagoscopy or EGD) Examination of the interior of a canal or hollow viscus by means of a special instrument, called an endoscope; the patient is sedated during the process.

Epidural catheter: A small tube placed under the skin through which medication can be administered to a patient, via a pump mechanism either at a low constant dose or when the patient presses a button, according to the physician's prescription.

Esophagectomy: The surgical removal of part or most of the diseased esophagus and part of the stomach, and then rebuilding a new esophagus using tissue from stomach or the small or large intestine.

Esophagus: A portion of the digestive canal, shaped like a hollow tube, which connects the throat to the stomach. Controlled muscle contractions propel food and liquids into the stomach, and muscles at the stomach form a valve (esophageal sphincter) that prevents the stomach contents from coming back up into the esophagus.

Esophagitis: Irritation, inflammation, or damage of the esophagus caused by regurgitation of the acid gastric contents.

External beam radiation therapy: A type of x-ray therapy that comes from a machine outside of the body, usually delivered daily in a specific series of treatments.

Feeding tube: A flexible tube passed through the nose and into the alimentary tract, through which liquid food is passed.

Fistula: An abnormal passage from a hollow organ to the body surface or from one organ to another.

Fundoplication: Suture of the fundus of the stomach completely or partly around the gastroesophageal junction to treat gastroesophageal reflux disease.

Gastroenterologist: A physician with special training in the function and disorders of the gastrointestinal system, including the stomach, intestines, and related organs of the gastrointestinal tract.

Gastroesophageal junction: Located where the stomach and esophagus meet, also known as the cardia.

Gastroesophageal reflux disease (GERD): A syndrome due to a structural or functional inability of the lower esophageal sphincter to prevent gastric juice from flooding back into the esophagus.

Gastrostomy tube (G-tube): A type of feeding tube that is inserted directly into the stomach; procedure is done surgically and requires sedation.

H-2 blockers: Type of pharmaceutical drug used to treat GERD and Barrett's esophagus; examples include Tagamet, Pepcid, Zantac, and Axid.

Hiatal hernia: Where part of the stomach protrudes through the esophageal opening (esophageal hiatus) of the diaphragm.

Helicobacter pylori: A specific type of curved or spiral microorganism (bacterium) that colonizes on the surface of mucus-secreting columnar cells, secretes urease, which causes infection and along with other dietary factors leads to gastritis and peptic ulcer disease of the stomach. It may play a role in the development of dysplasia and metaplasia of gastric mucosa and distal gastric adenocarcinoma.

Incentive spirometer: A device used to help the patient inhale and expand the lungs.

Glossary

Intravenously: Injection or infusion of liquid, usually medication, directly through the skin into a vein.

Jejunostomy tube (J-tube): A type of feeding tube that is placed through the skin directly into the small bowel; this is a surgical procedure that will require a hospital stay.

Laparoscopy: A type of surgery using a laparoscope, comprised of fiber optics and low-heat halogen bulbs that aid the placement and use of other surgical tools. One or more tiny incisions enable precise incision, drainage, excision, cautery, ligation, suturing, and other surgical procedures.

Laser surgery: A surgical procedure using a device that concentrates high energies into an intense narrow beam of nondivergent monochromatic electromagnetic radiation; used in microsurgery, cauterization, and diagnostic purposes.

Lower esophageal sphincter (LES): A muscle located at the top of the stomach that opens and closes to keep stomach acid and bile from backing up into the esophagus.

Malignant tumor: A rapid growth of abnormal cells that replace normal cells, invade other tissues and organs, may recur after attempted removal, and is likely to cause the death of the host if left inadequately treated.

Metaplasia: Transformation of an adult, fully formed cell of one kind into an abnormal cell of another kind; an acquired condition (see Barrett's esophagus).

Metastasis: Transmission of cancer cells from an original site to one or more sites in the body.

Minimally invasive surgery: An operative procedure that results in the smallest possible incision or no incision at all; includes laparoscopic, laparoscopically assisted, thoracoscopic, and endoscopic procedures.

Multi modality: The use of specialists in two or more disciplines to treat a specific disease; may include diagnostic testing, radiation, pharmaceuticals, or surgery.

Neoadjuvant therapy: Chemotherapy given before surgery to shrink or isolate the tumor.

Neoplasm: An abnormal tissue that grows by cellular proliferation more rapidly than normal, and continues to grow after the stimuli that initiated the new growth cease (see tumor, malignant, benign).

Oncologist: A physician with specialized training in the science of the physical, chemical, and biological properties of neoplasms, including causation, pathogenesis, and treatment.

Palliation: Used to reduce the severity or relieve the pain of a disease or symptom, but is not a cure of the underlying condition.

Pathologist: A physician who practices, evaluates and/or supervises diagnostic tests, using materials removed from living or dead patients, to determine the causes or nature of the disease change.

Patient controlled analgesia: Medication for pain that the patient can self-administer by pressing a button; after surgery while in the hospital, a small tube is inserted so the medication can be pumped into a vein.

Percutaneous endoscopic gastrostomy (PEG-tube): A type of feeding tube for those with an intact gastrointestinal tract, but unable to consume sufficient calories to meet metabolic needs; an ~30 minute procedure that requires local anesthesia.

PET (positron emission tomography) scan: A type of scan that measures positron-emitting isotopes with short half-lives that the patient has ingested to assess metabolic and physiologic function rather than anatomic structure.

Photodynamic therapy (PDT): A type of surgery that uses an injection of photosensitizing drugs to highlight the cancerous cells and laser light through an endoscope to kill them.

Photosensitizing: A type of treatment where target cancer cells are illuminated by bioluminescent drugs.

Polyps: A general term used for any mass of tissue that bulges or projects outward or upward from the normal surface level; is visible as a roundish structure growing from a mound-like base or a slender stalk.

Primary tumor: Location where the original tumor began.

Proton pump inhibitors: Type of pharmaceutical drug used to treat more complicated GERD (associated with bleeding or strictures); examples include Prilosec, Prevacid, Aciphex, Protonix, and Nexium.

Pulmonary embolism (PE): A blood clot that has broken away from the blood vessel wall and travels into the lung; a large clot can cause breathing problems and even death.

Radiologist: A physician specially trained in the disgnostic and/or therapeutic use of x-rays and radionuclides, radiation physics and biology; also trained in diagnostic ultrasound and magnetic resonance imaging and applicable physics.

Recurrence: When particular type of cancer has been treated, but later returns either in the same type of tissues or in other areas of the body.

Simulation: A process where the medical professional marks specific areas on the cancer patient's body, sometimes using computed tomography, in preparation for targeting the tumor(s) with radiation therapy.

Social worker: A degreed mental health professional who can provide counseling services to individuals and groups as well as help the patient network with community services and resources.

Squamous cell carcinoma: A malignant neoplasm derived from stratified squamous epithelium cells, such as those that line the esophagus.

Stent: A thread, rod or catheter that is inserted into the cell wall of the esophagus to keep it open.

Stricture: A narrowing or tightening of a hollow structure.

Transhiatal esophagectomy: Surgical type of resection of the esophagus where the incision is made from the cervical section of the neck from above and up from the abdomen from below.

Transthoracic esophagogastrectomy: Surgical type of resection of the esophagus through a thoracotomy incision (breast bone to the umbilicus, plus another incision on the right side of the chest).

Tumor: Any swelling caused by an increased number of abnormal cells.

Index

Index

Index